CHRIST
AND THE CAESARS

ETHELBERT STAUFFER

CHRIST
AND THE CAESARS

Historical Sketches

WIPF & STOCK · Eugene, Oregon

Wipf and Stock Publishers
199 W 8th Ave, Suite 3
Eugene, OR 97401

Christ and the Caesars
By Stauffer, Ethelbert
Copyright©1952 by Deitrich Stauffer
ISBN 13: 978-1-55635-818-0
Publication date 1/21/2008
Previously published by Wittig Verlag, 1952

FRATRIBUS PEREGRINANTIBUS

SALUTAMUS
VOS IN NOMINE VENTURI SECULI
UNDE PAX ADVENTAT
A CONSTITUTIONE MUNDI

1. ADVENT OF CONSTANTIUS CHLORUS
IN LONDON

CONTENTS

LIST OF ILLUSTRATIONS

AUTHOR'S PREFACE

THE Historical Sketches of which this book is composed were written in an apocalyptic time in which the demonic nature, the violence and the tragedy of the classical world, as well as the glory of Christ, pressed upon me with fresh power. I am deeply moved to read them now in the language of Shakespeare, and to witness their publication in the land of the British Museum. The English reader will readily perceive how much the author of these pages owes to the genius of Shakespeare as well as to the scholarly resources of the Department of Coins and Medals of the British Museum.

Although I have been asked several times to supply fuller references for various chapters or theses, I have decided not to do so. If the references were full enough to satisfy the expert, they would also be so full as to frighten off the non-expert. So may this book be a little help, in its English dress, in that struggle for the new picture of Jesus Christ which we need.

ETHELBERT STAUFFER

Advent 1954
Erlangen

I

LUX AETERNA

THE PEOPLES of ancient Iran celebrated the birthday of their sun-god Mithras at the time of the winter solstice. Devoutly and exultantly they celebrated the victorious resurgence of light as the symbol of the ultimate invincibility of the *lux caelestis* in this terrestrial world. Year after year they celebrated this event, and year after year the rise of light was followed by the onset of darkness in a *circulus vitiosus* which shattered every hope.

The Roman legions turned this nature philosophy into history and politics: 'make us a God to go before us'. They worshipped Mithras in the figure of the emperor, whose tent was in their camp and who rode at their head against the dark barbarian hordes in the east and north. At the moment of his victorious entry into vanquished London their general and Caesar Constantius Chlorus was glorified by them on a splendid gold medallion as the REDDITOR LUCIS AETERNAE, the Restorer of Eternal Light. The turning-point of the year had become a turning-point in history, Mithras had become a politician. But here we have more than Mithras. It is not just for a few months that our Caesar carries the light again into our world of darkness, but for all time. It is the eternal light which breaks in here.

The son of that Caesar, who grew up as a believer in Mithras and who was proclaimed as an essential manifestation of Mithras, Constantine the Great, when at the height of his career put the name of Christ upon his imperial standard, and beneath it the words, SPES PUBLICA, the hope of world history. From that time the peoples of his empire celebrated in the days of the winter solstice neither the turning of the year nor a turning-point in political history, but the turning-point of all history, which is both more revolutionary and more unobtrusive than any other revolution, and fulfils all that was meant in those other turning-points. From that time the Church sings, 'The eternal light breaks in here, and gives the world a new brightness.'

Such was the course of faith in the classical world, when drawn in a single line. The historical sketches which are brought together in the following pages will, I hope, make some of the scenes and problems of this development a little clearer.

II

MYTH AND EPIPHANY

'Now when Jesus was born in Bethlehem of Judaea in the days of Herod the king, behold, there came wise men from the east to Jerusalem, saying, Where is he that is born King of the Jews? for we have seen his star in the east, and are come to worship him.'

With these words the Gospel according to St. Matthew begins its account of the historical encounter between myth and epiphany.

For as far back as the memory of man reaches, the East has been the land of wise men, the home of myth. For myth is wisdom's last word. For millennia there was handed down among the wise men of the east the myth of the divine king who would redeem creation from its primeval curse. For millennia the guardians of the ancient myth searched the stars in order to learn the day of the redemptive epiphany. Generations came and went. Then there arose the age of the great emperors, whose brightness streamed from the Roman west far out into the east, to be mythically transfigured and returned: Sulla, Pompey, Caesar, Antony, Octavian. The promises mounted, the disillusions too. . . . Then in the days of king Herod God's sign appeared in the heavens, and the star of the epiphany pointed to Bethlehem in Judaea. And the wise men saw the star and rejoiced. They followed it and found the child. They fell down and worshipped. In the presence of Jesus Christ the witnesses of the ancient myth became the chief witnesses of the epiphany. That is the historical and theological meaning of the story of the wise men from the east.

The dogmatics, art and liturgy of the Old Church grasped the whole depth of this meaning. The theology of our time has scarcely any use for the 'Three Wise Men', despite the Manger and Twelfth Night. But the self-same theology debates *ad infinitum* the relation between myth and revelation. Perhaps we should give the speculative discussions a rest, and betake ourselves to the study of world history in the light of Matt. 2.

For the story of the wise men from the east contains a whole programme of historical theology. First, it calls for a history of the mythical spirit, as it penetrates ever more deeply into the terrible mystery of the world and watches with ever greater need for the saving act of God. Second, it calls for a history of the divine revelation which led the People of God through the law and the promise to the epiphany of Jesus Christ. Last and most of all it calls for a history of the encounter between myth and epiphany—that encounter which began in the wise men's homage to the Christ-child, was fulfilled in Christ's interpretation of Himself, and has found its permanently valid canonical expression in the Church's confession of Christ.

To carry out this programme would take a lifetime's work, perhaps the work of a whole generation of scholars. What I want to present here can only be the mere sketch of a preliminary study of the total historical and theological picture which has to be worked out in the spirit of Matt. 2.

I

What is 'myth'? Myth is the speech of religion. It is perhaps the speech of all religion. It is at any rate the speech of ancient religion.

How does ancient myth speak? It speaks of heavenly things in an earthly way, and of earthly things in a heavenly way. More precisely, myth speaks of other-worldly realities in this-worldly categories: God is enthroned in heaven above in the council of the gods. And myth speaks of this-worldly realities in other-worldly categories: God has given us a child, or He has set a goal to our course. That is the form in which myth is expressed. But this form is not to be understood as a naïve,

careless or unscientific confusion of divine and human things;
it is to be taken seriously as the expression in speech of an
objective correlation of other-worldly and this-worldly events.
Ancient religion makes use of the language of myth in order
to assert a definite understanding of reality. The basic motif
of this relation of reality is that there exists a mysterious interaction between divine and human things. The concrete appre-
hension of this interaction, however, has taken many different
forms. In the course of the millennia preceding the victory
of Christ it had a magnificent and tumultuous history. The
apostles and fathers of the Church knew of this history of
myth. And recent research daily brings new material to light.
It is not possible to unfold this history of ancient myth here.
But at least we may try to sketch the three chief morpho-
logical types of the mythical understanding of reality and
their place in the history of ancient life.

First we must speak of the myth of natural history. We all
know the individual motifs. The visible objects and events of
nature appear to some extent within a mythical nimbus, which
lends them an other-worldly relation: the heavenly bodies,
thunder and lightning, trees and springs, fruitfulness and
drought, birth and death.

Through these individual motifs there runs a tendency to
universal forms. The mystery of 'dying to grow' is seen as the
mythical world mystery, the course of the years is seen as the
universal form of the world's life. There arises on a mythical
background an organic picture of the world, which reaches
its finished form in the teaching of the circular course of the
world and the eternal recurrence of things. To live in this
biological myth means to triumph in the spring—'Life is victorious'—and in late summer to say, 'Autumn is upon us, it
will break my heart.' And when in the evening of life the
old might of Eros comes over them once more, then as in
a Dionysian ecstasy they say, 'Once more there falls into my
lap the red rose of passion.'

This natural myth is actualized in the festival of the new
year, in those timeless and varied new year festivals in which
ancient man celebrated the winter solstice and the new rise

of life. I take as an example of all these the old Anatolian festival of Sandon, when in the midmost winter night an enormous pyramid of wood was built, the scaffold of Sandon, the god of the year's course, of fruitfulness, of the intoxication of life, of the light of heaven. The women of the whole land streamed together bewailing the lovely, young, well-beloved Sandon, who would that day reach his end on the scaffold. But above the ball of fire an eagle rose up into the heavens, symbol of the immortal god who rises through the killing and quickening flames to new life, dragging all nature with him. Then the weeping of the women was changed to an orgiastic exultation and frenzy, and the whole people celebrated the victory of the god of the year in one great erotic carnival. And to call it a carnival points to the dark shadow lying over this tumultuous life of the knowledge of the great Ash Wednesday which no one can escape.

That is the biological myth of ancient man in its universal and actualized form. We have called it the myth of 'natural history'. But we must realize that when we speak of it as history it scarcely deserves the name, and is as it were history of the first degree. For there is nothing really new under the sun. All that happens in heaven and on earth is regarded as a natural occurrence, and this whole natural occurrence appears as an element in a cosmic circle, a gigantic *circulus vitiosus*. The myth of natural history thinks in circular forms.

This circular thinking is shattered in the myth of historical fate. This myth dates from the time when it is seen that there *is* something new under the sun, which enters the eternal succession of growth and decay and does not disappear, which enters into the substance of the world on a specific occasion and then cannot be got rid of, a factor in our earthly existence whose traces do not vanish in countless aeons. What kind of factor is this? It is guilt. All the passion of ancient men for life, for the ecstasy of Eros, as well as the ecstasy of battle, and of the cult of beauty, is in the last resort the passionate reaching-out for eternity. 'For all passion longs for eternity, for the deepest eternity.' It is a passion of despair, and at its end lies resignation. But eternity, which ancient man sought in vain in the passion of life, meets him, more, becomes his—in guilt. For guilt in the ancient myth of fate is not an individual matter. It is a mythical factor, whose presuppositions and implications reach to the uttermost regions of heaven and hell, of past and future. It is in this sense that Shakespeare speaks in his most profound sonnet of heaven which casts us into hell. In this sense, too, Immermann's devil points to a horde of god-seekers and says to God, 'They wanted to be with You—and they're with me!'

A *daimon* took hold of Xerxes, and filled him with the greatest idea that a statesman of the ancient world ever had—to unite land and sea, east and west under *one* sceptre. Like a man possessed, Xerxes acted under the compulsion of this *daimon*. So Aeschylus tells us. Like a god Xerxes was enthroned above the mighty parade of the peoples at the Hellespont, for days the troops marched past his dais, the fleet lay on the blue sea, stretched out further than the eye could see. There, at the height of his life, a height reached by no mortal man before him, he was overwhelmed, as by an enemy, by the bitter realization of the fragility of everything earthly, and the great king burst into tears. So Herodotus tells us. And again Herodotus tells how the Persians were banqueting with their allies the Thebans, and drinking to the coming victory. One of the Persians turned quietly to his Greek neighbour: 'Friend, you see these Persians at this table, and the army we have left in camp. In a short time only a very few of them will still be alive. Many of us know this very well. All the same we follow our king as the gods have destined. And that is the bitterest pain which men can know, to have great insight and no power.' Thus he spoke, and burst into tears. And Aeschylus again says, 'The *daimon* which has lifted the Persian king so high casts him but the deeper into the depths, and with the king's fall there will fall also the armies and the peoples.' Xerxes's premonition and his general's words were fulfilled. Thousands fell in vain. But Xerxes survived, and bore with him for the rest of his days a guilt rooted in world history.

This is the classical myth of fate and guilt. Gyges deceives and slays his good king and ascends his throne, and all goes well. But the fifth generation of his line had to pay for the guilt of his ancestor, and lost both throne and kingdom. Tantalus does wrong, and carries the curse with him into history, and the guilt of prehistoric time swells like an avalanche down the generations. That is guilt in the sense of the classical myth of fate. You must first grasp the reality of guilt if you are to know what history is. History, which is more than a natural course of events, is always in some way or other the history of guilt. That is why guilt is never a private matter, which can be settled privately, but is always a public matter. And this is the affliction of history, that man can know guilt, but not purity—can kill, but not make alive. That is why human guilt is always a historical matter.

For like the myth of natural history the myth of historical fate presses on towards a universal form, and is completed in a tragic view of life. The myth of historical fate was born when man grasped the eternal implications of guilt. The tragic view of life is born when man realizes that guilt cannot be evaded. This is when the history of Xerxes or Tantalus ceases to be a pitiful tale of distant times or places, and becomes a parable of all human history, a paradigm, to use the words of Aristotle, which rouses our pity and our fear.

When and where does this happen? According to Aristotle, it happens when you see classical tragedy. For in tragedy the myth of historical fate, which has reached its universal form in the tragic view of life, is actualized. It is in accord with this that Aeschylus took the Dionysian choruses, whose roots strike deep into the primitive layers of natural myth and cult, and created the classic form of classical tragedy, the canonical expression of the tragic view of fate held by Greek man— and not by Greek man alone. In accord with this, too, Aeschylus presented the story of the house of Tantalus in his *Oresteia* and the story of Xerxes in his *Persians*. So, too, the people of Athens gathered at their festivals as in a temple, not in order to sing an ecstatic lament, which would turn into an orgiastic revel, but in order to hear man's song of destiny, which offers no solution or consolation. So men in all generations have gathered to see tragedy, and this is the West's confession of belief in the myth of historical fate. Friedrich Hebbel once explained why tragedy is more than an art form of Greek poetry and is a sign of metaphysical significance. 'Tragedy', he wrote, 'is the deeper reconstruction of world history.'

Does this mean that the myth of historical fate reaches a final understanding of history? The cosmic circle is only history of the first degree. History of the second degree is that of guilt and the curse, which run like a red thread through the whole story. Does this mean, then, that tragedy is the last word about human destiny? Classical man says no. The myth of historical fate is only penultimate. Wisdom's last word is the myth of the Empire.

The myth of fate begins with the realization that guilt creates something new in history, which does not grow old. The imperial myth begins with the confession that man is sent to create something new, which is not a curse but a blessing, or at least that *one* man is commissioned to overcome the curse of history by a work of blessing which creates a new situation in the world. Who is this man, this chosen one, who by his deeds is to refute the witness of tragedy? He is the statesman. And what is the work of blessing to which he is called? His work is the Empire.

Classical man was intelligent enough to see that such an achievement needed more than a man. So his hope was founded not on the theory but on the myth of Empire. The Empire which was to resolve the tragic affliction of the world, had to come straight from heaven. Myths of gods and heroes which had long since faded quicken to fresh life in the historical figure of the saviour, the coming founder of the Empire. He is the child of the gods, the hero of light, the slayer of dragons, he and none other.

He desires power, and must desire it, since he will bring salvation by way of power. The coins of A.D. 69, the year of the four emperors, especially the coins of Galba, give expression to this myth. They include the coin on which the old cavalry general is greeted as the divinely promised lord of the world by the Spanish sibyl (the same sibyl whose promise was taken to refer to himself by the Spanish Charles V fifteen hundred years after Galba), and the coin on which Galba proclaims the goal of his struggle and his programme of government to the peoples of the world: SALUS GENERIS HUMANI—the Salvation of the Human Race.

We understand how powerful was the movement towards a universal form in this imperial myth, from the Sibylline Fragments, Virgil's Fourth Eclogue, Horace's *Carmen Seculare* and other products of classical secular mythology. Here the whole of history, in nature and in humanity, in heaven and on earth, appears as the history of the Empire, concentrated on the Ruler, whose power does not yield to the compulsion of the stars or the curse of man because he is not 'only' a politician, but both priest and saviour. Here one can see how the imperial myth as it were takes up into itself and dissolves the myths of nature and of fate. The mythical history of the Empire is revealed as the highest power of all historical happenings, as history of the third degree.

The imperial myth is born of the affirmation of historical action. Hence it is completely actualized not in a cultic orgy, nor in tragedy, but in a political deed, an act of advent: he comes, for whom the generations have waited—he is here! In the semi-official account of Vespasian's entry into Rome, that ceremonial entry which signalled the end of the bloodshed and confusion of the year of the four emperors, we read: 'The leading citizens of Rome did not wait in the city, but hastened out to meet him far beyond the walls. The ordinary citizens, too . . . streamed out, till the city was almost deserted. When the emperor's approach was at last announced, and those who had gone out to meet him praised the friendly and humane spirit in which he greeted everyone, the whole populace wanted to receive him on the way. Where he passed, his mild countenance inspired the masses with such enthusiasm that they called out to him, greeting him variously as Giver of Grace, Saviour, and the only worthy Ruler of Rome. The imperial capital was so bedecked with garlands and so heavy with incense that it almost looked like one great temple . . . the city of Rome, which had received Vespasian in such a friendly fashion, entered on a state of mounting prosperity from that hour.'

Can a more concrete and historically powerful form of the classical myth be imagined than this of the imperial myth? Can there be a more concrete form of the imperial myth than this advent ceremony? The basic concern of the classical myth is expressed here with elementary power—the correlation, namely, between the divine and the human world. In the person of the divine emperor this basic concern receives its fulfilment. The divine and the human have become one. The history of the age-old curse is at an end. The history of salvation can begin.

But it does not begin.

Dozens of rulers before Vespasian, dozens of Roman emperors after him, were received in just the same way as he, just the same way and yet differently. And everything remained the same. The form of the world did not change. The vicious circle of natural events went on as before. The basic tragedy in human history was not overcome. A modern historian has said that mankind is like a man sick to death, who as he lies on his bed of pain is filled with the need to turn constantly from one side to the other. And a popular modern book begins with the assertion that history is really a hell in which the damned are tortured in eternal repetition, endlessly and purposelessly. This is the last word of classical myth; but it is not the last word about human history. God has spoken. Let us hear that Word.

II

'I am the Lord thy God, which have brought thee out of the land of Egypt, out of the house of bondage. Thou shalt have no other gods before me. Thou shalt not make unto thee any graven image, or any likeness of any thing that is in heaven above, or that is in the earth beneath, or that is in the water under the earth: Thou shalt not bow down thyself to them, nor serve them: for I the Lord thy God am a jealous God, visiting the iniquity of the fathers upon the children unto the third and fourth generation of them that hate me: And shewing mercy unto thousands of them that love me, and keep my commandments' (Ex. 20.2-6).

These words still mark the greatest revolution in the history of the human spirit of ancient times. They have an immediate connexion with classical myth. But this connexion is negative, or rather, it is polemic. For the denial which the Decalogue opposes to myth is no clear and cool denial, but filled with zeal and jealousy; not a smiling but a threatening denial. The Old Testament takes myth so seriously that it utters a curse upon it.

'I am the Lord thy God. Thou shalt have no other gods beside me.' That means that the world is emptied of gods. It means an end to the mythological nimbus round the creature, whether in heaven above or the earth beneath or the water under the earth, it means a break with every religious transfiguration of what lies above us, within us, and beneath us. But I repeat that mythologizing and transfiguring of this kind is in the eyes of the Decalogue not a stage which has been overcome by the progress of the human spirit, but a temptation in the history of man. Worship of the creature is disclosed not as an error but as a misdeed, a deed of hate against God, as the chief sin, bringing the wrath of God upon it, and bringing ruin upon generations to come.

The religious transfiguration of the creature is the *proton pseudos*, the first error of mythology, which is brought to light by the Decalogue. Classical myth confounds and confuses this world and the other. The Decalogue makes this quite clear. The revelation tears apart the false mythological web which tries to bind the divine and the worldly together. Let the world be the world, and God be God. It reveals the spurious otherworldliness of the mythical world of the gods, and reveals the reality of God in its pure and genuine otherworldliness. This is the cathartic, directing, purifying and liberating service which revelation performs for classical myth.

'I am the Lord thy God, which have brought thee out of the land of Egypt, out of the house of bondage.' This wholly other, remote, and other-worldly God is Lord of the world, of history, and of human destiny, Lord as none of the mythological deities ever were. He is at the Archimedian point where the world can be shifted from its axis—He, and none other. This is the correlation between this world and the other. He leads His people, He makes history, as no nature God, or power of fate, or saviour-king makes history. That is the genuine correlation between the world of heaven and the world of earth. Revelation clearly takes myth seriously, not only in its error but also in its real concern. It tears away the false correlation in order to establish the genuine correlation between the really other-worldly God and the really this-worldly world. From this correlation history in a new sense arises, a history of which the classical myth has no inkling, the revelation-history of the Old Covenant.

The distinctive mark of this history is that it has a future. The natural myth of the classical world knew no future, but only perpetual recurrence. The classical myth of fate knew no future, but only the insuperable past. The classical imperial myth knew no future, but only the old wine in new skins. The revelation-history of the Old Covenant knows a genuine future. For it knows the God who shows mercy. And the presence of mercy makes an end to the past and its guilt, and opens the way to the future. All revelation-history is directed towards the future, and that is why it is revelation which first really and definitively leads out beyond the circular view of history, which was established by the natural myth and never really overcome either by the myth of fate or the myth of empire. Revelation is the first to lead to a radically linear view of the course of history. This is history of the fourth power.

Here you gain insight into the basic historical character of all reality. The whole of creation is on the way to the goal of God. So once more the concern of classical myth is taken up, taken seriously, and the happenings of the history of nature, of fate and of the Empire all find their place in the great course of universal history, as it is guided to its goal by the Creator of all and the Lord of history.

Need we speak of how this theology of history attained a universal form, of its falling heir to the kingdoms of the world in their movement towards the kingdom of the Son of Man which is not of this world? We turn to the actualization of revelation-history in the life of Christ.

When Mary and Joseph came to present the Child Jesus in the Temple, old Simeon took the Child into his arms and said: 'Now lettest thou thy servant depart, O Lord, according to thy word, in peace; for mine eyes have seen thy salvation, which thou hast prepared before the face of all peoples; a light for revelation to the Gentiles, and the glory of thy people Israel.' And he blessed the parents, and said to Mary, 'Behold, this child is set for the falling and rising up of many in Israel; and for a sign which is spoken against' (Luke 2.29ff.).

In order to grasp the mysterious destiny of the Old Testament people of the covenant and the divine meaning of the Old Testament history of salvation, one must first establish what this people was *not*. This people of the Old Testament was the one people in ancient times which was never brought into line with the rest of world history. The succession of ancient empires passed it over. And in consequence of this it endured untold suffering. Every people has its day in history. But this people never had its day. Is this really so?

It did have its day, says old Simeon. It was that day when Mary in Bethlehem brought forth the Christ of God to the world for the glory of her people. On that day this people reached the divine goal of its history, and Simeon's time of waiting was at an end. Now the servant of God can depart in peace. So Simeon sees the history of his people. The whole history of Israel is the prehistory of Jesus Christ. This people was created by God and led through the ages in order to bring forth Mary. That was its purpose in world history. When it has performed this historical service for mankind it can depart in peace. But this people does not see, in this its time, what belongs to its peace. Simeon expresses this in the prophetic words, 'This child is set for the falling and rising up of many in Israel, and for a sign which is spoken against.' The Baptist, who proclaims the eschatological Christ, is offended by the historical Jesus. This is the tragedy in the historical fate of Israel. It is destroyed by the Christ who came out of its midst.

Israel is the bow, and Christ the arrow, Franz Werfel once said. The arrow flies off—and the bow is broken. And the arrow flies far out into the world.

III

God's Saviour, prepared before the face of all peoples, becomes a light for revelation to the Gentiles, and they see Him with their eyes. 'And the Word became flesh, and dwelt among us (and we beheld his glory, glory as of the only begotten from the Father), full of grace and truth' (John 1.14). This is God's answer to the classical myth and its problems.

God takes myth seriously. The Old Testament revelation fights against myth. It opposes the spurious correlation between divine and worldly reality. It ensures the genuine transcendence of the reality of God, and the genuine relation between the transcendent Creator and Lord on the one hand and creation and history on the other. The revelation of the God who has become man overcomes the myth. For this is the manifestation of the true relation between the other world and this world, the genuine transcendence of the reality of God is manifested in genuine this-worldliness. This is the mystery of the Incarnation of which the Gospel speaks.

It is easy to show that Jesus and the apostles speak the language of myth. But the decisive question is, Why do they speak the language of myth? Is it simply because the men of the New Testament are bound to their time and place in history? This is what was taught a generation ago. Today we would say rather that the men of the New Testament speak the language of myth because they want us to hear, in the epiphany of Christ, God's final answer to the ancient myth with its problems and illusions, its concerns and demands. This is the seriousness with which God's revelation addresses myth. In the revelation the meaning of myth is fulfilled and at the same time the myth is dissolved; Christ's coming is to bring God's affirmation or denial of the open questions of all history. We shall make this plain by three examples.

27

Jesus called Himself the Son of Man. What does this mean?
Running through the myths of the Near East there is a
mysterious tradition of the man of heaven, who in various
embodiments through the ages determines man's fate. This
man of heaven makes his first appearance as the king of paradise whose primeval kingdom collapsed after the Fall. His last
appearance will be as the saviour-king of the last age, whose
kingdom endures for ever.

Against this myth the Old Testament sets the history of
the great empires in their succession. They are all branded by
the primeval Fall. Alike in their beginnings, their heyday, and
their end, they are full of bloodshed and violence. So 'the
rule of the world passes from one nation to the next in law-
breaking and violence' (Ecclus. 10.8). It is of no avail, things
become worse and worse, violence and deceit increase from
one empire to the next. How long? Till the coming of the
last kingdom of the earth, a monster with iron feet which
trample every land, and a little horn which speaks great things.
'And I beheld, and the same horn made war with the saints,
and prevailed against them; until the ancient of days came,
and judgment was given.' The Lord of history gives judgment on the lords of the earth. 'I beheld at that time because
of the voice of the great words which the horn spake; I beheld even till the beast was slain, and his body destroyed, and
he was given to be burned with fire.' Now the hour of the
heavenly ruler of the End has come, the 'Son of Man'. He
appears in the clouds of heaven and comes to the throne of
the ancient of days, and at his hand receives 'dominion, and
glory, and a kingdom, that all the peoples, nations and languages should serve him: his dominion is an everlasting
dominion, which shall not pass away, and his kingdom that
which shall not be destroyed'. That is the Biblical counter-
part of the mythical son of heaven and saviour-king, the Son
of Man from the seventh chapter of the Book of Daniel.

In Jewish apocalyptic the ancient eastern tradition of myths
meets the Old Testament history of revelation, sometimes
clashing with it, sometimes merging. The theology of the Son
of Man has played a great part in this apocalyptic. After the

time of Jesus it was bitterly contested by the rabbis, and so has come down to us only fragmentarily and indirectly. But we can still discern some elements in the apocalyptic view of the Son of Man, which we may with all reserve piece together into a picture of his course through history. First, he is Adam, king of paradise, who bears the name of Son of Man and is probably to be taken as the primal incarnation of the Son of Heaven. Elsewhere the Son of Man appears in the figure of the patriarch Enoch, who at the last is snatched away again to the throne of God. Other witnesses, again, speak of the Son of Man as a figure of suffering, who passes unrecognized over the earth, and dies at last, after much suffering and persecution, a martyr's death. All references to the Son of Man in pre-Christian apocalyptic, however, meet in the promise of the coming Son of Man as it is given in the Book of Daniel. When the history of human empire and the philosophy of power are exhausted, then the Son of Man will appear in heavenly brightness, and by divine power establish the kingdom that is without end.

Jesus grew up in these traditions of the Son of Man. He referred to them when He called Himself the Son of Man who now walks the martyrs' way and will one day come again on the clouds of heaven. These sayings about the Son of Man are among the oldest and most reliable elements of the tradition about Jesus, and everything indicates that Jesus considered this description of Himself to be more adequate than any other. In brief, the title Son of Man must be accounted a self-interpretation of Jesus. This means that in the centre of Jesus' witness to Himself there stands a mythical self-interpretation. Jesus chose an idea with a powerful mythological content in order to describe the mystery of His epiphany.

And by choosing this idea Jesus also indicated, silently but irrevocably, His attitude to the supreme and final form of ancient mythology in the myth of imperial history. All that can be said about the theme of Christ and the Caesars is contained in this one name of the Son of Man.

While the emperor in Rome exercises his right as lord and

is worshipped as the giver of blessings to the nations, the
Son of Man in Jerusalem goes the way of service, suffering
and death for the salvation of many—and in face of the epiphany of the Son of Man the myth of the emperor grows
pale as candles before the rising sun. For the Son of Man,
who bears the cross today, will bear the crown tomorrow.
He is the *Imperator futurus*, who will establish His kingdom
when the succession of the kingdoms of the earth has come
to an end. He is to stand forth as the *ultima ratio* of world
history, when the empires of this world in all their different
forms have come to an end. So the Son of Man enters the
goal of history; and the history of all peoples and all ages
finds unity and meaning in its relation to the *Imperator futurus*.
So the imperial myth of the ancient world finds its *telos*, its
goal. Every kingdom has its day. The day of the Son of Man
and His kingdom is the last day of history, the Day of Judgment. Then He who was before Abraham will appear on the
clouds of heaven, and those who pierced Him will see Him,
and all the generations of the earth will cry aloud. But the
children of the kingdom will lift up their heads. For the hour
of salvation has come. Jesus' mythical self-interpretation met
with a mighty response in the circle of the apostles. We open
the earliest Gospel, which is based on the message of the
earliest apostle, and in Mark 1.13 we read the earliest account
of the Temptation: 'And he was in the wilderness forty days
tempted of Satan; and he was with the wild beasts; and the
angels ministered unto him.'

'*Res magna est*', says Bengel on this passage. And rightly,
for all that can be said about the theme of Christ and nature
is contained in these few words.

The name of Son of Man is not used here. For its genuine
place is in Jesus' witness to Himself, not in the Church's witness to Christ. Nevertheless, something may be seen here of
the inexhaustible mythical content of the idea of Son of Man.
The picture of the primal man, the king of paradise, rises
again before our eyes, in the words of an old apocalypse:
'God created man and laid out paradise in the form of a city
and set man in it to be emperor and king over all, and Adam

established a rule of blessing.' The angels of heaven are subordinate to him, and he is a good shepherd to the beasts of the earth. But the Tempter brings the king of paradise to his Fall; the world of angels, his servants, withdraw, and the beasts rebel against the rebel. Paradise is lost, the harmony between heaven and earth is destroyed, the state of peace between man and beast is perverted to war of all against all.

But with the saviour-king of the last age the peace of the first age will return to creation. This is the promise of Biblical prophecy and apocalyptic; when God awakens the good shepherd who will make an end to the violent rule of the false shepherd, then will Jahveh establish a covenant of peace between heaven and earth and all creatures. A gracious rain will stream down from heaven, so that the earth will bear its fruit. And no beast on earth will rob and kill any more, so that man may dwell safely without any fear. Then the wolf shall dwell with the lamb, and the leopard shall lie down with the kid. Cows and lions will feed together, and a little child shall lead them. The sucking child will play on the hole of the asp, and the weaned child will put his hand on the basilisk's den. Then the devil will flee before the man of God, and the wild beasts will fear him, and angels will stand by him. 'For he shall give his angels charge over thee, to keep thee in all thy ways. They shall bear thee up in their hands, lest thou dash thy foot against a stone. Thou shalt tread upon the lion and adder: the young lion and the serpent shalt thou trample under feet' (Isa. 11.6ff.; Ps. 91.11ff.).

The cosmic hour of decision has come, says Mark (1.15). Here the epiphany of Christ is disclosed as God's answer to the natural myth of the ancient world: God has awakened the good shepherd. Straightway the Tempter rushes upon Him, to bring Him to a fall, as he brought the king of paradise in the first age to fall. But the Son of Man drives him back. And at once the beasts of the earth and the angels of heaven approach and assemble round the new King of paradise, who has overcome the Great Dragon, the ancient serpent, called the Devil and Satan. This is God's answer to the natural myth of the ancient world. This is a new beginning which is more than each year's beginning which was celebrated on new year's day by ancient man. It is an authentic beginning, at the decisive point in history, and thus a beginning whose influence stretches into the whole of history. Here the Gospel is revealed to all creatures. And angels and beasts bear witness to the epiphany for which the creation has waited since the days of the first age.

But at first they are the only witnesses. The epiphany of the Son of Man takes place far out in the desert, the revelation of the king of paradise is accomplished in deepest concealment. Nor can it be otherwise. For what happens here is only a sign of things to come—a fulfilment of an ancient promise, certainly, but a fulfilment full of promise, pointing beyond itself to the full revelation of the Son of Man in the peace of the creation made perfect.

So much for answer to the myth of imperial history and the myth of nature. What does the message of the epiphany of Christ say to the open questions of the classical myth of fate? We turn to the mysterious book of the last disciple, the Book of the Revelation, Chapter 5. All that can be said on the theme of Christ and fate is contained here.

The seer looks on the Ancient of Days, enthroned in the heavenly throne-room, in His hand a roll of writing with seven seals. In this parchment roll the Lord of heaven and earth has set down His eschatological will about the final fate of the whole world. But He has decreed that He Himself will not execute His will. Silent and unmoving He is enthroned, holding the roll of fate ready—for another.

The herald angel moved to the steps of the throne and proclaimed with a great voice, 'Who is worthy to open the book, and to loosen the seals thereof? And no one in the heaven, or on the earth, or under the earth, was able to do it.' Do we catch the echo of the opening words of the Decalogue? Thou shalt not bow down to them nor serve them, neither those in heaven, nor those on earth, nor those under the earth. Do we see how God's exclusive claim to majesty is here given its most realistic justification? No one was able to loosen the band of fate, no star in heaven, no emperor on earth, no spirit of the underworld.

And the seer wept, because no one was found worthy to
open the book and to loose its seals. Is there not something
of the weeping of Xerxes and of his general, something of
the Aristotelian shudder in face of the inescapable tragedy of
existence, in this weeping of the seer?

'But one of the elders said to the seer, Weep not: behold,
the Lion that is of the tribe of Judah, the Root of David,
hath overcome, to open the book and the seven seals thereof.'
A great victory has been won. The victory which no emperor
or king could win has been achieved by the Lion of Judah.
Now the book of fate, of world history, can be unrolled. We
listen and breathe again. For the frightening silence of God
is to be broken. His uncanny reserve is to end. The intoler-
able tension which burdens all creation is to be resolved.
God's fateful word is to be revealed, for judgment or grace,
for condemnation or acquittal.

God's Captain is long since home from the great victory,
back to the steps of the throne from which He went out. All
was ready for His reception, the Ancient of Days upon the
throne, and the eyes of all—His paladins, the heavenly Senate
and the myriads of ministering spirits—looked out to the Lion
of Judah, the noise of whose coming filled the spaces of
heaven. But He has already appeared, quiet and unrecognized,
and stands in the midst of the heavenly circle like a Lamb
that has been slain. And the Ancient of Days stretches forth
His hand and gives the sealed Book to the Victor of Golgotha. He who has ears to hear, let him hear! The Lord has
chosen the Crucified One to be the only Companion in knowledge, the Proclaimer and Fulfiller of His will for the end of
history. Now God's book of fate, the fate of the world, is
in His hand. Now the future of creation is put under the sign
of the Cross. So everything is decided. The need of humanity,
the curse upon our existence, the guilt which is our death,
the fate which tragedy could only exhibit not overcome, have
been overcome. Since the victory of Golgotha there is in truth
no more tragedy. That is the answer of the Gospel to the
ancient myth of fate.

The book is not yet unrolled, the creation does not yet

know what is in store for it. But it now knows who has been appointed steward of its fate, and that is enough. It falls down before the Lamb that has been slain, and sings a new song, that takes up into itself and resolves everything that has been sung from primordial times in the hymns to the sun and the songs of destiny and the heroic odes of the ancients. And the multitude of the heavenly hosts sing and worship in a liturgy of homage which comprises, and surpasses, every act of homage of which we have spoken: the homage of the wise men from the east, the homage of Simeon in the Temple, the homage of the beasts and the angels in the wilderness.

'And when the Lamb had taken the book, the four living creatures and the four and twenty elders fell down before the Lamb, having each one a harp, and golden bowls full of incense, which are the prayers of the saints. And they sing a new song, saying, Worthy art thou to take the book, and to open the seals thereof: for thou wast slain, and didst purchase unto God with thy blood men of every tribe, and tongue, and people, and nation, and madest them to be unto our God a kingdom and priests; and they reign upon the earth.

'And I saw, and I hear a voice of many angels round about the throne and the living creatures and the elders; and the number of them was ten thousand times ten thousand, and thousands of thousands; saying with a great voice, Worthy is the Lamb that hath been slain to receive the power, and riches, and wisdom, and might, and honour, and glory, and blessing.

'And every created thing which is in the heaven, and on the earth, and under the earth, and on the sea, and all things that are in them, heard I saying, Unto him that sitteth on the throne, and unto the Lamb, be the blessing, and the honour, and the glory, and the dominion, for ever and ever.

'And the four living creatures said, Amen. And the elders fell down and worshipped.'

We break off, and return once more to that historical act of homage of which we spoke at the beginning. What does Matthew say about the wise men from the east? 'And opening

their treasures they offered unto him gifts, gold and frankincense and myrrh.' They lay gold before Him as before a
royal throne and incense as before an altar. They do not offer
their homage to the dreaded king in Jerusalem, or to the
emperor who was worshipped in Rome, but to the Child in
Bethlehem, over whom the star of God is standing. In gratitude and adoration they lay at His feet the costliest products
of the east. And the Child from heaven does not scorn the
earth's dedications.

So classical man brought forth from the treasures of eastern
myth the most glorious things and laid them at the feet of
Jesus Christ, to glorify His epiphany. And the King of heaven
in the form of a servant did not scorn the gifts of gratitude
and adoration. Do we wish to rob Him of them? In the name
of the western spirit, or of modern man, or of science?

Surely we wish to do as the men of the east did, and to
lay at the feet of the Child of Bethlehem the greatest achievements of the spirit in our continent, in our knowledge of man
and the world and history, in order that east and west, the
classical world and the present, myth and science, may unite
in praise of His epiphany (Eph. 3.8ff.).

'Preach unto the Gentiles the unsearchable riches of Christ;
make all men see what is the dispensation of the mystery
which from all ages hath been hid in God who created all
things; to the intent that now unto the principalities and
powers in the heavenly places might be made known through
the church the manifold wisdom of God, according to the
eternal purpose which he purposed in Christ Jesus our
Lord: . . . to the end that ye . . . may be strong to apprehend
with all the saints what is the breadth and length and height
and depth, and to know the love of Christ which passeth
knowledge. . . .'

III

ART THOU HE THAT
SHOULD COME?

ONE of the earliest longings of mankind is the longing for
God to appear on earth. Egyptians and Persians, Greeks and
Romans, relate mysterious myths of gods who once walked
the earth in human form. In annual festivals they celebrated
the cult renewal of that mythical theophany—the epiphany
of Apollo, the advent of the sun-god, the birth of the heavenly
child of the Age, who was to lead in a new era of salvation.
With ecstatic cries and hymns they called on the god to appear:
'Come and do not delay!' For where the deity moves as a man
among men, the dream of the ages is fulfilled, the pain of the
world is scattered, and there is heaven on earth.

The readiness with which this longing for a mythical and
cultic theophany was expressed in contemporary and historical
form can be seen in the experience of the apostles in the city
of Lystra in Asia Minor. From earliest times the city had celebrated the epiphany of Zeus and Hermes with great pomp
(Acts 14.7ff.). When Barnabas and Paul approached the city,
and the fame of their miraculous deeds spread through the
streets, a tremendous wave of emotion ran through the people:
'The gods are come down to us in the likeness of men.' And
we are told how the priest of the temple of Zeus brought
oxen and garlands to the gates of the city, the people streaming after him, in order to welcome the gods Zeus and Hermes,
who were visiting their beloved city in the bodily form of the
foreign wanderers. But when the apostles saw what was happening they sprang forth among the multitude, crying, 'Sirs,
why do ye these things?'

This longing for a theophany was given a political form in

ancient Egypt which was to dominate classical culture and imperial history for more than three thousand years. The epiphany of the godhead, so runs the central dogma of this political philosophy, takes place in bodily form in the birth, the taking over of government, the entry of the Ruler. When the Pharaoh Thutmosis III had mounted the throne he summoned an imperial assembly, where he proclaimed: 'The god of heaven is my father. I am his son. He has begotten me, and commanded me to sit on his throne, while I was still a fledgling.' The assembled lords responded to this proclamation with the prayers and hymns suitable to a deity. When the Pharaoh appears at the 'epiphany window' of his palace, the people throw themselves on their faces and worship him in the words used in the worship of the sun: 'Hail to thee, O Pharaoh, god of the living, we see thy beauty once again.' And anyone summoned to an audience in the throne-room confesses in these words, 'A countenance is no longer afraid, when it sees thy countenance, and an eye that looks upon thee loses its fear.' When an oriental divine king assumes power, when the herald proclaims the gospel of the *parousia* of a Hellenist ruler, a new beginning is made with the reckoning of time. When the Assyrian Great King ascended the throne, there began for his peoples an age of salvation: 'Days of justice, years of righteousness, plenteous rainfall, good prices for merchandise. Old men leap for joy, children sing. The condemned are acquitted, the prisoners set free. The naked are clothed, the sick are cured.' When Demetrius, prince of the Diadoche, stepped from his chariot for the first time on to Athenian soil, it was as though a god had come from heaven, and at that memorable spot the Athenians erected an altar to commemorate the *katabasis*. In Palestine, when the emperor Titus appeared, fountains played again which had long been still. When the emperor Vespasian entered Alexandria the sick were healed; and when he made his entry into the imperial capital the people of Rome broke into spontaneous cries of enthusiasm, welcoming him as the fulfiller of every advent promise, who was ushering in the age of blessing. Evangel, katabasis, epiphany, parousia, advent—the whole ideology and formal idiom of the

37

classical expectation of a saviour have been given a political form. Who is the heavenly saviour whose coming the peoples have awaited? The emperor!

The official expression of this political philosophy is the classical coin. On the obverse of the coin we see the portrait of the ruler, decorated with the marks and emblems of deity, and framed in titles of divine dignity. For the ruler is the god who has become man. The reverse of the coin usually depicts the most symbolically potent event in the life of the ruler, his *advent*. Like a sign of things to come there appears on the coins of the Persian satraps the portrait of the Great King in solemn ascent, his hand raised in greeting and blessing. The *condottieri* of the late days of the Roman Republic show a more realistic outlook when they have the picture of their own arrival in some hard-pressed city or province depicted on the coins. But it was in the age of the emperors that the political advent philosophy reached its heyday. The first to have the word ADVENTUS inscribed on the coins was Nero. A Corinthian coin of Nero's reign, from the year 67, has on the obverse the type of the emperor in divine nakedness, adorned only with the laurel wreath of Apollo, and on the reverse the flagship with the imperial standard and above it the inscription ADVENTUS AUGUSTI, the Arrival of the August One. The divine Apollo once came by sea to the Greek mainland. The Roman emperor now makes his entry into Greece by sea, in order that he may be worshipped as Apollo incarnate. That was a year before the divine emperor's violent death. Two generations later the emperor Hadrian made a journey through the lands of his extensive empire, and wherever he went the people rejoiced and prayed and offered sacrifices, and even heaven blessed the fortunate earth which carried the emperor, by sending down rain upon it again. Hadrian commemorated this brilliant journey with an equally brilliant series of coins which glorify the ADVENTUS AUGUSTI in the different provinces. But these are imperial advent-coins, not Greek city coins as Nero's were. They show the patron goddesses of the provinces, surrounded by children carrying palms, welcoming the approaching emperor with a sacrificial offering. Among these coins is one with the 'Arrival of the August One in Judaea'. In fact Hadrian was received in Gerasa with a triumphal arch whose votive inscription has recently been recovered. But the entry into Jerusalem did not take place. For just at that time there raged a violent insurrection against the emperor and his advent philosophy.

The Epistle to the Hebrews makes a reference to the despairing repetition of the old ritual of sacrifice (9.8ff.). Each new sacrifice on the altar is a proof that the previous sacrifice, all previous sacrifices, were inadequate. Therefore every sacrifice bears in itself the mark of inadequacy. Yet the sacrifices are repeated, again and again. For each new sacrifice is a renewal of man's call for a sacrifice which will once for all, finally and fully, overcome the need which drives us to sacrifice. We cannot help thinking of these things as we survey the three thousand years of classical imperial history, with its monotonous repetition of its advent proclamation. Again and again the hope of the nations is kindled by some promising ruler, and again and again this political eschatology is thwarted. But the disillusioned peoples recover, and raise once again the old advent cry. And every new advent proclamation is the renewal of the demand which in the end is to be fulfilled once for all—the longing for God to become man. That is the despairing repetition in the political advent hope of the classical world.

The triumph of the *civitas dei* was to be reached by the self-exaggeration and self-destruction of the *civitas terrena*. The self-exaggeration and self-destruction of the classical advent philosophy was completed in the third century A.D. This is the century of which the schoolboy learns nothing because no young mind can bear the knowledge of what happened then. It was the century of the assassination of the emperors, of the sarcophagi of the dance of death, of the systematic persecutions of Christians, the century of twisted titles. Magnus, Maximus, Maximinus, Magnentius, Maxentius, Maximianus, Maximilianus, are the names given to themselves by those who wanted to be accounted important. In this century the political eschatology on which men had been nourished for thousands of years ran amok through the Roman world. About the year 260 Gallienus struck a coin with the inscription, 'The genius of the Roman people has entered the capital of the empire'. This patron spirit was incarnate in himself, the emperor Gallienus. In the same decade the imperial genius was murdered. In the year 275 Aurelian was celebrated as 'god and lord from birth'. In the same year the divine lord was murdered. The following year the emperor Probus ascended the blood-girt throne and struck a series of coins with the famous inscription ADVENTUS AUGUSTI and the portrait of the emperor riding up with his hand raised in greeting and blessing, led by the goddess Victoria. In the year 282 Probus was murdered. In 287 a coin of the emperor Carausius appeared, and on it we see Britannia greeting the emperor, as he arrived from the Continent, with the advent greeting EXPECTATE VENI, Come, Thou Longed-for One. In the Advent hymn the words are 'Thou Longing of all the world'. Carausius was murdered, and not long afterwards the emperor Constantius Chlorus entered the British capital. On his gold advent medal a kneeling female figure, symbol of London, receives him with raised hands as, just disembarked from his admiral's ship, he rides into the city, robed in his imperial garments. Above the figure of the emperor are the words REDDITOR LUCIS AETERNAE. It is the time of the sacred solstice, which ushers in the great revolution of all things. The heavenly sun-hero has appeared, who celebrates his epiphany on December 25 and leads the creation up out of the night of death and destruction into light. His entry is an epiphany of cosmic significance and the final victory of eternal light. In Christian hymn-books we call it 'Brightness of eternal dawn'.

This medallion is the most pretentious advent coin that was ever struck. But Constantius was the sixty-fifth emperor of the third century—and the father of Constantine the Great, who was great enough to grasp and to accomplish the will of history, who put the name of Jesus Christ upon his helmet.

The time is ripe. A new century, a new epoch, is on the way. An illusion of three thousand years has been shattered. The dream of the classical age, that God would be incarnate in the emperor, that political man is of divine origin and can bring salvation, is at an end. The political advent gospels, from the time of the Pharaohs to Constantius Chlorus, promised more than any emperor could fulfil. The political eschatology of classical times has broken up in the apocalyptic storms of the third century. The eternal light was not to be seen there.

The way was free for the revelation of the eternal Gospel, which fulfils the earliest demand of mankind, once for all; for the message of His Advent, His incarnation, His Kingdom. The eternal light breaks in there, and nowhere else. The ancient festivals of theophany disappear, driven out by the threefold festival which glorifies the epiphany of the One God: Advent, Christmas, Twelfth Night. The ancient dates and eras of advent disappear. The Advent of the One becomes the first date of a new reckoning of time, a new understanding of history. All previous history is the prologue to the Christmas history. All history since then is pre-history to the *Parousia* of Jesus Christ at the end of time.

'Who is worthy to open the book, and to loose the seals thereof?' cries the angel of the Apocalypse (5.2). No one was able, in heaven or on earth or under the earth, except the One who is mighty over heaven and earth and hell: EXPECTATE VENI.

IV

JULIUS CAESAR'S POLICY OF CONCILIATION

In the year 133 B.C. the Roman tribune of the plebs, Tiberius Gracchus, started an extensive scheme of land reform, which was to provide a healthy basis for the social life of the masses. In the same year he was assassinated by his conservative opponents, and along with him there were slain three hundred of the popular party. That was the beginning of a hundred years' civil war.

Ten years later Caius Gracchus took up his murdered brother's proposals, but he too was murdered, and with him three thousand of his friends. For some years the reactionaries possessed absolute power, by means of which they carried out a policy of hatred and destruction. 'The consul made the most unscrupulous use of the senate's victory against the party of the plebs', writes the contemporary historian Sallust, and he goes on: 'So the senate made ruthless use of its victory, removing many by execution or exile, but increasing rather public fears than their own power. In this way great State structures have always been destroyed, for one party wishes to conquer the other completely and then to take all the more ruthless revenge on the conquered section.' Sallust spoke from a full experience.

In the year 87 the opposition party came to power with the consul Cinna and the great soldier Marius as its leaders. The conservative senate was so naïve as to ask the new rulers to treat the citizens mildly. But of course the request was in vain. There was a reign of terror directed against all who belonged, or were accounted as belonging, to the opposition party, and it raged without bounds until the senate's commander, the experienced soldier Sulla, destroyed the legions of the popular party in a desperate campaign.

In the year 82 Sulla was appointed dictator by the senate. He rescinded every social law of the past fifty years, and launched a war of extirpation on the popular party which put all previous efforts of the kind into the shade. Thousands had fallen in battle. Many thousands more were put by the dictator on the so-called proscription lists. He proclaimed a state of emergency, and issued endless lists of the proscribed. Everyone whose name appeared on this black list was outlawed and condemned to death without trial or appeal. This was the new form which Sulla gave to the war of extirpation. After three years of this bloodthirsty rule Sulla resigned the office of dictator and withdrew to the country. But his proscription lists remained in the memory of the survivors like a sinister image of terror, and Sulla's ambiguous fame was proclaimed on his tomb with the words: 'He did good to his friends and evil to his foes like none before him.'

In the year 65 B.C. Julius Caesar began his official career, as aedile, in charge of the games for the Roman people. He sprang from one of the oldest noble families of Rome, which counted kings in its ancestry and traced its origin to the goddess Venus. His nature was royal, both in thought and in life there was greatness, and with the extravagant splendour of a king he organized for the people the games which were the most popular part of his duties. The year 65 was a great and splendid year—like a ceremonial overture to a new and better time after seventy years of violence and bloodshed. The Roman people never forgot that year, and ever afterwards the phrase *munificentia Caesaris* was used by them to mean a time of festival and rejoicing.

This royal figure became the leader of the popular party. What led him to that position? He despised the narrow and reactionary spirit of the senate clique, and he was convinced that their historical role was at an end. He loved the idea of the sovereign great kingdom in the sense of Alexander the Great, and believed that the problems alike of domestic and of foreign politics could only be solved by the establishment of a universal monarchy of a new kind. But above all he had a passion for having splendid men around him. Julius Caesar had the most royal passion of all: the passion to make men happy. That is why he lavished enormous sums from his own estate upon the great public games, and made the people's cause his own. That is why he wanted power. There are other interpretations of Julius Caesar, but none great enough to fit this truly great man.

Plato once said that 'the law is just, but the king is good'. Julius Caesar was a royal nature in this deepest sense of the word. He wanted power in order to practise goodness, in order to heal the world by *clementia*. Julius Caesar believed in a policy of clemency.

But he was no romantic enthusiast; on the contrary, he was an accomplished expert, even a virtuoso, in *Realpolitik*. He knew how to instil into the best men in his party his own belief in clemency. With his summons to clemency he showed his party new ways of work. And with this word *clementia* as propaganda he enormously strengthened the attraction of his party. From this time onwards a man of the popular party and a man of *clementia* were interchangeable ideas. What did Caesar desire? He desired appeasement, mercy. And what did the popular party desire? It desired a general amnesty. These strains had not been heard in Rome before. It was a new age.

Julius Caesar was in earnest about the new principle. In the domestic policy of the sixties and fifties a whole series of individual cases could be recounted in which the leader of the popular party showed that he was indeed the man of clemency. We take a single example. In the year 60 Caesar formed along with Pompey and Crassus the first triumvirate. In 59 Caesar became consul for the first time. That same year the ultra-conservative Marcus Junius Brutus struck his first coins of freedom, which are simply the defiant protest of the reactionary senate against the monarchist trend in the popular party.[1] But Caesar did not touch a hair of the young Brutus's

[1] The most important of them is a silver coin with the heads of the first consul Brutus and of Servilius Ahala, the murderer of the tyrant. This coin must not be confused with the gold coin in the *Münzkabinett* at Vienna which is made on the same model, but in 1863 was shown to be spurious.

head. In the same year Brutus was suspected of a conspiracy against Pompey; but Caesar saved him.

In 58 Caesar assumed the command in Gaul, and in the eight years of the Gallic War he had continual opportunities to work out the principle of clemency in the sphere of military and foreign policy. We know how passionately devoted the legions were to this Roman Napoleon. But we know too in what a masterly fashion he succeeded, in virtue of his clemency, in making a political conquest and friend out of the enemy who had been defeated in the field. He himself, at any rate, makes frequent reference in his war memoirs to this policy of conciliation in enemy country. Again and again he relates how the emissaries of the subjugated tribes appeal to his clemency: 'Deal with us in accordance with the mildness and magnanimity which are peculiar to you.' 'If you will treat us in accordance with the mildness and generosity which we have heard from reports of other tribes is peculiar to you, then leave us with our weapons.' We can see how Caesar's clemency has already become an international idea, a fixed formula in diplomatic language. Caesar himself replied to such pleas in these words: 'I will spare the town, less for its merits than for the sake of my custom.' And on another occasion he reported how in the name of the Roman people he extended pardon to the conquered tribe, instead of annexing its land.

Caesar's *Bellum Gallicum* is not the memoirs of an old man, willing to live the remainder of his life on proud memories of war, but it is a highly political work, written in the tumult of events and published just when Caesar was moving towards the decisive stroke of his political life, on the eve of the civil war. The Roman people were to be left in no doubt about the spirit in which Julius Caesar planned to conduct the struggle for power—and that was the spirit of clemency. But the public could also see, and were meant to see, from many an example of ruthless campaigning, that Caesar was no mere romantic weakling. The treatment of the Usipetes and the Tencteri, or the case of Vercingetorix, were sufficient illustration of this. So there were many people in Rome to whom the leader of the popular party and the conqueror of Gaul was

still a profoundly ambiguous or sinister figure. The historian
Sallust, for instance, sent a letter in the year 50 to Caesar in
which he besought him not to follow in the tracks of the
bloodthirsty Sulla.

In the last days of December of the same year the Roman
consul handed to the conservative Pompey the sword for the
defence of Rome against Caesar. And now the whole world
awaited with bated breath the unrolling of events.

In January of the year 49 the die was cast. Caesar marched
into Italy. One town after the other capitulated, one legion
after the other went over to him. Pompey fled from the
capital. By February Caesar was outside the town of Corfinium, east of Rome. He forced its capitulation, but let
Pompey's occupying forces go free. The news of this signal
act of clemency ran like wildfire through the Roman world.
The Caesarians seized on it for their propaganda, and in
speeches and letters praised the humanity and conciliatory
spirit of the conqueror and his abhorrence of every kind of
cruelty. His enemies, too, were given food for thought. Corfinium was the beginning of a moral victory for Caesar which
was no less successful than his military campaigns.

Meanwhile Caesar continued his march southwards, driving
Pompey before him. At the beginning of March, 49, he was
in Apulia, where he wrote an open letter to his friends, in
which he said: 'I heartily rejoice over your words of approval
of what I did in Corfinium. I will gladly avail myself of your
counsel, and will the more gladly do what I had already decided
to do of my own accord, to be as mild as possible and to
make every effort for a reconciliation with Pompey. In this
way, if it is possible, we want to try to regain everyone's trust
and enjoy a lasting peace. For our predecessors, in virtue of
their cruelty, were not able to escape hatred, and could maintain their victory for but a short time—with the exception
of Lucius Sulla, whose model I do not intend to follow. *Haec
nova sit ratio vincendi, ut misericordia et liberalitate nos muniamus*
—let this be the new way of conquering, that our strength
and our security lie in pity and generosity. How to realize
this in very deed is a subject about which I have many thoughts,

and there are many ways still to be discovered for its accomplishment.'

The conciliation of Corfinium, and these words about the new way of conquering, together exhibit the same spirit and the same man, and they did not fail of their effect. Even the sceptical Cicero succeeded in uttering a few appreciative words. Caesar took him up at once, and wrote: 'You have interpreted me aright, for you know how nothing is further from my nature than cruelty. Nothing is dearer to me than to remain true to my character and the Pompeians to theirs.' But Cicero's mind was too small to grasp properly the greatness and newness of what Caesar's actions proclaimed. He was too pleased with his clever scepticism, and as late as May 49 he was having witty conversations with his friends about Pompey's Sullan cruelty and the *insidiosa clementia*, the insidious clemency, of Caesar—conversations devoid of understanding, and stuffed with mistrust and fear. When a decision had to be taken one way or the other, Cicero decided for Pompey.

Meantime Caesar and Pompey armed themselves, both morally and militarily, for the final struggle. A classical historian gives the following account: 'Caesar showed marvellous moderation and clemency in the conduct of the civil war. Pompey declared that he would treat everyone as an enemy who was disloyal to the cause of the republic. Caesar proclaimed that he would account mediating statesmen and neutrals as his friends. Every officer whom he had appointed on the recommendation of Pompey was freely permitted to cross over to Pompey's camp. When the conditions for capitulation were being negotiated in Spain (at Ilerda), and in consequence a lively traffic arose between the two camps, the enemy leaders Afranius and Petreius suddenly turned round and had every soldier of Caesar's who was in the Pompeian camp seized and slain. But Caesar could not bring himself to repay this perfidy in kind' (Suetonius).

In the autumn of 48 Caesar gained the decisive victory over Pompey at Pharsalus. After the battle countless prisoners fell at the victor's feet and besought him with tears for their life. Caesar replied with a few words about his lenience (*de lenitate*

47

sua) and pardoned them all without exception. So Caesar himself relates. A Roman historian of the time of Christ calls this act of mercy a *munus misericordiae*, a work of mercy. And the sober Pliny writes: 'Caesar's special and most profound characteristic was his royal clemency, with which he conquered and converted all men. So he showed the example of a great spirit, such as cannot be seen again. . . . But the genuine and incomparable height of his all-conquering heart is seen most clearly at Pharsalus. For when the coffers with the Pompeian papers fell into his hands, he caused them to be burnt, *optima fide*, without so much as casting a glance at them.'

In the same spirit Caesar declared in 47 in the Alexandrine War, 'I do nothing more gladly than grant an amnesty to those who plead for mercy.' In the same style he conducted the moral and military campaign in 46 against Cato and the last of the resistance in Africa. We hear how the defeated general encouraged his anxious troops with the words, 'I have great confidence in Caesar's clemency.' His confidence was not misplaced. 'Caesar's clemency towards the defeated was the same as in earlier instances', says a classical report. And Pliny recounts how Caesar had all the enemy papers destroyed unseen, precisely as at Pharsalus. Similarly the defeated Pompeians in Spain appealed to Caesar's clemency, from which they hoped for every security, and in fact experienced it. At the same time Caesar won the heart of the pusillanimous Cicero, granting him unmolested return to Rome and complete freedom of action.

In March 45 Caesar defeated the last of the Pompeian party in Spain. Now he was master of the Roman world. Now the twelve last and most royal months of this royal life began, exactly twenty years after he had launched his political career with the unforgettable games and the programme of conciliation of the popular party.

The first and fundamental action of the conqueror was the establishment of a total amnesty which far surpassed even the most unlikely promises of the years of war. It is not possible to give in detail the contemporary witnesses to this unique work of amnesty. We quote only three summary reports from

classical historians. Velleius Paterculus says: 'Caesar returned
to the capital city as conqueror over all his opponents and
—incredible though it may seem to us—proclaimed a general
amnesty for all who had taken up arms against him. Such was
the clemency exercised by the great man in all his victories.'
Suetonius reports: 'Finally, in the last year of his life, he permitted everyone, without exception, who had not yet received
an amnesty, to return to Italy and enter on the highest government offices and military posts. He even had the statues of
Lucius Sulla and Gnaeus Pompeius, which had been torn
down by the populace, made new and set up again. And he
preferred to hinder than to punish hostile plans and utterances
which were later directed against his own person. Thus he
prosecuted conspiracies and secret meetings which were un-
masked, simply by delivering edicts that he knew all about
them. When men spoke spitefully about him he was content
to warn them in parliament not to do it any more. Even the
hurt done to his name by the lies of Aulus Caecina and the
libellous verses of Pitholaos he bore with urbanity (*civili
animo*).' And Dio Cassius writes: 'By releasing from any
punishment those of his opponents who had survived, and
pardoning them all on the same conditions, even advancing
them to government offices; by returning their marriage-
portions to the widows of the fallen, and giving the children
a part of their father's inheritance—in these ways he showed
up the infamous practices of Sulla, and earned the greatest
praise not only for courage but also for mildness, difficult
though it generally is for a man to behave the same in peace
as in war.'

We mention only one example of Caesar's liberal policies,
again the example of Marcus Junius Brutus. In the year 46,
at the close of the African war, Cato, the fanatical enemy of
Caesar, committed suicide in order that he might not survive
the downfall of the conservative cause. In 45 Brutus (his
nephew and adopted son) married his daughter Porcia and
composed an address of homage to the memory of the great
fighter for freedom. Caesar left him alone, and appointed him
praetor urbanus for the year 44, that is, president of the Roman

49

senate and supreme court of justice, and deputy chief of police.

Cicero was overwhelmed. That was more than he could understand. He felt himself all the more clearly called to play in his own way the philosophical accompaniment to Caesar's historical deeds. 'We do not find with you what we have found with every victor in civil war. You are the only one, Gaius Caesar, at whose victory no one has lost his life, except in battle.' So he addresses the dictator. In dithyrambic speeches he praises the *clementissimus dux*, the most-merciful leader, his 'unique and unheard-of', his 'wonderful and praiseworthy *clementia*'. With wise insight he speaks in letters to friends of Caesar's 'unique humanity' and 'incredible generosity', of his 'mild and good nature'. And again he turns to Caesar himself, this time with upraised finger: 'Do not weary of saving the good nobles, who have suffered a fall through no selfishness or evil in themselves, but in fulfilment of a supposed duty, fools perhaps, but not criminals.' One can imagine how thankful Caesar was for these political lessons. 'It is astonishing what Caesar let people say to him', writes the modern historian L. Wickert. Probably the dictator was content with an ironical smile. But Cleopatra, his peer in greatness of spirit, let the wordy Cicero know in her own way what the general opinion of him was. When the wise politician made his entry into her Roman salon with much bowing and scraping, she stepped up to him and greeted him with the ambiguous words, 'How happy I am to get to know personally the greatest virtuoso in words in Rome.' Cicero blinked for a moment, a little uncertainly, but soon recovered and continued his hymn of praise without any sign of embarrassment.

The senate too was carried away by the general attitude, and made a unique decision in honour of the unique historical moment. It appointed Caesar as father of his country and decreed that a special temple should be built for the *clementia Caesaris*. There Caesar and his divine *clementia* were to be set up and worshipped, and on the pediment of the temple a globe of the world would proclaim that the clemency of Caesar spanned the whole world.

Caesar himself celebrated festivals as never before, and with him the whole people. Seventy, a hundred, years later tales were told of the fantastic October festival in the year 45. 'He filled the city with the most magnificent gladiatorial games, with sea-battles, cavalcades, elephant-fights and other spectacles, and celebrated a mass banquet which lasted for days.'

It was not only the capital which was to know of these things, the whole Roman world was to unite in celebrations around the festal figure of the man who was setting mankind free from need and hatred and fear. So coins were struck with the type of Caesar with the inscription PATER PATRIAE, or the temple of mercy with the words CLEMENTIA CAESARIS, and reverse in both instances a riding-scene from the October festival. These coins were intended as good tidings, messengers of the man who was filled with the royal passion to have joyful men and a joyful world around him.

It is well known that Beethoven dedicated his Eroica Symphony to the consul Napoleon Bonaparte—and then later tore up and trampled on the dedicatory page. He could have dedicated his Ninth Symphony to the memory of Caesar, and would not have had to withdraw it. For Caesar strode and stormed and danced his way through life like Beethoven's symphony. The last twelve years of his life are like a single song to joy—

Joy, thou lovely spark divine, daughter of Elysium,
Drunk with fire we near thy holy presence, O thou heavenly one.

And again—

Grief and poverty must come, and joyous with the joyful be,
Revenge and grudges all forgotten, enemies forgiven be.
Annihilate your book of debts, be with the whole world reconciled!
Joy is sparkling in the beakers, in the ripe grape's golden blood. . . .

And once more—

Joy, thou lovely spark divine, daughter of Elysium.

That breathes the very spirit of Julius Caesar, the spirit of reconciliation, the spirit of free and festal life.

On March 15, 44, Caesar was assassinated by a band of reactionary senators. The moving spirit in the conspiracy was

Marcus Junius Brutus, the Roman Judas. When Caesar saw him push forward with naked dagger, he uttered only the three Greek words, *kai su teknon?*—You too child? Then he covered his face, and collapsed beneath twenty-three wounds. So relates the old tradition in Suetonius and Dio Cassius. It is not possible to present the historical tragedy of this moment in more simple human fashion. Throughout his life Caesar believed in the political evidence of his clemency, in the persuasive and winning power of his policy of forgiveness. 'I will rather be slain than feared, and build upon the clemency which I practise', he was in the habit of saying when pressed to adopt a policy of armed security. Marcus Brutus betrayed the confidence and mocked the faith of Caesar's life. That was the serpent's sting which destroyed Caesar.

Cicero put it in this way: '*Clementia* became the dictator's fate, his generosity became his destruction.' The classical historians agreed with him, and the Christian historian Orosius wrote: 'He was destroyed in the effort to build the political world anew, contrary to the example of his predecessors, in the spirit of clemency.'

The Roman people glorified the dead Caesar in a unique passion-liturgy, which echoes the ancient eastern laments for the death of the great gods of blessing, and many of whose motifs show an astonishing connexion with the Good Friday liturgy of the Roman mass. 'Those whom I saved have slain me', they sang in the name of the murdered man. And Antony declared before the temple of Venus, where the son of the goddess lay in state: 'Truly the man cannot be of this world whose only work was to save where anyone needed to be saved.'

The assassins of the Ides of March were wrong to suppose they could destroy Caesar's work, or mock the will of history. They had to pay dearly for the dagger-blow at Caesar's *clementia*. Caesar dead caused more trouble to his enemies than Caesar living, wrote a contemporary historian. Once more the bloodthirsty ghost of the proscriptions went through the land, and three hundred senators and two thousand knights were to die before the young Augustus resumed his father's policy of conciliation.

We have related nothing but facts, and only the most important of these. We have had to leave aside a great deal, and we have not entered into the passionate controversy which swings to and fro in judgment of Caesar and his *clementia*. We have thought it more useful to let Caesar and his contemporaries speak as far as possible in their own words.

From the history of Caesar's clemency three things may be learned.

First, this clemency of Caesar is embedded like a metaphysical postulate in the stormy history of that advent century before the turning-point of all time. The Christian knows how God Himself, and God alone, fulfilled that postulate. Caesar's work of conciliation fell to pieces. Christ's work of reconciliation was accomplished.

Second, Caesar's use of amnesty in *Realpolitik* is a legacy for all later political history. And mankind has had to atone bitterly for every neglect of Caesar's *clementia*.

Third, a Church which takes all these facts seriously must remind the peoples of the world, their politicians and their lawyers, with fresh courage and a fresh sense of responsibility, of the words which Caesar spoke two thousand years ago: 'Let this be the new way of conquering, that our strength and our security lie in pity and generosity.'

V

AUGUSTUS AND CLEOPATRA

DANTE speaks in the *Paradiso* of the eagle of world monarchy who rose in the East and in the course of history winged
his flight ever further to the West. Ancient history proves
that Dante is right.

Majestically the eagle of the *imperium mundi* rose over the
land masses of the Near East. For almost three thousand
years it circled round the great empires on the Euphrates and
the Nile. That was the age of the land empires of early antiquity. But a thousand years are in the course of history but
a day, and as the night when it is gone. The eagle of world
domination flew unceasingly westwards, appearing over the
Mediterranean, first over the Phoenician coasts, then over
Athens, Alexandria, Carthage, and finally Rome. For a thousand years it circled over the Mediterranean lands. That was
the age of classical antiquity.

So the general theme of classical imperial history is the
struggle for the mastery of the Mediterranean, the struggle
between the old East and the young West, a struggle of power
and a struggle of principle. And each time the end of the
struggle was the victory of the West over the East. For it is
not man's will which determines the destiny of the nations,
but the majestic will of history. The history-maker is the
man who recognizes this will and carries it out in free
obedience.

The struggle for the mastery of the Mediterranean was concentrated in two great decisive battles. The first was the sea
battle of Salamis, in the year 480 B.C. Athens fought against
Persepolis, and Europe won its freedom for thousands of
years. The second was the sea battle of Actium, in the year

31 B.C., when Rome fought against Alexandria, and won its leading position, likewise for thousands of years.

The drama of Salamis was written by Aeschylus, the founder of European tragedy, and himself a combatant in the great battle. And Herodotus, the father of European history, put Salamis in the centre of his History. The battle of Actium was celebrated by Rome's greatest poet, Virgil, in fifty-four apocalyptic verses, and he made it the centre of his epic. And indeed the spectacle which reached its climax at Actium was of fateful dimensions: two worlds clashed, a dying and a rising world. And each assumed flesh and blood in two persons who embodied and fulfilled the highest capacities of each world, and who entered on the struggle with the profound consciousness that they carried in themselves the life of their world, and that with them their world would live or die. These two persons were Cleopatra and Augustus: Cleopatra, an ageing woman, the last melancholy blossom of the dying world of the East, overshadowed by the tragedy of historical guilt and necessity; and Augustus, the youthful, incarnate genius of the awakening West, who ran his victorious course with the innocent brutality of a natural force. No ancient historian has fittingly depicted this unique encounter, but the two opponents have themselves left tokens of their struggle, official and original documents, which have been preserved unharmed, and which are more valuable than any literary product. By a study of these tokens it is possible to be an immediate witness of the great struggle of principles which was fought at that time between East and West, and to gain deep insight into the life of the two opponents.

These original documents are the coins which were minted by Cleopatra and Augustus.

Coins of ancient times are not to be compared with the insignificant coins of modern times. A modern coin is nothing more than a means of payment. An ancient coin is a political weapon, it is at once the newspaper, the radio and the news-reel, serving the politicians for the spreading of their news and their ideas, the proclaiming of their programmes, and the winning of adherents to their side. The politics of

ideas, wars of ideas, were not unknown to them. They created
the type of the political coin, and with the aid of portraits
and inscriptions they bombarded their opponents with deliberate propaganda which was as exciting as a modern newspaper war. In this art of war by means of coins the first great
masters were Cleopatra and Augustus. The coins which were
struck at that time not only developed into a first-rate political
instrument, but they made no small contribution to the clari-
fication, sharpening and conclusion of the great struggle of
principle between East and West. A large number of these
coins have survived and may be seen in European collections,
as splendid as on the day they were minted.

Cleopatra wore the crown of Egypt, the oldest crown of
history. We must not forget this for a moment, for Cleopatra
herself never forgot it. Four thousand years B.C., when the
women of Europe still sat in their lake-dwellings and painted
their pots of clay, there flourished in the women's apartments
in the palaces of Egypt a refined courtly culture with all the
arts of a sophisticated civilization. The height which this civilization had reached may be imagined when we learn that
there is in the Museum in Cairo a make-up palette which is
one of the oldest Egyptian works of art, whose lines and
workmanship are as fine as the Old Berlin powder-box in
Sanssouci, the gift of Frederick the Great to his friend Voltaire.
About the year 3200 B.C. the Pharaoh Menes founded the
Egyptian empire, the first world empire.[1] At that time the
tribal chiefs of Europe were still fighting one another with
stone axes. The Pharaohs lived in palaces on the Nile built
like temples, and were laid to rest finally in pyramids as tall
as Strasbourg Cathedral, surrounded by temple buildings for
the perpetual worship of the glorified Pharaoh. For the
Pharaoh was of divine origin and dignity, and his race was
holy. Only his sister could be his wife, and she alone could
be laid beside him in the heart of the pyramid. So in Egyptian royal history women played a quite special part. About
1500 B.C. the 'divine wife' Hatsheput was enthroned in the
temple palaces of Egypt, and lorded it over the peoples of

---

[1] We shall not discuss here the controversies about this date.

the empire as well as over her little brother Thutmosis, who for twenty years filled the role of prince consort. After her death, however, Thutmosis discovered a unique talent for sovereignty, and became the greatest Pharaoh of all time, creating the Egyptian world empire, dominating the whole civilized world from Tunis and Ethiopia to Asia Minor and Mesopotamia, and the Mediterranean from Malta to Crete and Cyprus. At the same time the first modest beginnings of the Chinese empire were developing on the Yangtse-Kiang.

Almost a hundred years later the heretical king Amenophis IV ruled in Egypt with his sister-wife Nofretete. By this time the Germanic tribes were pushing along the Rhine in wretched little boats made of hide. About 600 B.C. the twenty-sixth dynasty was reigning on the Nile. About that time the founder of the Japanese royal house flourished, and the kingdom of the Maya in Central America arose; the first Indian empire came still later. In 331 B.C. the Greek Alexander conquered the land of the Pharaohs. The Egyptian priests cleverly welcomed him as the son and emissary of Ammon the god of heaven. Alexander determined to make Egypt the base for a new world empire, and founded a new city on the delta of the Nile which he intended to make his world capital. This was the origin of Alexandria. Alexander carried his campaigns into Asia, and died in Babylon. But he was buried in Egypt, first in the ancient capital of Memphis, and later in Alexandria. One of his generals, the Greek Ptolemy, ascended the throne of the Pharaohs, becoming the founder of a new dynasty, the thirty-first to reign over the ancient land of the Nile and for a time as far as Carthage and Babylon. Alexandria, dominating the sea-routes, was his capital. Once more as in the days of the Pharaohs the kings of Egypt were enthroned as gods in human form. Once more in accordance with the ancient custom they married their sisters, and more than one of these proud women held undisputed sway in Alexandria. The last of that brilliant line was Cleopatra, the seventh queen of that name, with a genealogy reaching back to the ancestress of Alexander the Great.

Cleopatra had the dominating spirit of Hatsheput and the

nobility of Nofretete, but she was greater than either of them. She inherited a national kingdom, and set before herself the aim of creating an empire greater than the empires of Thutmosis and Alexander, a Mediterranean kingdom stretching from Gibraltar in the west to Babylon in the east, with Alexandria as its centre. To this end she used every means which lay in the power of a highly intelligent woman. She has become a legendary figure among the nations, the great mistress, enthroned upon many waters, playing at love with the kings of the earth, and intoxicating the world with the story of her loves. 'And I saw a woman sitting on the scarlet-coloured beast that comes up out of the abyss and goes to perdition. And the woman was arrayed with purple and scarlet, and decked with gold and precious stones and pearls, having in her hand a golden cup full of abominations, even the unclean things of her fornication, and she is called the mother of the harlots and of the abominations of the earth.'[1] Only the language of the Apocalypse is great enough, only a view clear of bourgeois prejudices is impartial enough, to do justice to this elemental figure. Cleopatra was greeted by the Sibyl as the divinely commissioned avenger of the East on the impious capital of the West. A Coptic bishop of the seventh century called her the greatest woman of all time: 'She was great, and she did great things.' Historians of the late classical age have written at length of the magic of her beauty. A book about beauty culture—and one thinks of that early Egyptian make-up palette and of the highly sophisticated appearance of Nofretete —passes under the name of Cleopatra. In modern times Arthur Brome Weigall has broken a lance for Cleopatra. But the preponderant historical tradition treats of this demonic woman with horror, and in schoolbooks she appears as a vicious figure. Certainly, it is true that this great seductress did not possess conventional beauty. She was of the number of those women in whose presence men tremble—not brilliant in beauty, like Helen, but rather with the quality of the melancholy Kundry. She was neither given to unbridled lust, nor ready to sell her

[1] It seems to me that the prophecy of Jeremiah 51.13 first referred to Cleopatra before it was transferred, in Rev. 17.8f., to Rome. See pp. 188f.

love to the highest bidder. She was a figure of majesty, like Brunhilda, who could love only the strongest natures, and as thanks for her love received crowns like dedicatory offerings. It was in the nature of things that it should be a Roman whom this last queen of the East loved with such a fateful love.

When Cleopatra's ancestor ascended the holy throne of the Pharaohs the little country town of Rome in Central Italy was at war with the neighbouring towns. When the Ptolemies ruled from Alexandria, the young city of Rome was struggling with the ancient Phoenician sea capital of Carthage for the mastery. Rome triumphed, and from that time there were two great sea-powers in the Mediterranean, Alexandria in the East and Rome in the West. But Rome had the last word, even in Egyptian affairs. When Egypt was threatened by Macedonia, Rome took under its protection the young king of the Ptolemies in Alexandria. When the king of Syria fell upon Egypt, he was met before the walls of Alexandria by a Roman officer, who summoned him in the name of the senate to depart. The king asked for time to take counsel. The Roman drew a circle in the sand round the wavering king, and said brusquely: 'Take counsel here!' The king accepted the ultimatum, and the triumphant Syrian army yielded to a single Roman. For the second time Alexandria was saved by Roman intervention. That was in 168 B.C. Not quite a hundred years later, in 69 B.C., Cleopatra was born. At that time Pompey was the greatest figure in the Mediterranean world, and the protector of the Ptolemies. The father of Cleopatra died in May, 51, and she inherited the throne. So at the age of seventeen a girl inherited the most ancient crown in the world. The traditional marriage to her brother, Ptolemy XIV, was no more than a formality, for he was only a child of ten. The civil war between Pompey and Caesar broke out two years later, and the young son of Pompey appeared in Alexandria to seek help for his hard-pressed father. He obtained sixty grain-ships for his father, and, it is said, the love of Cleopatra for himself. In 48 Cleopatra was driven from Alexandria by power-seeking friends of her brother, and the little Ptolemy was set on the throne. In the same year Caesar defeated Pompey, who sought asylum at the court of Ptolemy. But Ptolemy betrayed Pompey, and sent the victorious Caesar the head of his rival as a token of homage and a plea for favour. By this time Caesar was the acknowledged master of the world. He was expected to confirm the boy-king Ptolemy on his throne. He landed at Alexandria and took up quarters in Ptolemy's palace. Cleopatra, however, rapidly sized up the situation and took action in her own way. Rolled up in a carpet, she had herself smuggled into Alexandria, into the palace, into Caesar's room. Confucius once said, 'In this world there has never been so much done for justice as for a pretty face.' Cleopatra knew this, and it was her fortune. The elderly Caesar fell hopelessly in love with her. By the next morning he was convinced of the young queen's right to the throne, and he had her restored immediately. In the ensuing struggle the young Ptolemy was slain in battle, and his eleven-year-old brother Ptolemy XV became Cleopatra's 'husband' and partner on the throne. But now, Cleopatra took an independent course, and began to strike coins with her own head on the obverse and the coat-of-arms of the Ptolemies, the eagle, on the reverse; she was the first of the Ptolemies to strike coins in her own name and with her own portrait. So we know what she looked like at that time, the deified mistress of the deified man, lording it secretly over the lord of the world. In the summer of 47 she bore a son, the only son Caesar ever had. He was given the names Ptolemy Caesar. The two names together announce a programme: the child was to inherit Roman might and Egyptian tradition, he was to be the universal heir of the old empires. For he was a divine child, born to divine parents. For millennia the courtly art of Egypt had loved to depict the divine origin of the Pharaoh. We can see the annunciation of the child of promise in the council of the gods, the coming of the sun-god in human form to the queen (as in a relief in the nativity temple of Der el Bahri), the birth of the divine child, its nourishment and upbringing by goddesses, and even how, like the young sun-god himself, the child sucks his thumb. In perfect accord with this tradition the Egyptian people believed that the sun-god Ra had come to the last of the line of the Pharaohs in him the whole people. Seventy, a hundred, years later tales were told of the fantastic October festival in the year 45. 'He filled the city with the most magnificent gladiatorial games, with sea-battles, cavalcades, elephant-fights and other spectacles, and celebrated a mass banquet which lasted for days.'

It was not only the capital which was to know of these things, the whole Roman world was to unite in celebrations around the festal figure of the man who was setting mankind free from need and hatred and fear. So coins were struck with the type of Caesar with the inscription PATER PATRIAE, or the temple of mercy with the words CLEMENTIA CAESARIS, and reverse in both instances a riding-scene from the October festival. These coins were intended as good tidings, messengers of the man who was filled with the royal passion to have joyful men and a joyful world around him.

It is well known that Beethoven dedicated his Eroica Symphony to the consul Napoleon Bonaparte—and then later tore up and trampled on the dedicatory page. He could have dedicated his Ninth Symphony to the memory of Caesar, and would not have had to withdraw it. For Caesar strode and stormed and danced his way through life like Beethoven's symphony. The last twelve years of his life are like a single song to joy—

Joy, thou lovely spark divine, daughter of Elysium,
Drunk with fire we near thy holy presence, O thou heavenly one.

And again—

Grief and poverty must come, and joyous with the joyful be,
Revenge and grudges all forgotten, enemies forgiven be.
Annihilate your book of debts, be with the whole world reconciled!
Joy is sparkling in the beakers, in the ripe grape's golden blood. . . .

And once more—

Joy, thou lovely spark divine, daughter of Elysium.

That breathes the very spirit of Julius Caesar, the spirit of reconciliation, the spirit of free and festal life.

On March 15, 44, Caesar was assassinated by a band of reactionary senators. The moving spirit in the conspiracy was

and the birth of the new
official nativity temple at
of the legend. The votive
imaged, is from the year
nded by goddesses, above
fother of Ra'. Above the
e symbol of the scarab,
Caesar as the god of the
ebrate Cleopatra as the
e child in her arms into
yptian pantheon, Venus
, inscriptions and papyri
in Alexandria as late as
was worshipped as the
leopatra carry on their
ouble rule of the new
louble cornucopia sur-

e East followed Caesar
ved in a garden palace
Iber. On every hand in
red Egyptian shrines.
rum to his ancestress
e goddess with Cupid
child who is sucking
oung Ptolemy Caesar,
stress in person into
atue of the goddess,
olden statue of Cleo-
yle of the Alexandrian
t a copy of this por-
in the marble head
by Ludwig Curtius
e from the realm of
anny because it acts
of choice and will;
it is Shakespeare's
d in Rome a small

silver coin, the reverse type the familiar horn of plenty with the diadem, set over the world, and the obverse a smiling winged child: doubtless this is an imitation of the portraits of Cupid in the new temple of Venus, and very likely also an allusion to the growing child of heaven, the future divine ruler of the world. About this time Virgil probably received the first impulses for his Eclogue on the Saviour-child who was to come—that Advent song in which the 'Egyptian' motifs play so marked a part. In the same year Caesar drafted a law which was to permit polygamy for himself, thus making Cleopatra his legal consort and Ptolemy Caesar his legitimate son.

Cleopatra's stay in Rome was of enormous significance for imperial politics. Her magic took effect. For in those months there came to maturity in the Roman Caesar the great idea of a world monarchy of the Eastern style, sanctioned by his marriage with the heiress of the Pharaohs, and glorified by the divine honours paid to the reigning monarch; a world empire stretching from Gibraltar to Persia and turning the Mediterranean into a lake—just as Cleopatra herself had dreamed in her youth. Caesar began his preparations for the decisive campaign against the Parthians, who held the mastery of the Euphrates and the Persian Gulf. In the Eastern tradition, and quite contrary to Roman custom, his likeness was already appearing on coins. His portrait was being decked with emblems of divinity. The diadem was within his grasp. On March 15, 44, he was assassinated by a band of Republicans of old Rome, who preferred freedom to world dominion under an autocratic divine king. The daemon of Cleopatra had destroyed its victim. Some weeks later Cleopatra herself fled to Egypt.

There were three possible successors to Caesar: the three-year-old Caesarion, as Cleopatra's son was popularly called; the nineteen-year-old Octavius, called Octavianus, and later Augustus, grandson of a Roman banker and grand-nephew of the dictator, his adopted son and legal heir; and finally, the forty-year-old Antony, Caesar's most popular general, who had first made a name for himself as a young cavalry captain

Judas. When Caesar saw
gger, he uttered only the
—You too child? Then he
ath twenty-three wounds.
onius and Dio Cassius. It
al tragedy of this moment
hroughout his life Caesar
his clemency, in the per-
licy of forgiveness. 'I will
upon the clemency which
g when pressed to adopt
Brutus betrayed the con-
sar's life. That was the
r.
ia became the dictator's
ction.' The classical his-
istian historian Orosius
t to build the political
of his predecessors, in

ad Caesar in a unique
nt eastern laments for
, and many of whose
with the Good Friday
om I saved have slain
red man. And Antony
where the son of the
nnot be of this world
e needed to be saved.'
re wrong to suppose
ck the will of history.
low at Caesar's clem-
to his enemies than
rian. Once more the
nt through the land,
usand knights were
d his father's policy

in a forced march upon Alexandria, when he had overwhelmed the Egyptian frontier post of Pelusium, and was now the most powerful man in Rome.

Cleopatra took the little Caesarion with her to Alexandria. There she had her young brother and husband destroyed, raising her three-year-old son to share her throne, as PTOLE-MAIOS HO KAI KAISAR THEOS PHILOPATOR KAI PHILOMETOR, Ptolemy Caesar, God, and Beloved Son of his Father and Mother. Henceforth this was to be his official name. The name tells the whole story. It contains the claim to a divine kingdom and to world dominion, and it reveals the will of an almost omnipotent woman. It was not long before the whole world could see what this will was able to achieve. Cleopatra at once set about building a great fleet, and she conducted in person the first manœuvres of this fleet in the Mediterranean, while the battle for power in the Roman world swayed hither and thither.

The young Augustus, as we shall now call him, had meantime built up a mercenary army, drawing upon his private resources, and was coolly and calculatingly establishing his power in Italy. He was a true Roman, not storming triumphantly onwards, but 'stubbornly pressing on', and never yielding any ground. This was the fashion in which Rome had established itself in the centuries-long struggle of the Mediterranean powers, and now it was the fashion in which this nineteen-year-old Roman established himself in the long-drawn-out struggle of party leaders and *condottieri*.

Antony withdrew to the East, and there this first marshal of the empire succumbed to the ancient magic of the Orient. Kings came to meet him, and queens competed for his favour with their beauty and their love. He forgot Italy. It seemed strangely small to him now, and its civilization ridiculously young and poor, like a half-grown girl. He forgot Fulvia, his wife, waiting for him in Italy, and busy with politics on his behalf. It is true that at that time he had coins struck in Syria and elsewhere which bore Fulvia's as well as his own portrait —and they are the first coins to carry the portrait of a living Roman woman. But this was all he did for her. There are

other coins which show more clearly than the somewhat bourgeois double portrait the things which really engaged Antony's
whole heart. For instance, there is one showing his head and
that of the sun-god together, and the two heads are remarkably similar. Such a coin is both a confession and a programme. The East was his world, to which his affections and
his whole life were given. The sun was his primal image, he
wanted to rise like a sun-god and to reign like a sun-king over
the peoples of the East. It is in the East that such thoughts
arise, and in the East that they find their response. Plutarch
relates how Antony was received in Ephesus with divine
honours. The people streamed to meet him, in a festal procession of nymphs and bacchantes, and they celebrated his
advent in the capital city of Asia Minor with ivy wreaths and
ecstatic dancing to the music of the harp, welcoming him as
the reincarnate Bacchus and Father of Joys. It was in Tarsus,
the native town of the Apostle Paul, that he met Cleopatra,
and there his fate was sealed. In Plutarch or in Shakespeare
we may read how the Eastern goddess of Love made her
ceremonial entry into Tarsus on a galley with purple sails,
silver rowlocks and stern and canopy of gold, surrounded by
nymphs and cupids, sailing to meet the new Bacchus. As a
twenty-eight-year-old captain of cavalry Antony had once seen
the fourteen-year-old Cleopatra in Alexandria, and never forgotten her. Now at the height of their careers the two met
again, the forty-year-old Roman and the twenty-seven-year-
old Egyptian, and in Dante's words 'they felt the power of
courtly love'. They had found one another and their lives
were joined together, the marshal of the East and the queen
of the East. Their united power threatened young Rome and
the young Augustus in the West.

Now Antony turned against Italy, and Augustus came out
against him. Once again there was an agreement. They divided
the Mediterranean power between them. Augustus took the
West, Antony the East. The demarcation line ran between
Greece and Italy, Corfu and Brindisi, approximately the same
line as that which later divided the two parts of Diocletian's
empire, and which today divides the Roman and the Greek

64

2. MARCUS BRUTUS

3. CLEOPATRA

church. There was a ceremonial treaty, sealed by marriage. Antony, recently a widower, married the sister of Augustus, the young widow Octavia. She was perhaps the greatest, certainly the noblest, of the women of her time. With all the passion of a pure heart she took upon herself the office of reconciliation which was now her lot, mediating between two hostile men and worlds. Such a position involved great self-denial. This is clear from the coins which were issued to celebrate this political marriage. The Roman Octavia is seen beside her husband Antony, looking quite un-Roman with the ivy wreath of the wine-god Bacchus on his brow and a face shining with wine, while on the reverse he appears as the ecstatic Bacchus himself with the divine sceptre and the great beaker. This was the world in which the Roman matron had henceforth to live. But her sacrifice was in vain. Octavia's fate was that of every noble and pure-hearted person in this ugly and infected world. Antony longed for the flesh-pots of Egypt, he went back to Cleopatra, and events took their appointed course.

For almost ten years the two Mediterranean capitals armed for the great struggle of power and of ideas. In Rome the preparations went on quietly. Augustus did his utmost to create order once more, and to encourage commerce of every kind—rejoicing the heart of the little man. He restored the reputation of the ancient Roman officials, rejoicing the heart of the Senators. With the support of his admiral-in-chief, Agrippa, he also created a navy which destroyed the Pompeian fleet in Sicily, and in several campaigns subjugated the Germanic tribes on the lower Danube. Nor did he neglect to proclaim his measures and his successes to the peoples of the empire by means of coins. These special issues in gold and silver were so worded that the simplest could understand that every victory for Augustus was a victory for Rome, a victory for the Roman spirit and Roman power. The bust of warlike Roma is portrayed, or the goddess of victory in her chariot—the centuries-old symbol of Rome's victorious career. These were proclamations dear to the heart of the old Republicans. Or the death-mask of Julius Caesar is depicted, or the Roman goddess of Fortune with her helm of world dominion and her horn of plenty, promise of a new era of blessing. These were war aims dear to the heart of the new imperialists. Or the sceptre of world monarchy is displayed along with the standards of the army and the plough of the colonist. This was a programme dear to the heart of the veteran, fighting beneath the victorious banners of the *Imperator* the last battles which were to usher in the final triumph of the *Imperium Romanum*, leaving him to end his days as a landowner in some little settlement. And the head of Augustus also appears on these coins. The nations of the earth were to get to know the appearance of their future lord. This head usually has the beard of mourning, or the inscription CAESAR DIVI FILIUS, Son of God, that is, Son of eternal Caesar. He wants to be nothing more than Caesar's avenger and heir—or should we say, nothing less? Augustus's propaganda does not neglect the equestrian statues which were erected in his honour. One of them depicts him with the emblem of sacred power, the *lituus*, in his hand. Another bears the inscription 'By command of the people'. A third has, 'By resolution of the Senate'. To sum up, the content of Augustus's proclamation to the peoples of the empire was that he was the favourite of the gods, the executor of his divine father's will, the confidant of the Roman Senate and people, the chosen leader of Roman victory and Roman *imperium* and Roman peace—for a blessing to the whole world.

The critic who heard these large promises with scepticism was bound to notice one detail. During the crises of foregoing decades there had been a great deal of inferior currency. But Augustus, the grandson of a money-changer, issued his *denarii* in solid silver. That was propaganda which made no sound. But it meant a great deal. It won the confidence of the judicious more than the most splendid symbols of welfare and horns of plenty.

The mobilization of arms and propaganda in Alexandria was a much noisier affair. Cleopatra was more than ever the heart and soul of every enterprise. 'As certainly as I will give judgment from the Capitol', was her favourite oath—and she was, as she said, 'the first person, save for Hannibal, before whom Rome had ever trembled.' Her beloved Antony thought he could solve the problems of world politics in a way that was as simple as it was pleasant—by marriage and the breeding of children. Making use of the Eastern despot's privilege of polygamy, he took Cleopatra officially to wife—though he was married to Octavia—and attained thereby to a legitimate place on the throne of the Ptolemies. The problem of the succession he explained after the manner of Caesar as follows: 'My first ancestor Hercules did not confine his succession to the fertility of a single woman, nor fear marriage courts and paternity suits, but he aimed at founding many families. In this way he hoped to spread and increase his children and descendants in many royal families.' Cleopatra, however, had larger thoughts than this. Plutarch tells a delightful story about the manner in which this still attractive woman mobilized her infatuated consort for her far-reaching plans. The first soldier of the age is sitting by the water's edge, like any week-end tripper, and fishing. He catches nothing, but, wishing to impress Cleopatra, he secretly engages several divers to attach some good fish to his hook. A catch! Cleopatra of course realizes what is going on, and just as secretly she sends a special diver into the water; and as Antony once again is lucky and lifts his rod, a salted herring is hanging on the end. Everyone bursts out laughing and the great marshal is covered with embarrassment; Cleopatra, with her irresistible smile, says to him: 'Come, dear, give me the rod, and do you catch kings.' The conflict with the Parthians was overdue. They were the successors of the ancient Persians who had established a powerful kingdom on the eastern confines of the Roman empire. About 54 the Romans had been at war with the Parthians, and had suffered destructive defeat, with the loss of standards and prisoners. Ten years later Caesar was arming for a campaign of vengeance against the ancient enemy in the East, when he was assassinated in the midst of his preparations. Then Antony sent his generals to the East. They had already had promising preliminary successes in Syria and Palestine. Then he himself set out with a grand army of more than a hundred thousand men, and Cleopatra accompanied him as far as the Euphrates. But the promising enterprise ended in complete failure, and when Antony returned to Alexandria in 34 his only success was the subjugation of Armenia and the capture of its king. But this did not prevent him from celebrating his victory with a bombastic triumph in Alexandria, and from formally proclaiming a few days later the inauguration of the divine kingdom and world empire of the East.

Cleopatra was enthroned on a raised golden throne, arrayed and worshipped as Isis incarnate; beside her the prince consort. At their feet were Cleopatra's children: Caesarion the god and beloved son of his parents, and the three children of Antony, Alexander Helios, heir of Alexander as well as the incarnate sun-god, Cleopatra Selene, heiress of Cleopatra and the incarnate moon-goddess, and Ptolemy Philadelphos, heir of the Ptolemies and the beloved brother. Now followed the partition of the world, for everyone to see. As later in Byzantium, acts of State in Alexandria were often proclaimed in the form of theatrical performances. Antony made a fine speech from his stage-throne, proclaiming Cleopatra as queen over all kings, her young son and co-ruler Caesarion as Great King, and both together as rulers of Egypt, Libya and Cyprus. The younger children received only the title of king, but also quite respectable portions. Alexander Helios was decked as a Persian king and was to rule as sun-king in Armenia and Parthia (when it had been conquered, as Plutarch pleasantly adds); Cleopatra Selene received Cyrenaica, and Ptolemy Philadelphos, who appeared in the royal attire of ancient Macedonia, received Syria and Asia Minor. Antony had once shrewdly explained that 'the Romans show the greatness of their lordship not so much by means of conquests as by their gifts'. But this was only partly true. For the Parthian kingdom which he was giving away had not yet been conquered; while Asia Minor and most of the other lands which he was apportioning he did not have at all. They belonged to the Senate in Rome. And yet the infatuated fool stood there like Father Christmas on the stage at Alexandria and rubbed his hands together. He seemed to have forgotten himself completely, and there are good reasons why, despite his marriage, he is not once shown on all his many coins as wearing the royal diadem of the East. Probably the truth was that he looked on himself as Lord Protector and god of gods above all the swarm of kings, and rejoiced to be glorified in temple inscriptions and statues as the incarnate father of the gods. The temple was later dedicated to Augustus, and the statues overthrown. But one of them has more or less survived, depicting the foolish creature in divine nakedness, decked only with the long sceptre and fleece of the father of the gods.

It was Antony's special concern that the turn of events in the East should be properly recognized and appreciated beyond the limits of Alexandria. To this end coins must play their part. In the forties Antony had changed the name of Eumeneia, a town in Asia Minor, to Fulvia, in honour of his wife. The town had issued copper coins with the new name and a portrait of Fulvia. Now the town abandoned its new name, withdrew the Fulvia coins, and had the name of Fulvia overprinted. An example of these overprinted copper coins has survived and may be seen in the British Museum. At the same time the loyal town issued new copper coinage with a little picture of Cupid, a graceful compliment to Antony's new queen in Alexandria. In Egypt and elsewhere there now appeared coins of Cleopatra with the eagle of the Ptolemies, coins of Antony with the same august symbol, as well as coins depicting the crocodile of the Egyptian kingdom, and the ship's prow of Egyptian mastery of the sea. As a matter of course the glorious subjugation of the Jews and the heroic defeat of Armenia were celebrated by special victory medals. The great proclamation of the year 34 was spread abroad by means of a special medal.

What was the appearance of these two, then in the heyday of their brilliance, before whom the whole world trembled? Samson and Delilah on the throne! If one looks at the double portrait then despite every feeling of awe at the tragic majesty of the great queen, one cannot quite suppress an Old Testament proverb, which was also current in the lands ruled over

CHRIST AND THE CAESARS

by Cleopatra—'A man who runs after a loose woman is like an ox that is led to the slaughter.'

Antony, of course, intended to rouse quite different thoughts by his series of pictures. On the obverse of one coin there appears the head of the prince consort, with a tiny Armenian tiara and the proud inscription, 'Antony the Conqueror of Armenia'. So the coin keeps alive the memory of the triumph in Alexandria in celebration of the victory over the Armenians. On its reverse we see Cleopatra with the royal diadem of her ancestors and a ship's prow—Heiress of the Pharaohs and Queen of the seas. The inscription runs 'Cleopatra Queen of kings and kings' sons'—the content of the proclamation of the gymnasium, reduced to the briefest possible formula. These political proclamations received the expected response. Throughout the East coins appeared with the names and portraits of the two. In the past the princelets of the East had added to their names Philoromaios, Friend of the Romans, in this way hoping to secure to themselves the favour of Rome. Now one of the vassal kings of Asia Minor coined the formula, 'Tarkondimodotus, Friend of Antony'. The female rule in Alexandria was of course a thorn in the flesh to many in the East. Nothing could be done about it, but the cynical citizens of Antioch took their revenge by portraying the ageing Antony and his faded partner with unexampled realism. They are not courtly portraits, but caricatures in the spirit of a Daumier. But they are extraordinarily valuable for us, arising as they do from direct study of their subjects. For Antony and Cleopatra spent the winter of 37-36 carousing in Antioch. One sees in the portrait of the early fading southerner how the cosmetics and beauty aids and all the jewels of Egypt are of no more avail.

> a morsel cold
> Upon dead Caesar's trencher; nay, you were a fragment
> Of Cneius Pompey's,

says Shakespeare. This is the intention of this unchivalrous likeness on the coin from Antioch. What Cleopatra had lost of human graces was now made up by superhuman titles.

The mint-masters hastened, with the utmost respect, to add those titles to their mocking portraits of the ageing woman: 'Queen Cleopatra, the new Goddess.' But apparently the portrait continued to lose in appeal, for finally copper coins appear without any portrait, but simply the proud title, 'The new Goddess'. Antony, too, was not content with the role of Roman official or Imperator, or with that of Alexandrian prince consort. He wanted to be more, and the coins were used to tell the whole world. Thus there appeared a gold coin which celebrates him not only as Imperator of land and sea, but also as the Star and Lion of the East. Even more pretentious is another gold coin, the climax of Antony's coinage. The god Aeon is represented, the Inaugurator of the new age of salvation, and in the style of Hellenistic statues and coins he unites in himself the attributes of the most diverse deities. All the fullness of the godhead dwells in him bodily, all the good spirits of heaven are united in this splendid genius of the new age. The age-old longing for salvation, which at that time was especially strong, stirring the deep spirits of the age—the desire of the enervated peoples for an advent—was politicized by Antony and turned to his own uses. The prince consort in Alexandria appeared before the world public as— to use an ancient Assyrian formula—'the Desired of the Great Gods'. He is the Fulfiller of the ancient hopes of the East, the world Saviour who was to come and to usher in the Golden Age which was foretold by prophets and sibyls.

The peoples of the East might listen, but the Roman legions became restive. The more un-Roman Antony's behaviour, the more restless was his wooing of the soldiers' favour. He did all he could to detach their loyalty from his office and to attach it to his person. Then he (or was it the inventive Cleopatra?) had a clever idea: he issued his own coins for circulation in the army. There was no sign on them of oriental symbols of salvation, but the famed standards of the Roman army, and for each legion its own series with its number, the Guards division heading the list. That was an honour dear to the hearts of the Romans, like the mention in daily orders or the winning of a decoration. But soon the rumour spread round

71

the canteens that the coins were base—copper with silver gilt, which no farmer or merchant would handle—and the forger was none other than Antony himself. It was all a fraud—the new money, the eastern empire, the golden age—all unreal, unreliable, counterfeit. The saviour of the world with inflationary currency—it was bad propaganda.

Augustus followed events in the East like a lion awaiting his prey, watchful yet relaxed. He missed no opportunity of supplying his Romans with scandalous news from Alexandria, and he used his coins for a systematic education of the Roman people in the issues of the coming struggle. Was Rome or Alexandria to be the capital city of the world? Was the Roman people to dominate the Mediterranean lands as the imperial race, or was an oriental despot and divine king to lord it over an undifferentiated mass of peoples with equal rights, that is, equally without rights? Was Europe or Africa to have the leadership in the coming age? People in Europe looked on men and women and things in Africa as 'having a different spirit from us'. Augustus made sure that the war-weary soldier in the barracks as well as the peace-longing man in the street realized that no compromise was possible. Every victory for Antony was a defeat for Rome. For every victory for Antony was a victory for Cleopatra. A man who carried an Egyptian woman's train, who did not celebrate his triumphs in the capital, who gave away to foreigners Roman provinces and unconquered kingdoms—this was no true Roman. Augustus himself was certainly no Stylite. But the oriental manners and ideals of his brother-in-law Antony were most distasteful to his Roman heart. And the peoples of the Western world were as one man for the traduced Octavia.

In the late summer of the year 32 B.C. the Roman Senate and people declared war on Queen Cleopatra of Egypt. The thirty-year-old Augustus was entrusted with the conduct of the campaign. We know his appearance at that time from a bronze portrait.

Was he a pale young man, as Antony mockingly said? On the contrary, he was a remarkable and pitiless enemy, this young man with the cold gleam in his eyes. Antony and

Cleopatra were to learn the truth about him. This was the man who was now moving out against the arch-enemy in Alexandria, in the calm certainty that to his people belonged the judgment of the nations and the crown of the world, for the blessing of mankind. He was a Roman, take him for all in all. And his wife, Livia, whom he left at home, can be studied in the unfamiliar picture from a private house in Pompeii (p. 97). She became the wife of Augustus when she was nineteen, and at this time was twenty-five, just five years younger than her young husband. The two were probably the most handsome couple of the century, in the eyes of those, at any rate, who knew real beauty. So far we have said nothing about Livia, nor will there be occasion to say much. Thucydides says that 'the best woman is one of whom one does not speak'. Augustus thought the same. He never put her likeness on his imperial coins; whereas the infatuated Antony could never resist putting his latest love on his coins. Augustus wore the clothes which Livia had spun and woven and sewn for him at home. She was a Roman, take her for all in all. For him she was the epitome of the Roman matron's virtue and of the new universal civilization, she was the symbol of Mother Rome and of the world for whose victory he fought—the hidden opponent of the ageing empress in the East.

Antony and Cleopatra planned to land in Italy in the autumn of 32 and to take Rome by storm. But they were too late, and had to winter in Greece; there they passed the months in carousing, and issuing coins to celebrate their festivities. One of these coins depicted Cleopatra with the crown of Isis, glorifying the divine queen of Alexandria. Another coin of the same time shows the goddess of victory somewhat prematurely extending to Antony, Consul and Imperator, the victory laurel with the diadem, the Hellenistic emblem of divine kingship, which Caesar strove in vain to win, and which Antony, as we know, had hitherto avoided putting on his coins. One may term this advance payment of laurels.

Augustus entrusted his naval operations to his gifted commander Agrippa, who drove the whole Alexandrian fleet into the narrows at Actium on the west coast of Greece, and blockaded it there for months. Hunger, discontent, mistrust, quarrels and desertion weakened the striking power of the Egyptian fleet from month to month. Finally Antony resolved to engage the enemy, though the tactical situation was desperate. On September 2, 31 B.C., the die was cast which was to decide the destiny of the Mediterranean world and the future of mankind. Apollo confronted Anubis, says Virgil; Augustus fought in the sign of Venus, while Cleopatra flourished the sistrum of Isis. . . . The light cruisers of Rome defeated the heavy battleships of Alexandria. Cleopatra was the first to realize that the situation was hopeless; she drew the consequences without delay, and took to flight in her flagship *Antonias*. Antony followed, and together they reached the African coast. The date of the battle of Actium marked the beginning of a new era in Roman reckoning.

Why did Cleopatra break off the battle so suddenly? Ancient historians speak of headlong flight. Modern scholars see in her retreat a well-calculated but unfortunately abortive tactical manœuvre. The two men who knew her best, Antony and Augustus, thought differently. In her unexpected action Antony saw with fury, Augustus with amusement, the first step in a new direction—on the way from Antony to Augustus. I think they were right. In the turmoil of battle Cleopatra, with the clear vision of her *daimonion*, saw where the strongest man of the world was—not by her side, but on the flagship of the enemy. With the same suddenness as her vision she now cast all her love on Augustus—that love which could always love only the strongest.

When Childerich, the king of the Franks, had driven the Romans from his land, the queen of the Thuringians left her husband, went to Childerich, and said, 'I know now what a brave and splendid man you are, so I have come to be with you. If I knew of another man anywhere, to the furthest limits of the sea, I should have gone to him and joined myself to him.' So Gregory of Tours relates the story, and his apocalyptic account is filled with awe at the *daimonion* which drove the royal woman to the most royal man. One must know of this *daimonion* in order to understand the last of the Greek queens on the throne of the Pharaohs.

The whole of the last act in the drama of Cleopatra confirms this view. From the time of Actium there was a rift in the relation between Antony and Cleopatra, which in spite of well-meant efforts was never closed. Augustus with his unerring historical sense noted it at once, and in accordance with the true Roman principle, *divide et impera*, divide and rule, he took care that it became worse. So it came about that the defeated pair had to endure the bitter end of their destiny in a metaphysical solitude, Antony first, and then Cleopatra.

Plutarch has recounted the last scenes of this tragedy in a masterly fashion, to be excelled only by Shakespeare.

Formerly, in his heyday, Antony had founded a brotherhood of artists in living, an association of men who lived a life in the fairy palaces of sunny Alexandria which was like a single unending Bacchanalian festival. Now he founded in the same city an order of partners in death, an association of men who cast away both their hopes and their fears, and, prodigal of the richness and beauty of life in the face of death, lavished bread and wine on the inhabitants of this city of a million people, and gave games and festivals of a splendour such as only the East can achieve. Alexandria for the last time glittered in the brightness and enchantment of a dying age. Then these men went to their death as to a Dionysian dance.

Cleopatra shared officially in the celebrations. But behind her husband's back she was in touch with Augustus, and secretly sent him the crown of Egypt. Augustus demanded that she have Antony killed, and meantime moved steadily against Egypt, taking the same route as the young Antony twenty-five years before. When he had reached the frontier fortress of Pelusium Cleopatra secretly instructed the commander to capitulate. Augustus appeared before the capital, and established his camp at its gates. But Antony by an audacious sortie threw the enemy cavalry back into their camp. 'When the east wind blew, he was a man.'

The lord of Alexandria challenged the champion of Rome to a duel. It was a melodramatic and apocalyptic gesture. But

Augustus remained cool, and replied that there were enough ways open for Antony to die. As always, he was the lion awaiting his prey. Thereupon Antony gathered together the whole power of Egypt by land and sea, navy, cavalry and infantry, for the final decision. But one after the other left him in the lurch. He dismissed them regally, laden with gifts, the 'leapers', as their contemporaries called them, the political trick-riders who knew the moment to leap from one horse to another. Antony's last meal with his last friends was a last confession of faith in Dionysian living and dying—

> Well, my good fellows, wait on me tonight:
> Scant not my cups; and make as much of me
> As when mine empire was your fellow too,
> And suffer'd my command.

'And at midnight . . . there was a sudden harmonious sound of all kinds of instruments mingled with cries of jubilation and the sound of dancing, as when a noisy procession of devotees of Bacchus is passing by. The procession seemed to pass through the centre of the town, towards the gates, then out to the enemy camp, where the tumult reached its height and then died away. Those who tried to interpret this phenomenon said that the god whom Antony had ever tried to emulate had now abandoned him.' So runs Plutarch's account, a modification of the kind of legend of flying hosts which is often to be found in classical literature. In this case the story has a profound symbolic meaning. We have spoken earlier of the maker of world politics as the one who fulfils the will of history. It was the greatness of Augustus that he recognized and fulfilled this will of history. It was the tragic greatness of Antony that he recognized it, and despised it. Antony knew that Dionysus had abandoned his last and perhaps greatest apostle and had gone over to the camp of the well-tempered Augustus. The enchanted Dionysian world of the East was sinking, the orderly world of the Roman West was rising. Antony saw this clearly. But he loved the dying world with the drunken passion of a great heart, he fought for it with Promethean defiance of the gods, and he took with him to his grave the dream which the gods had despised, the dream of a great kingdom of the sun stretching from Babylon to Gibraltar. In his sovereign contempt for the gods and their historical will there lived again something of that defiance of the gods which was found in pre-Augustan Rome, filling men like Cato and Brutus, and women like Porcia; but now in Antony it was intensified to an un-Roman, an anti-Roman *daimonia*, and for a short time it even became a theomachy of transcendent dignity and universal range.

Outward events rushed to catastrophe. In the final battle Antony with his united forces faced the rising sun. 'The last of many battles', are Shakespeare's apocalyptic words for the day. Cleopatra had already issued her secret orders. The Egyptian fleet sailed out to meet the enemy, dipped its flags, turned, and sailed in unison with them against Alexandria. The Egyptian cavalry sallied forth, met the enemy, and joined forces with them. Finally Antony called out the infantry, his own legions which were no longer his. Unwillingly they went into the hated battle of Roman against Roman for a faithless Egyptian woman—and capitulated after a brief struggle. Such was the pitiful end of the great war. The betrayed leader raced back into the city, crying aloud in the streets, 'She has betrayed me to those against whom I fought for her sake'. But even though he was defeated, Augustus dared not let him live; he still stood in his way, and he still disturbed Cleopatra's plans. She sent her personal servants to him with the false news that she had committed suicide. So he followed her, as he had followed her purple sails from Actium, and fell upon his sword. He had time only to hear that she still lived, and he could not rest till he died in her arms: in the arms of his betrayer, whom he loved to the end. The loneliness of the great dreamer, cut off from god and man, is revealed in painful clarity.

The *daimon* of Cleopatra once seized upon Caesar and drove him to ruin. Now the great enchantress had triumphed again over the life and work of a Roman. Without hesitation she now stretched out her hand to the third and greatest of all, the heir of Caesar and the conqueror of Antony.

While her lover was dying she sent a special messenger to

77

Augustus inviting him to a personal conference. The victor hesitated for a long time, to the great distress of Cleopatra, who suddenly announced that the Jews were the cause of all the trouble, and that Alexandria could be saved only if she herself could slay every Jew with her own hand! At last Augustus came, and they confronted one another, the most powerful woman of the age, and the most powerful man. Now she played the last and greatest game of her life, the prize the mastery of the world and the possession of Augustus. But Augustus was cold. She fought for Egypt for her children. But Augustus did not respond. She begged for clear and reliable arrangements for her own future, and named, as though she would conjure their spirits to aid her, the names of Livia and Octavia, the two great women in Rome, whom she had hated all her life for their inaccessibility and invulnerability, and whom she was now ready to love and to appeal to. But Augustus made no definite promises, and departed. The great game was lost.

Napoleon had at least handed a rose to the pleading queen of Prussia at Tilsit. Matter-of-fact Augustus could not do even this. Once more, however, Cleopatra in her fallen majesty was able to attract the devotion of a young Roman, as in her early days at her father's court. The young nobleman performed for her the last service that was possible—he disclosed to her what her conqueror intended to do with her. She was to be led in his triumph as a spectacle for the Roman mob. This was what she had suspected, and now she was sure. The twilight of the gods had come. When the constables of the Roman emperor came for the prisoner, the empress of the East lay dead on her golden couch, decked with every ornament of her dignity.

There is an old story told of two society ladies who saw Shakespeare's *Antony and Cleopatra* and cried out in shocked tones at the end: 'The family life of our dear queen is very different!' We need not grudge Cleopatra a very different judgment. In Rilke's words we can speak of her as the one 'who ever comes again, when an age that is ending gathers together all its worth once more. . . .'

Augustus was now master of the world. He visited Alexander's tomb, and deposited a golden wreath on the sarcophagus. He was asked if he also wanted to visit the tombs of the Ptolemies. He only replied, 'I wanted to see a king, not corpses.' The young Caesarion was doomed to die. But the last plea of the condemned mother was not wholly in vain, for the other children found refuge in the house of Octavia, and this purest of women became their mother and guardian angel. The last Pharaohs, Antony and Cleopatra, were laid to rest in the shadow of the temple of Isis, in the last royal tomb built on the Nile.

Meanwhile Augustus celebrated his triumph in Rome, and as a substitute for his most precious booty had a wax effigy of the dead Cleopatra carried on a couch. A victory coin proclaimed the triumph to the world. The obverse has the Roman Victoria, as a deliberate counterpoise to the premature goddess of victory on Antony's last coin, symbolically set on a ship's prow. The reverse shows Augustus with the olive-branch of peace on his triumphal car. In Rome the temple of the war-god Janus was closed, and in the East a large silver medallion proclaimed freedom and peace among the nations. On the obverse Augustus is called the 'Liberator of the Roman people'. On the reverse stands the goddess of peace with the wand of Hermes in her hand, the symbol of blessing and peace. Other coins proclaimed step by step the consolidation of the empire. Egypt became an imperial crown land. The traditional crocodile was depicted with the triumphal inscription: Egypt taken. Augustus also took over for his coins the eagle of the Ptolemies. As 'heiress' of Cleopatra her more fortunate opponent Livia now appeared on the Egyptian coins. She was now the bearer of life for this land. The very dating of the Alexandrian coins of Augustus followed the ancient Egyptian custom, reckoning by the years which the kings of the land had reigned. So the beginning of this reckoning was August of the year 30, the month of Augustus's triumphal entry into Alexandria. Meanwhile the eastern frontiers of the empire were systematically rounded off and secured. Armenia was incorporated, and to mark this event there appeared a coin with the words 'Armenia taken', and the Armenian royal tiara, which Antony had once used on his triumphal coins, was conjoined with the portrait of Augustus. A small silver coin announced the news that 'Asia Minor is part of the Empire'. Once again Augustus made use of a coin of Antony, though the motif was an ancient one of Asia Minor. But instead of the reeling god Antony with the great beaker there. stands the victory goddess of Actium with wreath and palm-branch. Finally Augustus, favourite of the gods, attained by pure diplomacy what Cleopatra had always desired, what Caesar had planned and what Antony with his great army had attempted in vain: the Parthians returned the Roman standards and prisoners and sought friendship with Rome. Countless coins in every land and for many years celebrated this proudest success in the successful career of Augustus. SIGNIS PARTHICIS RECEPTIS—The Parthian standards returned —was the message on the *denarii*. For the first time in history the ring of lands round the Mediterranean was closed, and secured to the East. The Mediterranean was a Roman lake, and the first empire of European character arose. From this time Europe became the leader of the world.

4. CLEOPATRA

5. VARUS

VI

A PREMATURE ADVENT
CELEBRATION

IN the midst of the horrors that broke upon the Roman
world after the assassination of Caesar, the poet Virgil raised
a prophetic voice, saying, The turning of the ages is near at
hand. The iron age with its terrors is nearing its end. The
destined hour of world history is approaching. The divine
king of salvation, for whom mankind has waited since the
time of the Pharaohs, is on his way. He will at last fulfil the
promises which have not ceased to be heard among the Roman
people since the days of the Sibyl. He will annihilate the evil
of the past and free the peoples from unceasing fear. He will
establish a universal empire of peace and lead in the golden
age, for the blessing of a renewed humanity. And in nature,
too, all will be renewed. Poisonous plants and snakes will disappear, the fields will become a paradise, and the ox and the
lion will dwell together in peace. Gods who have been long
absent, ages of salvation which are long past, will return to
the earth. Saturn, the god of the primeval golden age, will
return to power. Apollo and Diana will hold protective sway
over the new age and its ruler. 'The time is ripe: enter on
thy high course of honour, great son of Zeus', cries the prophetic poet to the coming divine king. 'See how the whole
world, staggering beneath its burden, how lands and seas and
depths of heaven all rejoice at the inbreak of the new age.'

When after fourteen years of struggle Octavius, Caesar's
heir, offspring of Venus and favourite of Apollo, won the
victory at Actium which put an end to the internecine strife
of party leaders, legions and peoples, then all eyes turned to
him with the question, Art thou he who is to come? The

81

black lists were forgotten, with which the young Octavius had inaugurated his career. Two thousand three hundred political opponents had been destroyed, including old friends and near relations; and from the not inconsiderable property of the murdered men the rising saviour of the world had paid his troops and established his inexhaustible welfare treasury. No one desired (or no one dared) to mention these things. The temple of Janus was closed. It was a new era. Octavius himself went from success to success, from honour to honour. He subdued the frontier peoples to the north. He won a diplomatic victory over the old enemy in the east, the king of the Parthians, who 'voluntarily' returned the standards which the Romans had lost on Parthian battlefields. A temple was raised to Mars, god of war, to house the standards, a votive altar was built for the goddess Fortuna, and a triumphal arch for the returning emperor. The emperor was prouder of this bloodless victory than of any glorious deed in his life, for in his mind it stood for the beginning of a new era in world politics. From this time Rome was the centre of the world, the emperor was the judge of the nations, from Britain to India men listened to his words. After the successful issue to the Parthian problem the emperor concentrated his strength on domestic affairs. Laws affecting marriage and children were passed in order to call a halt to the serious dilution of the original Roman people, and to establish a basis for a powerful development of the imperial race.

In the fourteen years of reconstruction after Actium the Roman people was not slow to show its gratitude to its emperor. The priests accepted the conqueror of Cleopatra as one of the State gods, and addressed him in traditional prayers as the founder of a new race of gods. The Senate gave him the wreath of oak-leaves, the so-called 'citizens' crown', for saving citizens from mortal danger. As if that were not enough, the Roman parliament gave him the divine title of 'Augustus', which raised him, as Zeus incarnate and worshipful ruler, above mere human stature. In Asia Minor, Syria, Gaul and Alexandria temples were built and sacrifices and prayers offered to the goddess Roma and the god Augustus. And Virgil raised his voice again, celebrating Augustus's assumption of power as the fulfilment of his prophecy in the days of the civil war ('This is the man, the one who has been promised again and again'), as the universal advent (he uses the word *adventus*). It was Virgil's theological and political testament. He died shortly after the close of the Parthian conference. But his confession of faith lived on. It was the faith of his people and the confession of all peoples: Augustus is the world's saviour who was to come.

Augustus himself took his prophet at his word. He gave official sanction and fulfilment to the politicizing of the ancient hope of a saviour. In the year 17 B.C., when a strange star shone in the heavens, he saw that the cosmic hour had come, and inaugurated a twelve-day Advent celebration, which was a plain proclamation of Virgil's message of joy: 'The turning-point of the ages has come.' From documents known of old, as well as from some which have recently been discovered, from historians, poets, inscriptions, monuments and coins we have more reliable information about these days and their official significance than of almost any other happening of ancient history.

Heralds traversed Italy with their star-studded shields and the blessed wand of Hermes, and announced the invitation to the ceremonies. The Roman college of priests, with Augustus himself at their head, distributed holy incense to the masses for purification from past guilt. The people brought the fruits of the land for sacrifices to the chief gods of the festival, Apollo and Diana. The emperor inaugurated the ceremonies in the night preceding June 1, a night of full moon. As the divine and human mediator between heaven and earth, and the high priest of the Roman people, the emperor approached the altar in order to make a blood-offering to the goddesses of fate, with the prayer, 'I beseech you to grant the Roman people perpetual invulnerability, victory and prosperity and be ever gracious to me and my house.'

The second night he sacrificed to the goddesses of birth, the third to Mother Earth. The sacrifices by day were for the gods of heaven, the first day for the emperor's heavenly ancestor and image, Jupiter, king of the gods, the second day for Juno, queen of heaven. At this sacrifice one hundred and ten Roman matrons knelt and prayed for the growth, increase and blessing of the Roman people. The third day, the climax of the festival, Augustus presented, in the spirit of the new age, a bloodless sacrifice before the new imperial temple to Apollo and Diana, patron deities of the golden age and its ruler; the offering was prepared from the fruits of the land brought by the grateful populace. A double choir of twenty-seven boys and twenty-seven girls sang an advent hymn, composed for the occasion by Horace.

This hymn is a prayer to Apollo and Diana, who love the city of the seven hills. The sun-god, too (whose statue looked down from the pinnacle of the imperial temple upon the procession), was addressed—May Rome be the greatest sight that he has ever seen and ever will see in the eternal course of the ages! The goddesses of birth were called upon to protect the new marriage and child laws. Mother Earth was to pour out the blessings of paradise: a horn of plenty and a wreath of corn were to be the symbols of the blessed new age. Apollo and Diana were to scatter the riches of their grace on the bearer of life and the defender from death of the Roman world, Augustus, the offspring of Venus. The Parthians have bowed before his might, the nations of the far north and the far east bow before his judgment. From this time the irresistible hero of war will reign with clemency and forbearance over the conquered peoples as a saviour of peace. The genii of the blessed past, loyalty and peace, honour and discipline, courage and blessing, have returned to the earth. The emperor has brought the golden age to the world. May it last with increasing splendour from age to age, now and for ever. So the youths and maidens of Rome prayed in their advent hymn.

The Senate resolved that the words which proclaimed this festival—truly the proudest which proud Rome had ever seen —should be graven on a marble pillar and set up in the festival square. Fifty years ago the remains of this pillar were excavated on the very site.

Another monument tells us even more directly of the joyous

message of the coming of the new age—a marble statue of
Augustus, which makes use of the symbolic language of the
advent celebrations to glorify him as the saviour of the world
who has come at last. At the emperor's feet a little Cupid is
playing—a delicate allusion to Venus, the ancestress of the
imperial house. Augustus himself is wearing a breast-plate
with two shoulder buckles in the shape of the Sphinx, the
richest symbol of the time. For the Sphinx, like the Sibyl,
prophesies the future; it is the heraldic beast of Saturn, god
of the golden age, as well as the symbol of Paradise at the
end of the ages. It was popularized on Augustus's seal, and
can also be seen in the relief decoration on the double throne
of the gods, Roma and Augustus. The emperor's breast-plate
is richly decorated, the centre showing the State act which
was glorified by Horace in his Advent poem, the return of
the eagle standards by the Parthians, and the beginning of
the era of peace. To right and left the subjugated frontier
tribes of the north, the last to feel the weight of the emperor's
hand in war, are shown bemoaning their fate. This State act
is the political centre of a cosmic Advent drama which embraced history and creation, earth and heaven, men and gods.
On the ground is Mother Earth with her horn of plenty and
crown of corn. From each side there approach the patron gods
of the new age, Apollo and Diana. In the sky the sun-god is
rising, driving the gods of night before him with his quadriga.
The shadows of the past diminish, a new day is dawning for
the world. The god of heaven hovers over all these Advent
signs with the garment of the heavens spread out in protection and blessing. In this richly symbolic picture there is only
one figure absent, that of Augustus himself, the saviour of
the world. But this is deliberate, for his head towers high
above the whole scene and his countenance shines gravely
and mildly above the peoples like the divine countenance
itself. This is the emperor whom Horace addresses—

> When like the spring your countenance
> lights up over the people
> Then the day passes with more grace,
> and the sun shines more beautifully.

The finest means available to the Roman government for the spreading of news and ideas, a means of which Augustus in particular had learned to make such excellent use in the years of civil war, was the issue of coins. In the years about the time of this Advent celebration Augustus made exhaustive use of coins.[1]

After the successful issue of the Parthian affair Augustus struck innumerable coins in Rome showing a kneeling Parthian returning the standards. Others show the oak-leaves 'for the saving of the citizens', or honour Dionysos and Hercules, the pre-historic divine heroes whose deeds Augustus had repeated and excelled, or the goddess of fortune, who had led and protected the emperor, or the divine spirits ('Courage' and 'Honour') who have returned to the earth, or the sun-god who shines upon the new day which has dawned upon the world, or the half moon of Diana, or the lucky star shining on the life of Augustus, or Mother Earth herself with a triumphal car leading home not a hero of war but the blessing of earth itself, a basket of sheaves. These coins were to be found in every part of the empire, from the Rhine to the Jordan, carriers of the political ideas of Augustus. At the same time coins appeared from the mints of the great frontier provinces, with similar designs which lent support in their own way to the coins of the capital. In the East there were coins with the Sphinx, or the sign of Capricorn, under which Augustus was born, together with an allusion to the success over the Parthians. Ephesus issued coins with the triumphal arch, the sanctuary of the standards, and the double temple of Roma and Augustus. Alexandria, too, had the triumphal arch and the sanctuary of the standards. Antioch united on one coin the picture of the victory-bringing god of heaven and of the incarnate Zeus, the victorious Augustus, celebrated as 'worthy of honour', 'son of god'—SEBASTOS THEOU HUIOS. The many coins of these years between the victory over the Parthians and the Advent celebrations prepared the way for the

[1] We attempt here, for the first time, to follow the preparations for the idea of the Advent in coins struck from the year 21 to the year 17, then to demonstrate the effect of these coins of the new age upon the Roman and Greek coins from the years 17 to 12.

Advent idea in every part of the empire. With the celebrations this propaganda reached its climax. First the coins show the chief events: the herald with his starry shield, the distribution of the elements of purification, the arrival of Augustus at the Advent festival, the sacrificial ritual, and finally the commemorative marble pillar with the festival proclamation. Other festival coins have not come down to us in the original, but in later reproductions, showing the offering of the fruits of the earth, the sacrifice to the father of the gods, the praying matrons, the procession of the children's choirs, and the sacrifice to Mother Earth, reclining in the foreground with her cornucopiae and her sheaves (a clear echo of the Mother Earth on the breast-plate of the marble statue). In this way, then, the nations of the world and even succeeding generations were able to share the unique experience of the Advent festival.

This brilliant account in gold and silver did not fail in its political and propaganda purpose. In Rome, but especially in the provinces, there appeared in rapid succession a series of coins with old and new portraits, taking up in many variations and reproductions the leading motifs of the Advent proclamation. From Rome itself there came coins with the portrait of Augustus holding the programme of the festival, with the divine ancestress Venus, the imperial god Apollo, the sacrificial instruments, a votive legend for the welfare of the emperor, and an invocation for the increase and peace of the empire. From Corinth came Venus, the triumphal arch, and a goddess of victory above the earth. Alexandria struck coins showing the altar of the goddess of fortune, the sacrificial instruments, the half moon of Diana, the capricorn of Augustus, the miraculous star of the year 17, the goddess of fertility with the double cornucopiae, the bundle of sheaves and a lotus flower, indicating perhaps the flowers of paradise in the renewed creation. The Spanish coins of those years are a unique Advent doxology of the imperial saviour of the world. First there are the familiar pictures glorifying the Parthian success: the standards, the god of war, the sanctuary for the standards, the triumphal arch. Then there are the traditional

87

oak-leaves with the usual legend—'For saving the citizens'—
and the eagle standard with the decorations of victory and
the new title of honour—'Father and Preserver of the People.'
Here we find goddesses of victory with standards and symbols
of victorious peace, as well as the altar of the goddess of fortune, or a votive inscription for the welfare of the emperor,
on whom the welfare of the world depends. Frequently the
portrait is of his divine father Julius Caesar and his star—an
echo of the Roman herald's coins with a similar portrait and
the inscription 'Son of God'.

Two related coins from Spain direct attention to world
history. One is like a summary of the scenery on the armour
of Augustus: the sun-god is soaring up with his crown of
sun-rays and his outspread heavenly mantle, with the capricorn below, and between them the single word AUGUSTUS.
The other shows the capricorn again, this time with the
emblems of world dominion, the helm and the globe, and
above them the emblem of the king of paradise, the cornucopiae with the diadem, and again the single word AUGUSTUS.
The symbolic meaning is clear: a new day is dawning for the
world. The divine saviour-king, born in the historical hour
ordained by the stars, has come to power on land and
sea, and inaugurates the cosmic era of salvation. Salvation
is to be found in none other save Augustus, and there is
no other name given to men in which they can be saved.
This is the climax of the Advent proclamation of the Roman
empire.

The divine Augustus was still reigning in the fullness of
his glory, the broad spaces of the Roman empire were still
resounding with the imperial Advent proclamation, the Advent
coins were passing from hand to hand, when the Son of Mary
was born in a little corner of Palestine. It is hard to think of
a moment in world history in which the Advent of Christ
could seem more superfluous than precisely then. But the
Roman Advent message had promised more than any emperor
could fulfil. Fourteen years after the birth of Christ the imperial saviour died. Fourteen years after that his successor
Tiberius left his capital and retired to the solitude of Capri,

at odds with gods and men. It was in that state of affairs in the world that Christ died on the Cross, that the apostles raised their voices and put to the peoples of the Roman Empire the question which from that time was to agitate all history: Who is it, who should come? The emperor, or Christ?

VII

AUGUSTUS AND JESUS

AT the beginning of the Christmas story there stands the name of the emperor Augustus. The fact that the two most significant figures of history, Augustus and Jesus, appeared in the same generation, was a subject for thought even in the writings of the Fathers. Augustine's *Civitas Dei*, in the last analysis, circles round the foci of Augustus and Jesus. Christian art till the Reformation returned again and again to the same double theme. And rightly so. For to follow the course of events from Augustus to Jesus yields an insight into the way of God in history. Let us look, then, at this decisive act in the drama of human history.

It is not possible here to do more than indicate the issues. For the theme of Augustus and Jesus is inexhaustible. Viktor Gardthausen has published six volumes on *Augustus and His Time*, and the Fourth Gospel closes with the words: 'And there are also many other things which Jesus did, the which if they should be written every one, I suppose that even the world itself would not contain the books which should be written.' And that is not the greatest difficulty. When is a man old enough, when is humanity mature enough, to speak about this overwhelming theme? To look at it makes a man very small. But perhaps that is just the kind of historical work of which the Bible speaks—that we should feel small, when we look at Augustus, at Jesus, at Him who sits upon the throne and judges the nations and dashes them to pieces, till the Day of the Son of Man is come.

I

One must go far back in time, in order to grasp the historical significance of Augustus—to the beginning of the age of the Pharaohs, about 3000 B.C.

It was then that a new type of man appeared in history, the *homo imperiosus*, imperial man, the man who embodied the will of history to create an *imperium*, and brought it to realization in his own achievements. Since the Pharaohs united the crowns of Upper and Lower Egypt and raised the Egyptian people to be the first imperial race, imperial man has controlled the history of the nations. It is since that time that Napoleon's words, politics is destiny, have been valid. For imperial man bears life for his people and defends them from death, he bears destiny in his hands for all the nations.

For two thousand years the kingdom of the Nile was the leading power in the ancient world, first in Africa, and later in Asia as well. Then the leadership passed to the Assyrians, who extended their civilization of the two rivers as far as Egypt. The imperial leader was replaced by another, and a new imperial capital arose. But the empire itself remained, and maintained its leadership of international life. The symbol of dominion changed. The Pharaohs ruled with the royal scourge, the Assyrian kings ruled with the cudgel. But the effect was the same. In both empires the *homo imperiosus* ruled the nations as a master rules his slaves.

He rules like a tyrant—this was the cry which arose in Greece, the voice of Europe. And the Greeks confronted the type of imperial man with a new type, autonomous man. Since the re-birth of humanism it has often been said that it was the historical achievement of the Greeks to have discovered the dignity of man. So in the name of human dignity the Greeks protested against royal scourge and cudgel alike. In the name of human dignity they demanded free decision for the development of their own lives. This is the will to autonomy, which renounces imperial ambitions for the sake of freedom. It is the spirit of freedom, which has been justified at the bar of history by the classical creations of Greek science and art.

91

In 480 B.C. the Persians conquered Athens and reduced the ancient temple to ruins. In the same year the Greeks drove out the Persian king and his army of a million men. After this decisive liberation of Europe the city of Pericles and Phidias restored the ruined temple of Athene, making it more beautiful and more 'European' than before. For the unique sculptures which adorned the new Parthenon are not only a glorious manifestation of Attic art, they are also a political protest of Europe against the barbaric world of the scourge and the cudgel, they are the concrete confession of the Greek *polis* in favour of self-determination of civil life. This is symbolically expressed in a trait which is more than merely external. Every statue on the Parthenon, Athene herself, the long row of gods, heroes, kings, councillors and priests, the captains and soldiers and merchants—all wear the same garment. It is the *himation*, the precursor of the Roman toga, the philosopher's gown. The *himation* was the civil dress worn by the free Athenian citizen in public—whether he was a statesman or a poet, a professor or an officer. Where two or three—or five hundred —citizens met together in this dress, there the spirit of the *polis* was alive, they were a community which would tolerate no royal cudgel. There were sufficient unobtrusive distinguishing marks, in colour or ornament, to indicate status and rank. The *himation* was the clear expression, in its unceremonious arrangement and its dignified folds, of that grace and moderation which was common to all Greeks. At the same time the garment gave unlimited scope to its wearer to express his personal taste in the way he wore it. So from the time of the Persian wars until the age of Rome the *himation* was the characteristic dress of the Greek. One may even venture to say that if the royal cudgel is the symbol of the great empire of early antiquity, the *himation* is the symbol of the *polis* and its ideal of humanity in the classical Greek era, the emblem of civil freedom and an ordered political life.

Imperium and *polis*, direction and freedom, were the two principles which from this time on determined the course of classical history. The collision of these principles was at the heart of the struggle between the Persians and the Greeks.

The antinomy of the two principles was the problem which wrecked the empire of Alexander. Their encounter was the theme of Roman imperial history, which reached its climax in the person and work of Augustus.

Augustus was born in 63 B.C. Cicero was consul, and the passionate defender of the ideal of freedom as found in the ancient *polis* and the ancient Roman republic. That same year the *Imperator* Pompey entered Jerusalem and held sway in the lands of the East with the self-glorification of an oriental despot. These two figures appear over the cradle of Augustus like a fateful double star.

Augustus's youth was filled with the struggle between Cato and Caesar: Marcus Porcius Cato, of plebeian origin, with a proud ancestry of consuls and tribunes, who was always to be found in the thick of the battle for the dignity, freedom and rights of the Roman citizen, as well as for the defence of the provincials. His friends called him 'the only free and unyielding man'. And on the other hand Gaius Julius Caesar, sprung from the kings of the early Roman age, a *homo imperiosus* of almost demonic genius, obsessed by the desire to eliminate from the free Roman State its obsolete college of Senates ruling Rome, Italy and the imperial provinces of three continents by means of the government apparatus of an aristocratic local council, and to transform it into a world-wide military monarchy, with himself at its head, ruling with autocratic power. Cato fought Caesar's ominously increasing power with the intrepidity of an upright character and with every legal means in his power. But his methods were unsuccessful. In 46 B.C., in Utica, he fell upon his sword, while Caesar's advance troops were entering the city. 'Victrix causa diis placuit, sed victa Catoni'—'the victorious cause pleased the gods, the defeated cause pleased Cato.' Caesar was proclaimed as a demi-god, and as life-long dictator. But the spirit of Cato lived on, and his nephew and son-in-law Brutus continued the struggle for freedom with fresh resources. Two years after Cato's death Caesar fell beneath the conspirators' daggers. Brutus, however, was no Cromwell. He had the courage to destroy the most creative statesman of the age, in the name of freedom; but

93

he did not possess the constructive power to build up a new order in the name of freedom. The conspirators fled, leaving chaos behind, from which Antony alone was to derive any benefit. On his initiative Caesar was deified, and buried with the funeral chant, 'Those whom I savēd destroyed me'. Was the struggle between direction and freedom to flare up again? Would it rage till Rome and the Roman world were utterly destroyed?

It was at this moment that a nineteen-year-old student came into the forefront, claiming for himself, in the name of freedom, the direction of affairs. He was a grand-nephew of Caesar and his adopted son and heir. At the end of his long life Augustus wrote about the beginning of his career, 'At the age of nineteen, on my own initiative and with my own resources, I gathered an army with whose help I freed society from the domination of a power-group.' What Augustus expresses in the language of practical politics may be expressed in the language of political theory thus: direction and freedom go together. Direction without freedom is tyranny. Freedom without direction is anarchy. Only where there exists genuine direction can you find genuine freedom. This was the regulative principle of Augustus's politics. It sounds like the wisdom of an elder statesman. The remarkable thing is that it was the wisdom of a young man, which accompanied him unchanged through the fifty-six years of his activity, and that he did not once have to retrace his steps. He came on the stage as a finished statesman, which he remained till the end. The phenomenon of Augustus cannot be illuminated by psychological categories of development. He can be understood only with the help of historical and metaphysical categories. His statesmanly wisdom was the fruit not of long individual experience but the climax of generations. In him the history of imperial man reached its goal in the person of a leader who established an empire of freedom. His will, and the course he took, were not the arbitrary will and course of a calculating politician. But the course he took, step by step, was that which was marked out for him by the will of history. Hence his iron coldness and deliberation, his ruthlessness and

irresistibility. We shall note here the most remarkable moments
in this remarkable career.

His first step was to destroy the upholders of romantic
ideas of freedom. With Antony's help he prepared a list of
proscriptions, containing some thousands of names of Caesar's
opponents. A price of about £2000 was set on the head of
each of these men. Without delay the great massacre began.
Even Cicero was included in the list. He was an old man,
and tried to escape in a litter. But he quickly realized that
there was no escape, and bowed his head silently beneath the
swords of the murderers. So died, without a word, the man
who had written and spoken most in the late republic. 'The
rest is silence.' The grey head of the erstwhile consul was
impaled in the market-place in Rome. Those who could escape
betook themselves to Brutus, who was gathering an army in
the East, and on countless coins was summoning men to the
final battle for freedom. But the united legions of Antony and
Augustus won a complete victory at Philippi over the army
of the liberators. The dream of the old republic was finished.
Brutus committed suicide. His brother-in-law Cato, the last
of his house, was killed in the battle. Porcia, the daughter of
the elder Cato and wife of Brutus, put an end to her life by
asphyxiating herself with a handful of burning coals stuffed
into her mouth. For them a whole world was destroyed. The
victors divided the earth between them, Augustus taking Rome
and the West, Antony Alexandria and the East. The war-
weary peoples breathed once more. Virgil proclaimed the
return of the golden age: *redeunt Saturnia regna*. And when, in
the year 40, Augustus visited the colonies in Gaul which
Caesar had established or extended, there appeared in Gaul
a rare bronze coin with a Janus head, composed of the heads
of Caesar and his adopted son, and the double inscription,
'The divine Caesar—and the Son of God.' On the reverse
appeared the chariot of Saturn, the primeval king of paradise.
So an official memorial celebrated the arrival of the twenty-
three-year-old Augustus as the return of the king of paradise
and the coming of a new era.

The second mighty blow struck by Augustus shattered the

romantic legend of the Great King which had so intoxicated the royal lovers, Antony and Cleopatra, in Alexandria. The two had already begun to promise, on their coins and in other ways, the fulfilment of the empire of the Pharaohs and of Alexander in the form of an autocratic monarchy stretching from the Indian Ocean to Gibraltar. But Augustus put them to flight at the battle of Actium, and drove them to death in Alexandria, taking over Egypt as his personal possession. The autocratic dream was over. The official commentary on these events was provided by the coins which appeared throughout the East, celebrating the victor of Actium as the heroic ruler and divine saviour of the world, as the defender of Roman freedom, and as the guarantor of Roman peace.

After this victory Augustus ruled in Rome ostensibly as an official of the republic. All emergency laws and powers from the time of the civil wars were annulled. The son of Cicero, who had been on the black list and had only with difficulty escaped with his life, was made proconsul of Asia, and in this capacity he struck official coins of copper showing the head of his father—the same head which half a generation before had been exposed in the Roman forum. Augustus himself refused to be anything but *princeps senatus*, the first man of the Senate, the first to speak and the first to give his vote. But he could be confident that his voice would not be ignored. It makes an interesting study of a grandiose policy of pretence to see how the forms and formulas of the Senate's liturgy began to take shape at that time. Augustus refused to fill any office which was contrary to the constitution. But in the unprecedented accumulation of various offices, granted for life, his position as leader in the free State was certainly made highly effective. The LIBERTAS AUGUSTA, Augustan freedom, was the name given later by the Senate to this union of autocracy and autonomy. As a Roman among Romans Augustus steadily refused to be named dictator or the autocratic-sounding *dominus*, master. But the Senate and people found other metaphysical categories to express his unique authority. In the framework of an ancient liturgy he was invoked like one of the ancient national gods of Rome, he was given the title of

6. OCTAVIAN

7. LIVIA

Augustus (which means worthy of reverence or worship), and he was surrounded with such an abundance of religious honour that many people thought there was nothing left for the worship of the heavenly gods (Tacitus).

This was the way the Roman *polis* expressed its gratitude to Augustus for making them the free imperial nation of the earth. His political leadership, moreover, was meant to extend freedom to the annexed peoples as well. The Roman *imperium* and its *imperator* became the controlling centre of the life of the nations from the Thames to the Indus. Augustus had a masterly ability to make a moral conquest of nations. This is shown at its most splendid in a journey of several years' duration which he made to the East in the year 21 B.C. He restored their self-government to Tyre and other towns, he united the cities of Asia Minor in an association for the worship of Roma and Augustus, he endowed a daily sacrifice in the temple in Jerusalem for the welfare of the emperor, he settled affairs in the vassal kingdom of Herod, he received embassies from India and the region of the Don, he established his influence as paramount in the mighty continental empire of the east, the Parthian, without raising a single sword—where Crassus lost a battle and his life, where Caesar armed at all points and Antony time and again fought in vain. In the year 19, when Augustus returned to Rome at the humble request of the Senate, his arrival was celebrated like that of a god, and an altar was set up for Fortuna Redux, the patron goddess who had brought him safely home again.

Some years later Augustus undertook a journey to the north, accompanied by the prayers and vows of Rome, in order to study the military state of the Rhine frontier, to settle problems of government in the provinces of Gaul, and at the request of a British delegation to settle some political controversies there. To celebrate his return the Senate decided to set up an *ara pacis Augustae*, an altar in honour of the man who had established peace. For four years the chief artists of the empire worked at this altar, which is not only one of the loveliest works of the golden age of Roman civilization but also the first great monument of European imperial art. Many fine pieces

97

of this have survived, finest of all the marble relief on which Augustus himself appears, composed and dignified, the first citizen and servant and priest of the empire. He wears a toga, the *himation* of the free Roman citizen. All the figures on the altar, gods and heroes and men, princes and priests, soldiers and officials, wear the same dress.

If one compares this work of art with the oldest monument of imperial art, the pyramid and sphinx of Gizeh, and remembers Herodotus's description of how hundreds of thousands of slaves laboured at these tasks for thirty years, then one can appreciate the change which Augustus had brought about.

The last twenty-five years of his long rule were for the most part years of quiet, and this quiet is in fact the finest achievement which Augustus could have wished for his policies. The best politics are those which are unnoticed. That was the ideal of the age, and the way in which the almighty *princeps* governed. The people had bread and games. The emperor did not need much for himself. Antony and Cleopatra were prodigal of the riches of Egypt and the perfumes of Arabia for their mythological masquerades, in which they themselves played the chief parts—so they squandered the most precious weeks of history. Augustus wore the woollen toga spun and woven for him by Livia, and his only personal luxury was his two barbers who shaved him simultaneously when official business was pressing. Antony's head chef put another boar on the spit every ten minutes, in order to have a constant supply of crisp roast ready for his master. Augustus preferred coarse bread and cheese. Cleopatra died in the tomb built for her after the fashion of the Pharaohs, on a golden couch, surrounded by all her treasures. Augustus died in the bed where he had been born. He was a master of immanent asceticism; he knew how to possess everything as though he possessed nothing. And if the State treasury, or the purse of some friend, were empty, Augustus supplied the need from his own resources. So, for example, in the year 12 B.C. he paid the year's taxes for the whole province of Asia from his own coffers. In this manner he gave away enormous sums. Far away, beyond the German frontier, there was war. But the war was waged by the emperor's own mercenary troops. There was news of a heavy defeat suffered by Quinctilius Varus, a relation of the imperial house, which was taken very seriously by the now elderly emperor. But everything was smoothly settled by the clever strategy of the emperor's stepson Tiberius and his deliberate exploitation of Germanic domestic rivalries. Everything was in the best of hands. Augustus was a blessing to mankind. He was remembered at every prayer at table, and by men on their death-beds. The Senate designated him father of the fatherland. Poets honoured him as the father of the earth. Twenty-three years after his conquest of Egypt an inscription was set up on the island of Philae high up the Nile at the first waterfall: 'The emperor, ruler of oceans and continents, the divine father among men, who bears the same name as his heavenly father—Liberator, the marvellous star of the Greek world, shining with the brilliance of the great heavenly Saviour.' And decades after his death an Alexandrian Jew called him the great benefactor and in the style of a litany says, 'The whole of mankind would have been almost destroyed in internecine strife, if one man and leader, Augustus, had not appeared, who is worthy to be called the hero who averted disaster, who healed the common afflictions of the Greek and barbarian worlds. It was he who not merely loosened but burst the chains which bound and oppressed the dwellers of the earth. It was he who led all the cities of the earth to freedom, who made order out of chaos, who preserved freedom [and now comes a very sober statement], and gave each man his due (*suum cuique*).' Augustus himself expressed it even more soberly. 'It has been my endeavour', he said in an official proclamation, 'to be described in days to come as the creator of the *optimus status*, and to hope, when I come to die, that the foundations which I have laid will last immovably.' *Optimus status* we may translate as 'the best possible state of affairs'. The words have an Aristotelian sound. The great political philosopher of antiquity, whom Augustus no doubt had studied, had examined the history of nations and of constitutions in order to discover the best and therefore the most enduring *status* and had found it to consist in the

avoidance of autocratic and of autonomous extremes, and in
the union of direction and freedom. Now the great statesman
of antiquity had made this *status* into a political reality. So
he has become the classic exponent of European imperial politics and the political teacher of the whole world. More, he
made his age itself into the best possible in history, an age
of blessing such as war-ridden mankind has not seen before
or since. The age of Augustus may well be described in
Hölderlin's words as one in which 'fate for a while has been
pacified'.

But only 'for a while'. Augustus died fourteen years after
the birth of Christ. His successor Tiberius did not disturb the
foundations laid by Augustus, and he ruled the world with
excellent restraint and admirable tact along the lines laid down
by his glorified adoptive father. But the new master of the
world was filled with profound resignation, with a melancholy
like that of king Saul or the emperor Charles V. In the prime
of his life he spent a year as a hermit on the island of Rhodes.
He ascended the throne when he was fifty-six, and seven years
later he once more withdrew into solitude, and finally at the
age of seventy he retired to Capri where he cut himself off
completely from the world. He left the reins of government
in the hands of his commanders of the guard—and it was as
though God had given over the rule of the world to the devil.
Conspiracies, trials for lese-majesty, judicial murders, denun-
ciations, suicides, mysterious deaths in the imperial family,
gossip and wild rumours were the signs of the time. A bitter
rhyme went from mouth to mouth—

> Caesar, you have changed
> the golden age,
> For as long as you live
> it will be an iron age.

This was the fruit of Augustus's promising achievement. It
was as though every power of fate which he had expelled had
broken loose again, and the dance of death was beginning
again, worse than ever before. How could this happen in a
single generation? Even the great Augustus could only bind,

not conquer, the demons of history. He brought an armistice, not peace, to the world. This was the secret which was now revealed—what is possible and what is not possible to the perfect product of the *homo imperiosus*. This was what Augustus showed, and this is his historical significance. His achievement, which was the greatest possible, illuminated the tragic and ambiguous quality of all historical action. Something is not in order with history. Something has happened. Something has to be put in order, something has to happen. This is the problem which drove history on from Augustus to Jesus.

II

One must go far back in order to grasp the significance of Augustus. One must go much further back in order to understand the significance of Jesus, to the very beginning of human history.

The history of man is the history of guilt rolling through the ages like an ever-increasing avalanche. This guilt is the *daimonia* of self-glorification, which shattered first the community between man and God and then, with logical necessity, the community between man and man. From that time every historical community has been merely an emergency structure on a shattered foundation. Thus the greatest builder of community ever seen in history, the *homo imperiosus*, was only an emergency builder. He could only take emergency measures, which could never overcome radically, and therefore definitively, the original daemonic distress of human society. The *homo imperiosus* could bind the dragon; but he could not slay it.

These are not truths which lie open to the whole world. They are secrets which are entrusted to the people of Jesus Christ. But they are not the ultimate secrets. The ultimate secrets of history were entrusted to the prophet Daniel and his apocalyptic successors. The content of these secrets is that imperial man is and remains the bearer of history from one age and empire and imperial nation to the next. But the people to whom the prophets and the apocalyptists belong is excluded

from the succession of imperial peoples—until the coming of
the New Man, who comes down from heaven to make a new
beginning on earth, to gather together the people of the future
kingdom, and to establish an eternal kingdom. He will come
to the people of the prophets and apocalyptists, he will not
be recognized by them but will be persecuted and will give
his life, as the innocent servant of God, for an atoning sacrifice for his people and for the building up of the coming
kingdom in which there will be no more crying or pain. This
great stranger who will make an end to the primal cleavage
and establish the destiny of mankind on a new basis is the
Son of Man.

This was the spiritual background of the world in which
Jesus grew up. The political background must also be described.

The homeland of Jesus was almost the only region of the
Roman world where even the great Augustus was never able
to create complete peace. Herod the Great, king by the emperor's grace, was a bloodhound perpetually at war with the
Jewish nationalists and with the Messianic movements. In his
last years, by his own arbitrary policies, he lost a large part
of his royal powers, and the imperial legate for the East,
Quirinius, introduced a census of the population, at the request of Augustus, in order that in Palestine as in the rest of
the empire there might be a basis for the levying of the imperial taxes. The Galilean rebel and guerrilla king, Judah ben
Hiskiah, proclaimed a holy war, and established the party of
the Zealots, that is, those who were zealous for God and His
kingdom. And Joseph, the descendant of David, went with
Mary from Nazareth to the old royal city of Bethlehem, in
order to fulfil his duty as a vassal. This is the report of the
Gospel according to St. Luke. It was in this historical situation
that Jesus was born.

The census was carried out. But the unrest continued, and
the differing attitudes to Rome drove deep wedges through
the mass of the people as well as their leaders. The sons of
Herod and their followers, the Herodians, owed their power
to Rome alone, so that their policies were those of Rome.

The high-priestly group, the Sadducees, deprived of political power by the Romans, but with their priestly functions guaranteed, were the men who offered the daily sacrifice for the emperor's welfare and exhorted the people to submission and loyalty. There were the scribes, who were for ever discovering new laws in the Torah, and the Pharisees, who made it their lifelong task to fulfil these laws, in order that by their super-piety they might constrain the kingdom of God to come. If only *one* Sabbath were truly kept, they said, the Messiah would have to come and the kingdom of Israel be established. Then there were the Zealots, the party of Judas of Galilee, now a kind of secret society, which was arming for the struggle to establish a political kingdom of God. Their influence grew after the emperor Tiberius, in A.D. 26, had withdrawn for good to Campania and his prefect of the Guard, Sejanus, had appointed as procurator of Judaea a man after his own heart, the brutal Pontius Pilate, an implacable hater of the Jews, whose period of power, till the fall of his patron Sejanus in 31, was a mere series of provocations and pogroms. The people defended themselves as well as they could, and in their despair turned to each new sabre-rattler and miracle-worker who appeared. The serious-minded, however, attached themselves to John the Baptist, who was gathering round himself the holy ones of the last days, for the promised kingdom of the end. The call of Jesus took place at this historic moment.

For more than thirty years Jesus had awaited this call in quietness—and now there began the history of those four short years which can never be forgotten by men. Here we shall only mention a few of the facts.

The day of the call was followed by a time of temptations. The call of God was immediately confronted by another call. The Gospels speak of this apocalyptic event in apocalyptic pictures. The daimon of this world shows God's Called One all the kingdoms of the world and their glory and says to him: 'All these things will I give thee if thou wilt fall down and worship me' (Matt. 4.9). That is Jesus' great temptation: the temptation to go the way of the *homo imperiosus*, who with daimonic power seizes power for himself and wins the masses by miraculous bread and games—a new David, or Judas Maccabaeus, or Herod, a second Augustus, a greater than all of these together, yet just one more of a series who capitulate to the daimon of this world. If Jesus said Yes to this temptation, then everything would be as before. But Jesus said No. 'Get thee hence, Satan: for it is written, thou shalt worship the Lord thy God, and him only shalt thou serve' (Matt. 4.10). Then Satan left Him. Who was this who overcame the old wicked enemy, to whom no man had been equal since the days of Paradise? Who was this, who after his apocalyptic victory gathered about him a court of beasts and angels like the royal man of the first days? It was no man of this world. Jesus Himself gave the answer: It is the Son of Man.

The Son of Man came to His people, and grief seized Him on their account, for they were like sheep lacking a shepherd. He looked at the leaders of His people, and anger seized Him, for they were false shepherds, hirelings and wolves in sheep's clothing. They were men of violence, who tried to take the kingdom of God by force of arms or by their religiousness.

Jesus entered upon a struggle against the uncalled leaders of the people, a struggle for the soul and destiny of His people, who could not find their place in the kingdom of this world and time, for they refused to see and to fulfil their mission in the service of the coming kingdom. He called His disciples from every group of His torn people—twelve in all—and sent them out to the twelve tribes of Israel to proclaim His good news of the kingdom of God. The message of the kingdom was accompanied by the signs of the kingdom. 'Behold, I have given you authority over all the power of the enemy' (Luke 10.19).

But He Himself was the decisive sign of the kingdom, going about doing good, and healing all that were oppressed of the devil, going in and out among those that laboured and were heavy laden, promising mercy to the merciful, comfort to the mourners, and to the meek the earth. In the midst of a world full of barriers the Son of Man appeared, with room in His heart for good and evil, for joyful and sad, for Romans and

Samaritans, for children and animals. Where He was, there was the kingdom, in the midst of a world full of suffering and outcry.

He remained among His people, and did not leave them. He knew that He was sent to the lost sheep of Israel. He would not give bread to the dogs before the children of the house had had their fill. He came to cast fire upon the earth. But the place where it is to be kindled is the ground where His people dwells. For His people is the people of the Son of Man, the people of the kingdom of the future. Augustus proclaimed the message to his people: you are the people of the kingdom on earth. Jesus brought his people the message: you are the people of the kingdom of the coming world.

Jesus uttered His call in the name of God. But His people said No. Jesus knew this from the beginning. But He had to utter His call, and the people had to answer as they did, in order that the measure might be full.

After the decision had been taken, Jesus moved northwards with the little group of loyal followers to the source of the Jordan. A city had been built there by Philip the Tetrarch, called Caesarea in honour of his master in Rome. A white marble temple towered above the city, built by Herod the Great for the worship of Augustus. But the snow-capped Mount Hermon rose almost nine thousand feet above the temple. It was in this majestic scene that Jesus asked His disciples, 'Who do you say that I am?', and Peter answered 'Thou art the Christ'—and Jesus replied to him, 'The Son of Man must suffer many things'. Peter tried to contradict Him, but Jesus turned and said to him, 'Get thee behind me, Satan: . . . for thou mindest not the things of God, but the things of men' (Matt. 16.13ff.).

Once more the daimon of this world had tempted Him, once more the Inaugurator of the new humanity had carried off the victory over the ancient enemy. And now He entered on the sacrificial way, ordained for the Son of Man since the foundation of the world. 'Behold, I cast out devils and perform cures today and tomorrow, and the third day I am perfected. Howbeit I must go on my way today and tomorrow and the day following: for it cannot be that a prophet perish out of Jerusalem' (Luke 31.32f.).

So Jesus came to Jericho. This was an ancient fortress whose first walls were built not much later than the Pyramids, which was seen by the dying Moses from nearby Nebo, and first conquered by Joshua in the might of the Lord. Herod the Great had re-fortified the town with a citadel and a strong wall. Within the walls lay the palace in which he died, and the hippodrome in which the prisoners he had gathered to accompany him in death awaited the executioner. The whole of Jericho was like a sinister monument to a demonic will to power. In the shadow of the wall there cowered a blind man, like a symbol of the need of this world, which no power of this world can conquer. The march of history passed this man by. But when he heard the step of Jesus he cried, 'Jesus, thou son of David, have mercy on me', louder and louder, till Jesus spoke the word of release, 'Go thy way; thy faith hath made thee whole' (Mark 10.46ff.). The need of the world had found its Master. The angel of mercy traverses the world of violence.

The final encounter of the *civitas dei* and the *civitas terrena* took place in the city of God, which quietly looked upon itself as the future capital of the world, the city of the temple of Jahweh and of the palaces of the rulers, during the tense days of the Feast of the Passover, when the songs of the pilgrims and commands of the centurions mingled their echoes in the streets. Jesus made His entry into the Holy City as the powerless king of the divine kingdom of peace. The crowd hailed His advent as the fulfilment of their political hopes: 'Blessed is he that cometh in the name of the Lord: Blessed is the kingdom that cometh, the kingdom of our father David' (Mark 11.9f.).

Now events moved to an overwhelming climax. The political parties wanted to subdue Him in one way or another, either by winning Him over or by making His cause impossible; so they put the question which had divided His people since the revolt of Judah ben Hiskiah: 'Is it lawful to give tribute unto Caesar, or not?' (Matt. 22.17). The reply of Jesus is a confession of loyalty to the empire and a summons to the kingdom of God. To go the way of God in history includes loyalty to the emperor. To serve God's historical purpose means that God alone must be worshipped. This was a realistic negative to the nationalist and Messianic war policy of the Zealots, with its romantic hopes. Jesus spoke of this in a parable which was also a programme: 'Or what king, as he goeth to encounter another king in war, will not sit down first and take counsel whether he is able with ten thousand to meet him that cometh against him with twenty thousand? Or else, while the other is yet a great way off, he sendeth an ambassage, and asketh conditions of peace?' (Luke 14.31f.). This political parable has unmistakable apocalyptic overtones. As God, in the days of the Babylonian empire, proclaimed, 'And now I have given all these lands into the hands of Nebuchadnezzar the king of Babylon . . . and the nation and kingdom which will not serve him will I punish . . . until I have consumed them by his hand' (Jer. 27.6ff.), so now Jesus proclaims in the age of Roman domination that the struggle against the emperor is a mischievous and hopeless struggle against God who has called him, it is theomachy.

The emperor by God's grace is the ultimate historical source of all political legitimacy. Jesus spoke of this too, in another of the parables of the kingdom, that of the money entrusted to the servants—in its original form alluding to Herod Arche-laos's journey to Rome, in order to be confirmed in his rule by Augustus, in defiance of the protests of a Jewish delega-tion: 'A certain nobleman went into a far country, to receive for himself a kingdom, and to return. . . . But his citizens hated him (for he was an austere man who took up what he had not laid down, and reaped what he did not sow), and sent an ambassage after him, saying, We will not that this man reign over us. And it came to pass, when he was come back again, having received the kingdom, that he summoned these servants and said, "Howbeit these mine enemies, which would not that I should reign over them, bring hither, and slay them before me"' (Luke 19.27).

Jesus' attitude was clear. His break with the romantic idea

of a political kingdom was complete. His rejection of the
divine city, which neglected its historical mission in its obsession with utopian dreams of being a universal capital, and
which was moving steadily towards catastrophe, was final.
'If thou hadst known in this day, even thou, the things which
belong unto thy peace! . . . For the days shall come upon
thee, when thine enemies shall cast up a bank about thee, and
compass thee round . . . and shall dash thee to the ground,
and thy children within thee . . . because thou knewest not
the time of thy visitation' (Luke 19.42ff.).

Not long afterwards two sons of Judas Galilaeus were
crucified. Not many years afterwards an uncanny visitor
appeared at the temple festivals on Mount Zion, the apocalyptic Jesus ben Hananya, prophesying: 'Woe to Jerusalem.
A voice of the morning, a voice of the evening, a voice of
the four winds, a voice against Jerusalem and the temple,
against bridegroom and bride, against the whole people. Woe,
woe to Jerusalem!' And in the middle of the night the temple
doors sprang open and the priests heard a voice from heaven,
saying, 'Let us depart from here.' So the rabbinic tradition
tells how the Holy One left His sanctuary—how God left His
people. The theomachy of the people of God ended in a
terrible catastrophe. The last son of the hero of freedom,
Judas Galilaeus, led his people in a desperate assault on the
Roman legions. A forest of crosses arose round the destroyed
city of God. The survivors gathered in a little stronghold in
the mountains, 1960 men, women and children, the last fanatical upholders of freedom. They had only one hope left—
to die; one wish—to die together; one loving service to perform—to slay one another, so that none should be taken alive
by the victors.

These visions of the future hung over the farewell words
of Jesus to His people like a lurid sky. Jesus saw the Roman
eagle poised over Jerusalem like a bird of prey ready to strike.
'How often would I have gathered thy children together, even
as a hen gathers her chickens under her wings, and you would
not!' (Matt. 23.37).

The people of the Old Covenant had failed. But the kingdom

of God went on its way, and the Son of Man founded a
new people of God. He gathered His disciples for the Feast
of the Passover, and passed round the cup, and said, 'This is
my blood of the covenant, which is shed for many. Verily,
I say unto you, I will no more drink of the fruit of the vine,
until that day when I drink it new in the kingdom of God.'
The same evening He proclaimed the covenantal law of the
new kingdom: 'Ye know that they which are accounted to
rule over the Gentiles lord it over them; and the great ones
exercise authority over them. But it is not so among you:
but whosoever would become great among you, shall be your
minister. And whosoever would be first among you, shall be
servant of all. For verily the Son of Man came not to be
ministered unto, but to minister, and to give his life a ran-
som for many' (Mark 10.42ff.).

The next morning the Sanhedrin delivered the Son of Man
to the procurator Pilate and asked for Barabbas the rebel chief
to be handed over in return as a Passover gift. On the way to
execution Jesus addressed His last words to his people:
'Daughters of Jerusalem, weep not for me, but weep for your-
selves, and for your children' (Luke 23.28). Soon Jesus hung
upon the Cross, over Him the mocking superscription of the
Roman procurator: 'Jesus of Nazareth, the king of the Jews.'
And the people of Jesus celebrated the feast of the Passover
as though nothing had happened.

But the story of the Son of Man was not over. In the hour
of crucifixion it broke through the framework of national
history and became universal history. The Crucified has made
history. The Resurrected completed the work begun in the
days of the Passion—the founding of the people of the New
Covenant. The heavenly shepherd handed His pastoral staff to
the first apostle—'Feed my lambs' (John 21.16ff.), and sent
out His last apostle with the message of peace and the coming
kingdom to the ends of the earth.

Augustus spoke of the aim of his life, the hope he took with
him to the grave, as that 'the political foundations which I
lay may endure immovably'. His hope was wrecked. Jesus
said, 'Upon this rock I will build my church; and the gates

of hell shall not prevail against it' (Matt. 16.18). The promise of the Son of Man was not wrecked.

The new people lived and increased—not free from the demon of guilt, but in the grace of God, living by the Word of forgiveness and the sacrament of the divine covenant, and experiencing the miracle of a new relationship between man and man. It was the Church of the Cross, the symbol of the new situation in the world, which had been brought about by the Son of Man, and at the same time the sign of the kingdom He had promised.

For two thousand years the history of *homo imperiosus* had determined human destiny. For two thousand years man's history had been one of violence and illegality, with world dominion shifting from one nation to another. Then the secret redemptive history of God came to light, and the history of the divine people, politically disinherited, because destined to be the heir of the kingdom of God, sent its shining track across human history. The history of the Old Covenant lasted a thousand years, the span given to it by God to become ripe for its redemptive mission. Then the Son of Man appeared in the midst of the people of God, greeting the holy people of the Most High in the name of the coming kingdom, the source of peace since the creation of the world. But the people of God rejected the Son of Man. So He turned away—'I say unto you, ye shall not see me henceforth, till ye shall say, Blessed is he that cometh in the name of the Lord' (Matt. 23.39). Thus ended the first book of human history.

At the same moment the second book began. Jesus called the new people of God, which was destined to take over the redemptive function of the old: the Church, the people of Christ, who had heard the call of the Son of Man, and remained true through all the vicissitudes of time, proclaiming Christ's message of the kingdom through all changes in worldly powers as the ultimate *ratio* of history. The Church's gospel sounds through the noise of politics like the *ceterum censeo* of God, which cannot and will not be silent until human history has reached its final point—when all the peoples of the earth join in the advent cry of the divine people: 'Blessed is he that cometh in the name of the Lord.'

In the days of the Old Covenant Moses led the wandering people through the wilderness to the frontiers of the promised land, which he himself was not allowed to enter. He saw it from afar, and died. And God Himself buried the friend to whom He had to deny this last thing. Another led the people into the promised land—Joshua, whom the Greeks call Jesus.

In the days of the New Covenant Augustus led men to the limits of the blessing that imperial man can bring to mankind. And history has given to its chosen favourite, to whom it had to deny the last thing, the most honourable memorial among mortals. But the way into the land of promise was made by another, by the great stranger from the other world, Jesus.

VIII

THE STORY OF THE
TRIBUTE MONEY

THE oldest form of the story of the tribute money is probably
to be found in Mark 12.13-17. The accounts of Luke and
Matthew (Luke 20.20-26 and Matt. 22.15-22) do not differ in
any essential from Mark—a valuable illustration of the unity
of the primitive tradition. They provide us, besides, with the
oldest commentaries on the Marcan account.

In recent times there has come to light a fourth version of
the story in the Egerton Papyrus, discovered in 1934, and to
be dated at latest A.D. 140. The translation of this text is as
follows:

'They came to Him in order to question Him, and tempted
Him with the words, Rabbi Jesus, we know that Thou art
come from God. For what Thou doest bears witness beyond
all the prophets. Therefore tell us, Is it lawful to render to
the Caesars what one owes to the government? Are we to
render to them or not? But Jesus knew their intention, grew
wrathful, and said to them, "Why do you call me Rabbi with
your lips, and do not listen to what I say? Well did Isaiah
prophesy of you, saying, 'This people honoureth Me with
their lips, but its heart is far from Me. In vain do they worship Me, commandments. . . .' " '

The fragment is without any original historical value. The
clumsy form of address alone shows this. For the dogmatizing
combination 'Rabbi Jesus' comes neither from the synagogue
nor from the early Christian community. The plural 'Caesars',
moreover, is a suspicious anachronism, indicating the age of
the dual principate. The style of the harmonies of the Gospels
is to be seen in the abstract and common form 'intention',

8. THE TRIBUTE MONEY

9. THE TRIBUTE MONEY—*Reverse*

which tries to harmonize the concrete Synoptic forms of
'hypocrisy', 'wickedness', and 'craftiness'. These and other
signs indicate a text about two generations later than that of
Mark. What does its content offer us? At the beginning a
question which is no question, at the end an answer which is
no answer, and for the rest an unsuccessful mosaic of New
Testament reminiscences and forms—which is all, nevertheless, a very welcome proof that by that time not only Mark
but also the Fourth Gospel was generally known. It is worth
while comparing the papyrus text in detail with the words of
the Bible from which it is derived.

Papyrus: They tempted him. Matt. 22.18: Why tempt ye
me? Papyrus: Rabbi Jesus, we know that thou art come from
God. John. 3.2: Rabbi, we know that thou art a teacher come
from God. Papyrus: What thou doest bears witness beyond
all the prophets. John 5.36b: the very works that I do, bear
witness of me; John 5.36a: the witness which I have is greater
than that of John. Papyrus: to the Caesars. I Tim. 2.2: for
kings (the Caesars). Papyrus: to the government. Tit. 3.1: to
authorities (governments). Papyrus: to render what one owes.
Mark 12.17: Render. I Mac. 11.35: the custom which one
owes. Rom. 13.7: Render to all their dues: tribute to whom
tribute is due; custom to whom custom. Papyrus: Jesus grew
wrathful. John 11.33: Jesus grew wrathful (groaned). Papyrus:
Why do you call me Rabbi with your lips, and do not listen
to what I say? Luke 6.46: And why call ye me, Lord, Lord,
and do not the things which I say? Papyrus: Well did Isaiah
prophesy of you, saying, This people honoureth Me with their
lips, but its heart is far from Me. In vain do they worship
Me. . . . Matt. 15.7ff.: Well did Isaiah prophesy of you, saying,
This people honoureth me with their lips; but their heart is
far from me. But in vain do they worship me. . . .

Commentary is superfluous. Fictitious stories and speeches
about Jesus are just of this kind. The Marcan account is quite
different; it does not bear the marks of fiction. The scientific
significance of this papyrus is that it shows once more that
in time and place and matter the account of Mark 12.13ff. is
precise, rich and full. A comparison with the papyrus can

only strengthen our respect for the historicity of Mark's account: 'And they send unto him certain of the Pharisees and of the Herodians, that they might catch him in talk.'

They wanted to destroy Jesus. Why? Because He proclaimed God's authority. That was the reason, but it was concealed (Mark 11.27f.). They sought a pretext. His weapon was His words. Therefore His words must yield the pretext. But His words yielded nothing. For God's claim of authority is to be found where it is proclaimed purely, where neither the government nor the law can touch it. But still they waited for a word with which He would be 'beside Himself' and so settle His own fate. So now they tried to draw this word from Him:

'Master, we know that thou art true, and carest not for any one: for thou regardest not the person of men, but of a truth teachest the way of God.'

This is one of the most splendid witnesses to Jesus, an undogmatic judgment from the lips of His enemies, an objective statement like that of Mark 1.27, Matt. 7.28ff. and John 7.46. The first word means 'Teacher', and the last words also speak of teaching. They address Him in the forms customary for addressing one who is learned in the Scriptures. They ask for a professional judgment, for a competent exposition of Scripture. For He is 'true'. This does not mean something subjective, a truth that is in love with itself and pours forth unfledged truths. But it means objective truthfulness, which is bound to the truth and proclaims the way of God, which has been darkened by untruthful exposition of Scripture and the exegesis of the schools (John 7.15; Mark 6.2, 1.27). This truthfulness has a distinguishing mark: it is ruthless ('Thou carest not for any one'). And it has a presupposition: it is fearless ('thou regardest not the person of men'). The scribes ask to right and to left. But Jesus asks neither to the right nor to the left. Therefore He will come into conflict in the end, either with those on the right or on the left, or with both.

'Is it lawful to give tribute unto Caesar, or not? Shall we give, or shall we not give?'

Kēnsos is the word used by Mark and Matthew. Luke says

phoros, likewise Rom. 13.7*a* in the oldest version of the story. An ancient variant says *tributum capitis*. All three expressions are technical, and may be harmlessly translated as poll taxes, and still more harmlessly paraphrased as direct taxes in contrast with the *telos*, the indirect tax which was rented in bulk to the tax-farmers and collected by their despised tax-gatherers. But this interpretation loses the political note which is contained in each expression, and which is sounded for our ears quite clearly in the Latin word *tribute*.

The court artists of the Pharaohs depicted in gigantic triumphal scenes the reception by the divine Pharaoh of the delegations of the conquered peoples, bringing him tributes as offerings to a god. Herodotus makes us realize the views of ancient times about taxes: The ruling nation pays no taxes. Tax-paying is the duty of the subjugated peoples, it is the tribute which attests the loss of their sovereignty and the fact of their national subjugation. As formerly the Persian, and later the Hellenist Great King gathered taxes from the con-quered nations, so now the Roman emperor exacts tribute. In the homeland this was the care of officials of the Senate. But in the frontier provinces the system of taxation was con-trolled by personal representatives of the emperor, who directed the flow of tribute into the emperor's coffers in Rome. Syria was one of these frontier provinces. A few years before the birth of Christ Publius Quinctilius Varus ruled in Syria. The nature of his rule may be inferred from the laconic report of a Roman contemporary: 'As a poor man he went to a rich province, and as a rich man left a poor province.' His son, too, as Tacitus reports, was famed for his riches. With the money he brought back from Syria he may have acquired the costly silver vessels from which later, in the Teutoburger Forest, he ate and drank so unsuspectingly with Arminius, on the eve of the great battle. Next day they were the booty of the Germanic tribes, and today they are in Hildesheim, a warning to all unjust stewards.

Palestine was in a sense part of the province of Syria. A system of tribute had been introduced there by Pompey, the well-hated destroyer of Jewish freedom, the unforgotten conqueror of Jerusalem and profaner of the holy of holies. The Roman tax in Jerusalem was a constant reminder of the black day in the city's life, and a symbol of the heathen domination.

In the days of Varus Jerusalem was ruled by king Herod, of whom we read in the Gospel narratives (Luke 1.5; Matt. 2.1). He was a typical time-server, cringing before those above him, trampling on those beneath. How this puppet king ruled can be read in Josephus: 'The carrying-out of these measures was watched with bitterness by the people, as a destruction of their worship and customs, and they were filled with rage and fury. But Herod, faced with this situation, only increased his preventive measures. He deprived his subjects of all time or opportunity to rebel, and issued a special regulation that everyone should remain constantly at work. The inhabitants of Jerusalem were not permitted to meet in public assembly, or in private, whether at home or in the street. A constant watch was kept. Anyone who was caught was severely punished. Many were removed, openly or secretly, to the fortress of Hyrcania, and there destroyed. Wherever people met, in the city or in the streets, there were informers to spy on them. It was even said that the king himself joined in this work, disguised as a private citizen and moving about among the people by night, to learn what they thought about the government. The disaffected, who were stoutly opposed to his measures, he plagued by every means in his power. And the majority were bound to him by repeated oaths of loyalty and submission, exacted from them in servile fear. The independent opponents who were unable to conceal their dissatisfaction with his rule of terror were removed.'

Everything we know of Herod's fiscal policies bears out this general judgment. Herod was the legal functionary of Augustus and therefore exacted tribute in his name. In practice, however, he simply paid a lump sum into the imperial treasury—as had been customary in Palestine since the time of the Ptolemies—and exacted the taxes from his subjects in his own right. The greed and brutality with which he carried this out made him more hated than before; nor was this without political consequences. Six thousand Pharisees refused to take the oath of allegiance to the person of the emperor, and of submission to his vassal-king. Twice the imperial government compelled Herod to reduce his tax demands. But the miseries of the people were not abated, and there were constant messengers to the imperial court, carrying complaints about the oppressive burden of taxation and requests for a political change. Augustus responded in the end by prescribing a census and taxation of the whole people—that enrolment reported by Luke whose date is so difficult to determine. The effects of this on the people were of two kinds. We learn that the high priest advised unconditional loyalty, and we know that the parents of Jesus obeyed him (Luke 2). A contemporary of Joseph, on the other hand, the scribe Judas Galilaeus, looking on himself as the true teacher of the true way of God, in the sense of Mark 12.14, summoned his countrymen, in the name of God and Holy Scripture, to refuse to pay the tax, to passive resistance, and finally to a war of liberation from Rome. 'He called his fellow countrymen to revolt, and reproached them for patiently paying tribute to Rome, and trying to please mortal men next to God.' 'He reproached them for being submissive to the Romans next to God.' It is clear that the reason for this refusal to pay the tax was not only an economic protest by a plundered people, not only a political protest by a subjugated nation, but also a theological protest by the people of God against their heathen rulers and their emperor, against 'any confession of Caesar as lord'. And behind the protest there was a programme. Judas Galilaeus aimed at being the Messianic king and at raising his people to be the rulers of the earth. This promised man had established his headquarters at Sepporis, three miles north of Nazareth. The people streamed to join him, at their head the Pharisee Sadduk. The Romans crushed the rebellion mercilessly. 'Judas of Galilee . . . perished; and all, as many as obeyed him, were scattered abroad' (Acts 5.37). The enrolment was continued. In Judaea a Roman procurator took over control and was responsible for securing the taxes. The Sadducaean authorities, whose loyalty was proved again and again, were his agents. But the matter was not so easily settled. So it was taken over by the

procurators themselves, lesser government officials whose aim
was to renovate their own dilapidated finances in the style of
Varus. The emperor Tiberius, who was unsentimental and
far-seeing in matters of taxation, once replied to an official
proposal to increase taxation in these words: 'A good shepherd is one who fleeces the sheep without taking the skin off
their backs.' But in respect of Judaea, where questions of
taxation were not merely economic and political, but were
also mixed up with religious politics, he was not so exact in
his advice to his functionaries. Valerius Gratus, the first procurator to be sent by him, entered on his duties in A.D. 15.
In the year 17 an appeal reached Rome from the exhausted
province for an alleviation of taxes. But the emperor left
Gratus in office till 26, saying that his procurators were like
flies who must first suck their fill and they would then be
more moderate of their own accord. In the year 26 there was
a change in Rome: the emperor retired to Capri and left the
government in the hands of Sejanus, his prefect of the Guard,
who proceeded to fill offices with his own creatures. Sejanus
was determined 'to extirpate the Jewish people', and he sent
to Judaea a man of his own kidney, the procurator Pontius
Pilate, who ruled for ten years until he was recalled by the
emperor in person, and disappeared into obscurity. Pilate
inaugurated his official career in Palestine by an action which
provoked the whole population in respect of religion as well
as politics. Roman standards were adorned with medallions
portraying the reigning emperor. For the Jews, with their
prohibition of images, this in itself was abhorrent. But these
signa also played a part in the military cult: the image of the
emperor had to be worshipped. To the monotheist Jews this
was double abhorrent. Hitherto the Roman military commanders had magnanimously respected Jewish feelings, and
had the medallions removed from the *signa* before entering
Jerusalem. But Pontius Pilate thought otherwise. His troops
were brought by night into the holy city with their standards
complete, and the next morning the *signa* with the obnoxious
medallions were to be seen beneath the windows of the castle
of Antonia in the temple area—the 'abomination of desolation'

in the holy place. There was a tremendous agitation. Only when Pilate realized that even the fiercest threats were unheeded did he give way. But he never forgave the people their triumph. From that time he sensed revolution or lesemajesty everywhere, and omitted no opportunity of injuring or incensing the populace.

The story of the standards in the temple area has been often discussed, both in ancient and modern literature, and may be followed in a paper by P. L. Hedley in *The Journal of Theological Studies* (1934). Another of Pilate's measures was just as malicious and provocative, but more subtly contrived —and has therefore been little regarded by either ancient or modern historians. I refer to the new course which he adopted in the policy of coin issues. His policy may be studied in G. F. Hill's *Catalogue of the Greek Coins of Palestine* (1914). The procurators had the right to issue local copper coins to meet the unusual demand in Judaea for small coins. But it was their duty in choosing portraits and inscriptions for the coins to avoid offence—for example, by making use of portraits of the emperor. Valerius Gratus, in compliance with this, had issued coins with types of a palm-tree or ears of corn. But as early as 29 Pilate issued copper coins bearing the *lituus*, the priest's staff, or the *patera*, the sacrificial bowl—two symbols of the imperial philosophy which were bound to be obnoxious to the people. It was a deliberate provocation. Pilate could exasperate them as much as he pleased in this way, without any fear of noisy demonstrations. For even his most pious and uncompromising opponents had a bad conscience about coins, and Pilate had obviously realized this in his first three years of office. In fact the people who had been so roused by the matter of the *signa* accepted the provocative coins without open resistance. It was not till the fall of Sejanus (A.D. 31) that the matter was probably raised and the offence removed. For the issue of such coins suddenly ceased at that time. It appears that Pilate lost the right to issue any coins at all. His successors, who were certainly no angels, did not resume the obnoxious practice. Pilate's coins were even withdrawn from circulation, and the offensive sceptre was overprinted with an unoffending palm branch. There is a coin of Pilate's in the British Museum which has been overprinted by the procurator Felix in this way. It is possible from this kind of evidence to deduce that Pilate was, in this matter at least, the most unpleasant procurator whom Judaea ever had.

The New Testament, too, mentions several incidents in which Pilate and the people came into conflict (Luke 13.1; Mark 15.7), and a contemporary account catalogues Pilate's crimes as bribery, arbitrary action, expropriations, torture, insults, countless illegal executions, insatiable and ruthless cruelty. When we know that the secret organization of Judas the Galilean was spreading in those days under the leadership of his sons, we have some idea of the way in which Pilate handled the system of taxation, driving the people ever deeper into economic, political and religious tribulation. Praises of freedom and laments about the violence of the procurators were on the lips of all. Even in the circle of Jesus' disciples there was at least one zealot—that is, a follower of Judas the Galilean (Luke 6.15, 22.38).

In the commentaries Mark 12.14 is mostly related just to older works of reference and to some classical texts. But who looks up these references? That is why I have tried to sketch the story of the imperial tax. For one must know something of the previous history of this tax in order to appreciate the accuracy of the Marcan account and to understand the background as well as the subtlety of the question about tribute. In the eyes of His opponents Jesus is a new Judas of Galilee, a new teacher of the Law with messianic claims. He must say what He thought about the question which had kept a whole generation in ferment and had split the Jews into two camps. The question was put to Him in Jerusalem, where it was most acute, and in the Passover season, when the atmosphere was always most tense and at that time was more thunderous than ever before. Pilate had just entered Jerusalem at the head of his Roman troops, and Jesus at the head of the pilgrim procession. His questioners were the Pharisees and the Herodians, opponents of the tax and friends of the tax, old enemies, but united in the desire to lead Him into trouble in one way or

another. So they put Him the most dangerous question
possible, the question about tribute. The tribute-money went
to the emperor—this is the correct formula, for the land was
an imperial province, and in the palace of Herod sat the
emperor's representative who levied the taxes and sent them
to the emperor in Rome. That was the obnoxious thing, and
the reason for the double question, which however has been
preserved in its precise and proper form only in Mark. Shall
we give, or not? The Pharisees ask the question, and it is the
theological question of Judas of Galilee. The Herodians ask
it, and it is the political question of the Roman party. If Jesus
said Yes, He would be finished so far as the people were concerned, who were thronging around Him. For a Messiah who
came to terms with Caesar would be no Messiah in their eyes.
If Jesus said No, He would be finished so far as the Romans
were concerned, whose threatening troops were marching in
every street. For a man who attacked the law of Caesar was
in their eyes a rebel (Luke 23.2). What would He do?

'But he, knowing their hypocrisy, said unto them, Why
tempt ye me?'

Jesus' reply begins with a surprise, characteristic of God's
answer to man's questions. God takes our questions seriously.
But He is not trapped by the way we put our questions, He
is not led or prejudiced by them. He is not bound by the way
we formulate our ideas, or by the alternatives we put. His
answer may be a riddle for the questioner, or an offence, or
folly, it may be a repulse. God's answer may disclose the
injustice, or the true justice, of our question. Or God may
reply by silence.

Jesus' first words straightway re-established the proper order
of things. The men who wanted to treat Jesus publicly were
publicly exposed. They had put the question about the truth.
So He told them the truth. Their concern was not serious,
their question was not a genuine question, for it did not arise
out of genuine need. They had settled the question for themselves long ago, in one way or the other, as doctrinaire groups
have always settled all questions. They were simply playing
a part, and misusing the burning problem of the conscience

of their people as a malicious trick question. Jesus saw this
with the clarity of divine insight (Luke 22.48), and replied
with the majesty of divine wrath. They thought they had
finally caught Him in a dialectical trap. 'But he passing through
the midst of them went his way' (Luke 4.30). 'Bring me a
penny that I may see it. And they brought it.'

Jesus repulsed the questioners, and no one would be surprised if He just left them there (Mark 11.33; John 8.5ff.).
But He took up their question. That is the second surprise.
He took the question seriously for the sake of the objective
historical need which was in it—despite all its subjective wiles.
The way He led from question to answer is the third surprise.
He was addressed as a teacher of the Law, from whom a saying from the Bible, or an exposition from the Talmud, was
expected. They wanted to introduce a theological disputa-
tion, so that He might be driven into a corner. But Jesus did
not quote Scripture, as He usually was so ready to do (for
instance, in Mark 12.29). This surely means that in Jesus'
judgment there were opinions about this question in the Old
Testament, perhaps very significant opinions, but no answer.
Nor was He to be led into any exegetical deductions or discussions. There had been enough 'conversations' since the
days of Judas of Galilee, the 'problems' had been gone over
again and again. Jesus acted in an astonishingly untheological
way: He brought His people with their theological problems
down to earth in a thoroughly realistic way. Mark once again
has held to this point with unerring precision. Jesus asked
for a penny, a *denarius*.[1] Why? There were a great many
coins in the wide Roman empire which passed as legal currency, old and new, large and small, imperial and local, gold,
silver, copper, bronze and brass. In no country did so many

---

[1] A recent critic has doubted the historical credibility of Mark 12.15f. with
the foolish argument that coins with the emperor's portrait were unthinkable
in the Promised Land with its prohibition of images. But such coins were circulating in Palestine at that time in great quantities. Witness not only the coins
which have been discovered, but also the New Testament itself (Luke 7.41,
10.35; Matt. 18.28, 20.2; Mark 6.37, 14.5; John 6.7, 12.5; Acts 6.6), as well
as the Talmud, which uses the word *denarius* as a common foreign word, as,
for example, 'The money-changer must not go out [on the eve of the Sabbath]
with a *denarius* in his ear' (Jerusalem Talmud, Tractate Sabbath 3*b*).

different kinds of money circulate as in Palestine. But the prescribed coin for taxation purposes throughout the empire was the *denarius*, a little silver coin of about the worth of a shilling. (It can only be the silver *denarius* which is intended in Mark 12.16, Luke 20.24 and Matt. 22.19, not a gold coin as Titian supposed, in his representation of the tribute scene, nor a Herodian coin, as is often asserted; for the Herodian coins were not called *denarii* and were not tribute coins, but were local copper coins.) Jesus knew this, and so He asked for the silver imperial tax coin, using the Latin word, the Roman technical expression, which had become current in Palestine along with the coin itself. Bring me a *denarius*, He said. He did not produce one from His own pocket. Why not? The point now is not whether Jesus had such a coin in His pocket but whether His opponents had. With Socratic irony, he added: 'That I may see it.' Why? He had a maieutic purpose with his questioners, he wanted to deliver them, in the Socratic manner, not *a priori*, but *a posteriori*. Not their logical or moral sense, but their historical situation and attitude would bring the truth to light. Something is to be seen, and deduced, from the *denarius* itself.

'And they brought [it].' This laconic expression, found again in John 2.6, and indeed frequently in Semitic texts, is surely one of the finest sentence formations in the verbose literature of late Hellenistic times; for similar turns of language one goes in vain even to Caesar, Augustus and Tacitus. In brief and pregnant style Jesus' sovereign conduct of the struggle is shown, His complete mastery of the situation, as He drives His opponents into a corner, and they shamefacedly produce a *denarius*, like a *corpus delicti*.

The content of the accounts in Matthew and Luke is the same, but less sharply defined—and so the strange error has arisen, certainly never intended by Matthew or Luke, that Jesus was not clear about the matter, as though He lived in a 'supra-historical' dimension and took no notice of the political questions of his day. But Mark shows that Jesus knew very well how matters stood. This is clear from the following sentences.

'And he saith unto them, Whose is this image and super-scription? And they said unto him, Caesar's.'

Does Jesus ask because He needs information? Of course He knows what is to be seen on such a coin. His questioners know as well. But He wants them to say it. He wants to pin them down with their own answer—'Caesar's.'

Augustus issued several hundred different *denarii*, all of which were still current in the last year of Jesus' life. With very few exceptions, which do not matter here, they bear his image and a legend giving his most recent titles or honours.

But in the Gospel story we have clearly to do not with a *denarius* of Augustus but with one of Tiberius. For the emperor shown on the coin must be the reigning emperor. Tiberius had only three types of the *denarius* struck, all of them with his portrait and the appropriate inscription. Two of the types are rare, while the third is very common, being obviously the one preferred by Tiberius and continued throughout his reign with the conservatism peculiar to him. It was issued in great quantities from the imperial mint at Lyons for twenty years, with only minor stylistic variations, as the standard silver coin for the whole empire, including Palestine. Countless ancient forgeries confirm its validity as well as its popularity. It was at the same time the leading coin of the age, used far beyond the confines of the Roman empire; it was copied in Persia and India, while the original coins from Lyons circulated as far as the highlands of Deccan—as is proved by the discovery of one in Coimbatore in India in 1914. It was this *denarius* of Tiberius, then, which in all probability (as Madden, Reinach and Roller have maintained) played its part in the Gospel scene. The whole series of coins, together with the Asiatic imitations, may be studied in the *British Museum Catalogue*. Their interpretation has been greatly advanced in modern times by Alföldi's studies of the insignia and dress of the Roman emperors.

The coin has on its obverse a bust of Tiberius in Olympian nakedness, adorned with the laurel wreath, the sign of his divinity. The legend (given in full, without the abbreviations) is TIBERIUS CAESAR DIVI AUGUSTI FILIUS AUGUSTUS. How this was meant to be understood, and was in fact understood, in the East, we learn from contemporary Syrian provincial coins which carry the same text in Greek: TIBERIOS KAISAR THEOU SEBASTOU HUIOS SEBASTOS. This may be translated as 'Emperor Tiberius august Son of the august God'. The reverse concludes the description with the title PONTIFEX MAXIMUS= Archiereus=High Priest. Also on the reverse is a type of the emperor's mother, Julia Augusta (Livia), sitting on the throne of the gods, in her right hand the Olympian sceptre, in her left the olive-branch which indicated that she was the earthly incarnation of the heavenly Pax. The coin, in brief, is a symbol both of power and of the cult.

It is a symbol of power. For it is the instrument of Roman imperial policy (an emblem of the imperial supremacy throughout the *orbis Romanus*), of Roman currency policy (a uniform coin for all parts of the empire, and the norm for all local coinage), of Roman fiscal policy (the prescribed tribute coin for all provinces of the empire). So the inscription is in Latin, the official language of the Roman government. So the coin bears the portrait of the emperor, and also of the emperor's mother, whom Augustus had raised, in his will, to be co-ruler with her son; in Palestine she was accorded special distinction, her name appearing along with that of Tiberius on the procurators' coins. The Jewish nation had always been extremely sensitive about the symbolic significance of coins. This is clear from the First Book of Maccabees (15.6) and from the Rabbinic citations given by Billerbeck for Matt. 22.15ff. ('Coin' and 'power' were regarded as synonyms, so that the coin was the symbol of the ruler's dominance; so Mordecai struck coins which showed himself on the obverse, and Esther on the reverse.) But this is most clearly seen in the fact that every leader of the struggle for liberation in Hellenistic times, and in the reigns of Nero and of Hadrian, proclaimed their seizure of power by issuing their own coins with their own symbols of supremacy and Hebrew inscriptions.

The *denarius* of Tiberius was a symbol of the cult because it carried the portrait of the emperor. From the time of Alexander the portraits on coins had cultic significance. Thus the mint-masters of the Roman Republic were strictly forbidden to put their own likenesses on their *denarii*. Caesar was the first, in the last weeks of his life, to arrogate to himself the right, along with other divine honours, to have his portrait on the imperial coins. Caesar was assassinated. But his coins survived, and their cultic character was emphasized by mythological ornament and inscriptions. Tiberius was particularly strict in this regard and, as we learn from Suetonius, had everyone who did not handle the Augustan *denarius* with the requisite devotion executed as a sacrilegious criminal. The Tiberius *denarius* with which we are concerned was of a modest character, and it was typical of Tiberius's religious policy that he emphasized on this coin the mythological glorification of his parents. This lent to his own person an Olympian brightness. For one whose parents are both divine (a claim greater than the Church ever made on behalf of the Son of God and of Mary) is certainly of divine dignity and may therefore be represented in divine style, may be called Augustus. Suetonius and others say that Tiberius used the description of Augustus for himself very sparingly. It is all the more significant that this description appears on the imperial coinage in unabbreviated form as the last in the series of titles on the obverse: the August, the Image and Manifestation of the King of Heaven on earth. It is clear that the Jewish people would be highly sensitive to the mythological character of this coin (cf. Rev. 13.16f.). We know that in the time of Antonine (whose types were not for the most part any more pretentious than this *denarius* of Tiberius) Nahum of Tiberia, the Holy One, never looked on the image on a coin all his life. Similarly, Bar Kochba, the revolutionary Messiah of the second century, had the imperial *denarii* collected, the obnoxious portraits and inscriptions beaten out by hammers and replaced by Hebrew Temple vessels and inscriptions. This may be studied in Hill's *Catalogue of the Coins of Palestine*.

The Tiberius *denarius* is a symbol of power and of the cult. But it is not these things separately, but together, and that is the decisive point. This *denarius* becomes a symbol of the metaphysical glorification of policy which runs through the

whole of ancient imperial history, and which also determined
the Roman philosophy of domination from the time of Julius
Caesar. Though perhaps the most modest sign, this *denarius*
of Tiberius is the most official and universal sign of the apotheosis of power and the worship of the *homo imperiosus* in the
time of Christ.

We have already noticed a symbol with an identical significance—the portrait of the emperor on the standards of the
legions, which looked not unlike an enlarged *denarius,* and
showed the same synthesis of imperial policy and philosophy.
We have already remarked the uproar among the worshippers
in the Temple area when these imperial portraits appeared in
their midst. But the sensitive reaction to these standards was
not paralleled in the matter of the coins. There was compromise with the mammon of unrighteousness, not merely
casually and secretly, but quite officially. The Jewish money-
changers wore a *denarius* in their ear on week-days, as a sign
of their trade. The *denarii* of Tiberius must have lain on their
tables in the Temple area in great heaps. The Talmud tract
on idolatry tells how the patriarch Jehudah II (about 250)
was loth to accept the *denarius* on account of the emperor's
portrait on it, but was also unwilling to refuse it, lest he become politically suspect. A later addition to this tract lays
down the basic rule: The coin is acceptable. It is possible that
Jesus was present during the revolt of the Temple worshippers
against the imperial standards. He also knew what was on the
tables of the money-changers in the Temple, which He had
overthrown. He knew the ambiguous position of His people,
and He relentlessly exposed their hypocrisy. 'Whose image
and superscription is this?' He knew that this touched them
to the quick. To accept the symbol of Roman policy and
imperial philosophy meant to forgo the right to a conscientious
revolt against the emperor. The reply of His opponents was
as brief as possible, and grudgingly given: 'Caesar's.' They
avoided all the mythological and polytheistic titles used by
Tiberius on the coin itself, and chose the most harmless
designation which they could find—Caesar. But this word
was sufficient confession of the fact that in this question of

tribute to Caesar their integrity was spoiled. For they had the imperial money in their pockets.

'Jesus said unto them, Render unto Caesar the things that are Caesar's, and unto God the things that are God's.'

We must watch the choice and sequence of words in the Marcan text as carefully as possible. For again it is only Mark who gives an unvarnished account of how Jesus takes up the last word of His questioners in order to draw forth the inescapable consequences. The *denarius* with the image and superscription of the emperor is 'Caesar's', said Jesus. For portrait and official titles together provide, in the classical view, the evidence of the *signum* of the emperor. The *denarius* carrying this *signum* is on the Roman view the emperor's coin in the triple legal sense of majesty, guarantee and property. It is the imperial silver coinage in distinction from the copper coinage of the Senate and the local silver coinage of the eastern towns or provinces. It carries the imperial seal, which guarantees the full content and weight of the coin in the name of the emperor. It is the means of payment used by the emperor for his soldiers, officials and suppliers, which he thus sets in circulation but can at any time withdraw and melt down. This being the case, the emperor's tax has the character of a partial drawing-in of the coinage. The imperial *denarius* returns to its source as the tax *denarius*.

What is the legal basis for this partial drawing-in? Is it simply the brutal right of the mightier, or is it a moral right? The answer to this decisive question lies in the choice of words made by Jesus: Render, give back. The controversy about the tax here reaches its verbal climax.

To pay taxes was described in the *koiné* in Palestine as 'to give (or pay) tribute'. The correlative idea is 'to receive tribute'. Josephus as well as Origen afford many examples of this usage. The taxpayer said it. So too did Judas of Galilee, when he summoned the people to refuse to pay. The Herodian Agrippa II said the same, when he tried to mediate between Rome and the revolutionary party, and to persuade the rebels to pay their taxes again. The Pharisees and the Herodians took over this way of thinking as a matter of course, when they asked Jesus, May we give, shall we give? In Matt. 17.25 Jesus Himself used the same terminology, where the question is about payment of a tax to which no moral obligation to pay is attached.

A significant example of the opposite usage is to be found in the twelfth book of the *Antiquities* of Josephus. Josephus is describing how Ptolemy ceded to Onias the high priest the taxes of his kingdom, receiving as compensation an annual sum from Onias. This sum was not paid. A representative of the king arrived to demand his sovereign's legal rights. The matter had assumed the character of a debt, the word for paying taxes was 'give back', or 'pay back', and for receiving taxes, 'receive again', while refusal to pay was 'keeping back'. The same usage is to be found in Thucydides. Jesus uses the same terminology when He says, 'Render, give back.'

That is the first great surprise in this verse, and its meaning is: the payment of tribute to Caesar is not only your unquestioned obligation; it is also your moral duty.

Jesus, in answering His opponents, also corrected their ideas. Mark reports it clearly and objectively. The first readers and commentators on the text did not miss the silent correction. The other evangelists stress Jesus' surprising counterattack by their stylistic usage (the prefixing of the imperative by *toinun* or *oun*). Paul took over Jesus' term with all its presuppositions and consequences in Rom. 13.7: 'Render to all their dues: tribute to whom tribute is due; custom to whom custom . . .' Origen emphasizes the idea. An anonymous writer in the Greek Commentary on the Catenae writes on Matt. 22.21: 'Render to Caesar what is Caesar's. That is something different from "give".'[1] The Vulgate translates the Greek imperative by *reddite*, as do the Latin Fathers. Hilary paraphrases, 'Jesus decides that what is Caesar's must be given

---

[1] See *Gott und Kaiser im Neuen Testament* (1935), by the present writer, pp. 15f., 31; *Rom und die Christen im ersten Jahrhundert* (1942), by Martin Dibelius, p. 3, opposes this view on the grounds that the technical expression *apodidomi* is 'used of every payment within the framework of a relationship of debt'. The observation is just, but not new, while the opposition it intends to my view is not quite clear to me. For this is exactly what Jesus, Paul and the Church Fathers meant: 'You are in a relationship of debt to the State, and your payment of taxes is therefore the fulfilment of obligation to give back.'

back to him. It is not an improper demand that what is Caesar's should be given back to him, and that what is exclusively God's should be given back to God.' Other uses of *apodidonai* in secular and ecclesiastical literature agree with this interpretation. Stephanus in his *Thesaurus Graecae Linguae* gives the following equivalents: *reddo, retribuo, redhibeo, restituo, persolvo,* with numerous examples.

The Egerton Papyrus, too, takes the idea of 'giving back' seriously, and emphasizes it very strongly, though it introduces the greatest confusion with its eclectic and imitative zeal. It takes over from Mark 12.17 the technical term 'to render, give back', realizing that it indicates the performance of an obligation (I Cor. 7.3), and therefore connects the word with the accusative 'that which is befitting' (Philem. 8)—then introduces the whole phrase into the question put by the opponents of Jesus and thus fabricates the grotesque question: 'Is it lawful to render to the imperial government that which is befitting to it?' To a question which so childishly anticipates the answer, Jesus' reply is bound to be an empty one.

Jesus knew, and shared, the basic view of ancient times that tribute was a tax paid by subjugated nations (Matt. 17.25). He saw how the conquerors treated his own people (Luke 13.1, 19.14, 27, 22.25). But He made it clear that His questioners accepted the imperial *denarii* in payment, and that this meant that the people of God had accepted its subjugation to the Roman empire. By accepting imperial money they have profited by the financial, economic and legal order of the empire. In the past Palestine had suffered often enough from insecure or cramped conditions in these spheres, and could appreciate the stability which came from assimilation to the Roman economic system. In such circumstances, there was no real basis, whatever the practical grievances, for refusing to pay the tax on economic grounds. To refuse to pay would be parasitical. 'The lord of this land rightly says to thee, Live according to my laws, or leave my land. . . . And thou dost live according to the law of this city for the sake of thy property and other goods' (*Shepherd of Hermas*). 'If there is nothing remaining to us of what is Caesar's, then we are not bound to render him what is his. But if we enjoy his treasures, and profit from the order of his rule, then we are bound to give something in return' (Hilary). They use the imperial money, although it bears the sign of the emperor's sovereignty. So they have no right to withhold their tribute on political grounds from the head of the empire. They take this money into the temple, although they know that the image and the superscription are polytheistic in character. So they have no right to refuse to pay the tax on theological grounds.

So far we have spoken negatively of what was not permitted. But Jesus held up the coin before His questioners in order to give them a positive and imperative lesson about the duty which the people of God owed to the empire. This is not just a recommendation to be loyal to one's nearest superior (as the Talmud speaks of 'not attempting to evade taxes'). But it is an affirmation of the *Imperium Romanum*, of the foreign master-race with its polytheistic emperor, an unsentimental and undialectical affirmation in the true succession of the prophetic and apocalyptic theology of history. 'I have made the earth. . . . and I give it unto whom it seemeth right unto me. And now I have given all these things into the hand of Nebuchadnezzar the king of Babylon, my servant. . . . And all the nations shall serve him, and his son, and his son's son, until the time of his own land come: and then many nations and great kings shall serve themselves of him. . . . And the nation and the kingdom . . . that will not put their neck under the yoke of the king of Babylon, will I punish, saith the Lord . . . until I have consumed them by his hand' (Jer. 27.5ff.). 'Behold, we send thee silver', wrote Baruch from the Dispersion to Jehoiachim the priest in Jerusalem. 'Buy burnt-offerings and incense and food and offer it on the altar of the Lord our God and pray for the life of Nebuchadnezzar king of Babylon.' To pay the imperial tax means to fulfil God's will for history —and is at the same time a contribution to the prayers and sacrifice for the emperor. For the imperial tax clearly provided in the time of Jesus the means for the daily sacrifice for the welfare of the Roman emperor. In brief, the tax to Caesar was the contribution of the people of God to the maintenance of the empire which involved not only financial and political considerations, but also theological views about imperial history.

Jesus affirmed this relationship to Caesar. Did He then make reservations about the worship of Caesar, which was so clearly reflected on the imperial coinage? He affirmed the symbolism of power, but He rejected the symbolism of worship. But this reservation was not made as a negative statement, but rather as a positive command. 'Render to God what is God's.'

The same imperative, 'render', which was used with reference to Caesar is now used to refer to God. This is another surprising fact, which leads us to a highly concrete sense of the imperative. From a concordance to the Septuagint we may learn that the linking of the verb 'render' with the dative 'to God', the Lord, is a common technical usage for the ceremonial discharge of obligations in the cult. It appears about twenty-five times, with *apodidonai* as the equivalent for both *shalam* and *shub*. In Num. 8.13ff. we can see the presuppositions of the idea. Everything belongs to God. When we sanctify or give or sacrifice something to him, as a part for the whole, this is only an act of partial restitution (cf. the contributions to the building of the temple in I Chron. 29.9ff., and the rabbinic comment from the time of Trajan, in the Mishna *Sayings of the Fathers*, 3.7: 'Give God of his own, for you and yours belong to him'). Similarly, this imperative runs through the whole Old Testament: 'Thou shalt pay thy vows (*apodos*) to the Highest.' It is in the Psalms—that is, in the temple liturgy—which Jesus knew from countless festivals, that the sacral formula is most widely used. 'Vow, and pay (*apodote*) unto the Lord your God: let all that be round about him bring presents unto him that ought to be feared. He shall cut off the spirit of princes: he is terrible to the kings of the earth' (Ps. 76.11f.). Jesus is thinking of this when at the Passover season He says to the pilgrims, 'Render to God what is God's.' Jerome, in his commentary on Matt. 22.21, saw this clearly: 'Render unto Caesar the things that are Caesar's, namely, coins, tribute, money; and to God the things that are God's, namely, tithes, first-fruits, vows, sacrifices.' But the imperative needs to be understood even more concretely and

precisely. For the summons to render, to give back, has the
same meaning for both clauses, for the one about Caesar as
well as the one about God. The clauses are strictly parallel,
and of the same structure, in Matthew and Luke as well as
Mark. The interpretation must therefore also be strictly parallel.
'Render' in the first clause means the payment of the poll-
tax to the imperial treasury, and has nothing to say about
customs and similar dues. Likewise in the second clause there
is no mention of tithes and similar dues, but a summons to
pay the poll-tax into the temple treasury, that is, the annual
tax paid by every adult male Jew throughout the world for
the maintenance of the 'perpetual' burnt-offering. This temple
tax was paid in different currency from the imperial tax, and
amounted to two *drachmae* annually. It fell due in the spring,
was collected in the month of Adar and brought to Jerusalem
during the Passover season, about the time, that is to say,
when Jesus spoke the words of Mark 12.17.

The imperial tax was the practical expression of the fundamental relation of the people of God to the empire. The
temple tax expressed the relation of the people to the kingdom of God. All creatures are to join in the *glorificatio Dei*.
The world was false to this primal destiny, and in the time of
Christ had joined in the *glorificatio Caesaris*. But there was one
people in the Roman world whose meaning and historical
mission are summed up in the glorification of God, and that
was the people of Jesus Christ. There was one place in the
Roman world which was reserved for the glorification of God,
and that was the temple on Mount Zion. From every corner
of the earth there flowed into the temple the tax from God's
people. Out of the contributions of this tax there rose up the
sacrificial smoke of the burnt offering, compassed by the
trumpets of the priests, by the Hallels of the Levites—'I will
pay my vows (*apodoso*) unto the Lord in the courts of the
Lord's house' (Ps. 116.18, 19)—by the Amen of the worship-
ping people, and accompanied by the Shema rising from a
million voices at the same time in every part of the Roman
world: 'Hear, O Israel: the Lord our God is one God' (Deut.
6.5ff.). Liturgically, the temple tax signified a contribution to

the glory of God in the midst of a world that was filled with
the glory of Caesar. Theologically, the temple sacrifice signified
a prayer for the coming of the kingdom of God in which
creation will return to its primal destiny and every land be
filled with the praise of God. 'I will come into thy house with
burnt offerings, I will pay thee my vows (*apodoso*)' (Ps. 66.13).

'Render unto Caesar the things that are Caesar's.' Of course
this refers primarily but not only to the tax. 'Render unto God
the things that are God's.' Of course this refers primarily but
not only to the temple tax. Jesus had good reason for choosing the form of the riddle or *maschal* for His reply. He formu-
lated his concrete imperative so universally because the life
principle He here proclaimed has the validity of a regulative
principle for history, uttered as it was at the decisive hour
of all history.

'And they marvelled greatly at him.'

They left Him and went their way (Matt. 22.22). For He
is neither Pharisee nor Herodian, neither Zealot nor Sadducee.
There is no group or group doctrine in which He can be
classified. He is the Christ. His words about God and Caesar
are not a general human teaching like, for example, the words
'Fear thou the Lord and the king, and be disobedient to
neither' (Prov. 24.21), or the rabbinic rule 'that a man must
fulfil his duties to men as to God'—the counter-proclamation
to the pseudo-messianic mission of Judas of Galilee. Jesus'
words are a messianic proclamation uttered with messianic
authority in the messianic hour of history, in the city of the
Messiah, directed towards the people of the Messiah, in order
that the *via Dei* may be manifested in truth (Mark 12.14), the
way of God with His Messiah, with the people of His covenant
and His Church. This messianic proclamation says that the
imperium Caesaris is the way and the *imperium Dei* the goal
of history.

Here is clearly disclosed something of the paradoxical mystery of the way of Christ. At the beginning of this way there
is the great temptation of the Messiah (Mark 1.13). The Christ
of God renounced the way of the *imperium*, since it led through
the worship of power (Matt. 4.9). Now the temptation has

come to Him in a new form—the form which brought about the destruction of the pseudo-Messiah Judas of Galilee. Christ conquered this temptation afresh with His words about the double duty of obedience to the way and to the goal of history, to the kingdom of the world and to the kingdom of God. Mark 12.17 is spoken by Christ *in conspectu mortis*, in the sight of the messianic death. Holy Week is the existential exegesis of His words: submission to the dominion of Caesar, submission to the dominion of God—united in the acceptance of that monstrous judicial murder by which Caesar's most wretched creature fulfils *sub contrario* the work of God (Matt. 26.52ff.; John 19.11).

Christ goes the way of God and calls His people to follow Him. He knows that His people is destined to bear the yoke of the kingdom of the world until the hour of the kingdom of heaven comes. But Jesus calls in vain. They marvel—and leave Him and go their way. They do not want to know, on this their day, the things that serve their peace, and they go the way they themselves have chosen, disobedient to their historical mission, to God and Caesar alike, the way that leads to catastrophe (Luke 19.42ff.).

They left Jesus alone with His disciples. Who will follow Christ on the *via Dei*? The Church: it is the Church for whom those words about the kingdom of Caesar and the kingdom of God have become normative for all time, in life and in death. We therefore end our exegesis of the words about tribute with the four earliest witnesses in the Church—who unanimously confirm our exegesis.

'Render to all their dues: tribute to whom tribute is due; custom to whom custom; fear to whom fear; honour to whom honour', wrote Paul to the Rome of Nero about the year 57 (Rom. 13.7). Seven years later, in the same Rome and under the same emperor, he sealed by his death his witness to the worship of God alone.[1]

In the year 96 Domitian had some Davidists and pretenders

---

[1] Two new studies of Rom. 13 may be mentioned: W. Elert, 'Paulus und Nero' (*Zwischen Gnade und Ungnade*, 1948, p. 38ff.), and H. von Campenhausen, 'Zur Auslegung von Römer 13' (*Festschrift Bertholet*, 1950, pp. 97ff.).

to the throne from among the circle of Jesus' relations brought from Palestine to Rome. There he interrogated them closely about their life and beliefs. They told him about the modest land they owned, about their hard daily toil, and added emphatically these words, 'We pay our due taxes' (*tributa*, as in Luke 20.22 and Rom. 13.7). The Lord's word about the duty of paying taxes were not forgotten by the circle of Jesus' relations, even in the presence of Caesar. For the rest, these alleged messianic politicians confessed their hope in the heavenly kingdom of Jesus Christ which is to come. The emperor dismissed them this time (Eusebius, *Ecclesiastical History*, 3, 20, 4). But eleven years later Simeon, the honoured cousin of Jesus and bishop of Jerusalem, was denounced again, and this time was crucified for his confession of the coming kingdom. This happened in the reign of Trajan, and we know the precise way in which Christians who had been denounced were interrogated. They were commanded to sacrifice before the image of the emperor. 'For so far as we know, no Christian can be constrained to do this', wrote Pliny about the year 112 to the emperor Trajan. And Simeon did not let himself be constrained. Render unto God the things that are God's.

About 153 the Christian apologist Justin wrote in Rome to his emperor: 'The taxes (*tributa*) and dues commanded by you we hasten to pay before all others, following the Master's commandment, Render to Caesar the things that are Caesar's, and to God the things that are God's. So we pray to God alone. But in the other things we serve you gladly, and confess that you are kings and lords over the children of men, and pray therefore that you may be found to be such as possess, along with royal power, an understanding mind. But if you despise our prayer, it is not we who will suffer from it' (*Apology* 17). There is a tendency to treat the Apologists somewhat slightingly, as men who came to terms with the spirit of their time and with the mighty of this world. This criticism has been made most sharply by men who themselves have come to very good terms with the world. But Justin knew no compromise when his hour came, about twelve years later in the reign of the great Marcus Aurelius. Simply and unpretentiously the account of the trial is given (*Acta Justini,* 5 f.): 'Then the martyrs said, Do with us what you will. We are Christians and do not sacrifice to idols. And they praised God and went out to the place of execution and fulfilled their confession to our Saviour, to whom be the glory in eternity.'

In 180 the representative of the mentally deficient Commodus commanded the Christians in Carthage to swear by the divine spirit of the lord our Caesar. Then Speratus, one of the accused, said, 'I know nothing of the *imperium* of this world, but serve the invisible God. I have embezzled nothing. On the contrary, in every transaction I pay the due tax (*teloneum reddo*). For I know my Lord, the King of kings and *Imperator* over all nations.' Cittinus, another of the accused, said: 'We fear the Lord our God, who is in heaven, and nothing else in the world.' Donata said, 'Give to Caesar the honour that is his due—but fear God. *Honorem Caesarim quasi Caesari—timorem autem Deo.*' The governor sentenced them to death. Then the assembled martyrs praised their God with *one* voice and said, 'We thank Thee, thrice Holy one, and praise Thee, Thy kingdom endures through all eternity. Amen.'

IX

NERO THE WORLD SAVIOUR

THE emperor Tiberius was dying of old age. But he was not dying quickly enough for those around him. When he seemed to be recovering again from a collapse, Macro, his closest companion, commander of the imperial guard, dealt summarily with him by smothering him in his pillows. Then he turned round and saluted the new emperor Caligula. Caligula liked to appear with the radiate crown on his head as a sign that he was truly a god in human form. Four years later the young god was murdered by two officers of his guard. His successor was Claudius, an insignificant fool who was ruled by his wife of the moment. From his reign of fourteen years only one circumstance is worth noting. Immediately after ascending the throne he exiled the 'philosopher' Seneca,[1] who had been compromised by a scandal of adultery, in order to save him from the threat of capital punishment. But at the wish of his fourth wife, Agrippina, he later had him brought back, and made him tutor to her son Nero. The experienced master conscientiously introduced his apt pupil to all the vices,

---

[1] Some readers will perhaps find the portrait of Seneca, which is rather presupposed than outlined in the following pages, somewhat unusual. I depart from the traditional account only in thinking it necessary to take the actual facts of his life as seriously as the rhetoric of his 'philosophical' writings. The gulf between the two was described by an ancient historian: 'Not only in this [adultery] but in everything else his actions were sharply opposed to his philosophy. He condemned tyranny, and became the teacher of a tyrant. He despised those who curried favour with the mighty, and could not himself be persuaded to leave the palace. He attacked flatterers violently, and paid court to the empress and the freedmen of Claudius in a panegyric of which he was later so ashamed that he denied its authorship. He reviled the rich, and himself was a millionaire. He contracted a brilliant marriage, but amused himself with young boys, and encouraged Nero in the same courses, though at first he acted very puritanically and besought Nero to spare him kisses and common meals, in order that he might have leisure to philosophize' (Dio Cassius, 61, 10, abridged).

and soon the young prince looked as fat and self-satisfied as the old roué and amateur philosopher. In an October night of the year 54 Agrippina had her husband poisoned, in order that her son might reign. So at the tender age of seventeen Nero became the master of the world.

Seneca celebrated this new 'turning of the ages' by a piece of scurrility about his protector Claudius, which for hatred and meanness left nothing to be desired. At the same time he took the opportunity to laud his young pupil and master as the long-awaited saviour of the world. A new age has begun, an age of freedom and blessedness. The wretched Claudius is dead, and the chosen of heaven has come to power. The political picture of the saviour as drawn in the time of Augustus has now assumed the lineaments of Nero. Apollo himself accompanied the sisters of Fate with his lyre, when they spun the golden thread of the young emperor's life. The philosopher became a poet when he fabricated his prologue in heaven, which is the climax of the classical advent hope distorted to a courtly grimace: 'Apollo rejoiced, and praised the beginning. "Go on with your spinning, O sisters!" he cried. "He whose life I see in your hands deserves that his course run much further than that of other mortals. He is like me in much, in form and appearance, in his poetry and singing and playing. And as the red of morning drives away dark night, as neither haze nor mist endure before the sun's rays, as everything becomes bright when my chariot appears, so it is when Nero ascends the throne. His golden locks, his fair countenance, shine like the sun as it breaks through the clouds. Strife, injustice and envy collapse before him. He restores to the world the Golden Age." '

The historical commentary on this advent hymn is the life of Nero himself.

First the episode of the poisoning of Claudius, which was everywhere spoken of, had to be officially denied. So Nero declared the unfortunate Claudius to be divine, and arranged a funeral festival at which he himself held a funeral oration about the incomparable thinker and statesman. Seneca wrote the speech. His mother Agrippina, the murderess and widow, was made high priestess of the new cult. Five years later he had her stabbed to death for high treason. Seneca composed the accusation after the event, for the Senate, which hastened to thank the gods for the exposure of the traitress and the salvation of the empire. Then Nero tired of his young wife Octavia, had her executed on a charge of adultery, and had her head exhibited to his mistress Poppaea. The Senate made thank-offerings to the gods for this restoration of public morality. In July 64 Rome went up in flames. Nero ascended the stage of his country palace with his lyre, and there within sight of the burning capital he declaimed a song of the burning of Troy. He had this heroic occasion perpetuated on countless coins, with himself as Apollo playing his lyre. Even Suetonius speaks of these coins. Evil tongues declared that Nero was personally responsible for the burning of Rome, and that he did it for the sake of this theatrical display. No doubt he wanted to create space and opportunity for the grandiose buildings which he now proceeded to erect. He blamed the burning of the city on the Christians of Rome, and stirred up feeling against them—creating a new theatrical occasion for his dilettante moods. While he himself appeared as a divine charioteer ('how everything becomes gay when my chariot appears'), the Christians were covered with tar and set up in the imperial parks as living torches, while their women were shamelessly exhibited in mythological pantomimes before being devoured by wild bulls. Even the Roman mob was horrified. Nero's fury was not slaked. Now it was Seneca's turn. For a long time he had been a prisoner of the court. He had sought in vain to escape from the golden cage. The emperor's attempt to dispose of him by poison failed; but he was doomed, for he knew too much. In April 65 the imperial saviour of the world compelled his erstwhile prophet to commit suicide. At the same time he arraigned a number of officers for conspiracy before a military tribunal. Nero conducted the proceedings himself, prosecutor and judge in one, and asked an officer of proven worth, 'How could you forget your oath?' The accused (to use the words of the report) 'made his confession an occasion for clearing his honour', and replied: 'I hated you. No soldier was more loyal to you so long as you deserved love. My hatred began when you murdered your mother and your wife, and became a charioteer, an actor and an incendiary.' The emperor, 'unaccustomed to hear his actions discussed', immediately broke off the 'interrogation' and had the man executed. The Senate called for prayers of thanksgiving and offerings to the gods. Meanwhile Nero ruined the imperial finances by his building activities and other passions. In order to make good the deficit he despatched an expedition of treasure-hunters to Africa, and when that was of no avail he got rid of his debts by means of an inflation of the currency. The State treasury made its payments in inferior new currency, but insisted on receiving taxes in the undepreciated currency of the Augustan epoch. The emperor's creatures glorified their master in the court theatre as the imperial magician who conjured up the legendary treasures of the golden age. A few weeks later Nero kicked to death his former mistress Poppaea, now his empress and expecting his child—and straightway raised her to divine honours, to be celebrated as the mother of a divine child. The senator Thrasea, whose applause was considered too meagre, was condemned to death by the college of senators, and died with a prayer to 'Zeus the Liberator' on his lips. A year later the emperor travelled to Greece on an artistic errand. This journey was the climax of his theatrical career. Propaganda coins celebrated his Apolline advent in the Greek capital. He was received in Corinth like a saviour from heaven, and acclaimed in the sports stadium as 'Zeus the Liberator'. This was the fulfilment of the cry of the dying Thrasea.

Art thou he that is to come?

After one more year the fourteen-year reign of blood was over. The legions revolted, the Senate pronounced the emperor a State enemy, the court left him in the lurch, his bodyguard mutinied and advised him to commit suicide, and the emperor fled, bemoaning his fall with the words, 'What an artist dies with me', and stabbed himself before his pursuers caught him.

X

THE COURT PROPHET

DURING the Wars of the Maccabees the last great Old Testament prophet saw and described world history in grandiose visions: one empire would succeed another, till the last and worst of all, the kingdom of iron. Then the Son of Man would appear to establish the kingdom of God, which is not of this world. This is the theology of history to be found in the Book of Daniel.

During the reign of Nero, when Roman imperial glory had changed into a demonic grimace, the Jewish people had come to understand the prophet's promise of the kingdom of God in a political fashion, and had united it with the ancient eastern desire for world dominion. So it came about that wherever Jews dwelt—and that meant in every large city of the Roman empire—there was whispering about the coming world ruler, who would arise in the east like the sun. His advent could happen any day, and he would appear to waiting mankind in the mysterious land and people of the Hebrews and enter on his triumphal course. The romantic advent philosophy of Rome was confronted by a new advent hope, which was also political, and carried the Jewish sign.

Kindled by such dreams of the future, the Jews of Palestine rose in violent rebellion against the Roman dominion in the last years of Nero's reign. The spirit of the Maccabees was alive again, and a priest's son, called Joseph ben Matthia, who boasted descent from the Maccabaean heroes, quickly rose to eminence among the insurgents. He was given the military command in Galilee, and was probably imagining the moment when he could proclaim to his people, 'I am he that should come.'

The Jews were at first successful. Then Nero entrusted the former general Vespasian with the crushing of the rebellion. The decision was not an easy one for the emperor to take. For Vespasian had drawn upon himself the attention of the imperial secret police during the visit to Greece, by showing his boredom or by absenting himself when the actor-emperor made his appearances; and in consequence had been abruptly dismissed. But now Nero had to make the best of it. For Vespasian was the best soldier of the empire. With the emperor's pardon in his pocket he set out for Syria, accompanied by his son Titus, and was soon pressing the Jewish nationalists hard.

Joseph was able to withdraw into hiding with a small remnant of his forces. But the situation was hopeless, and the beleaguered troops were left with the alternative of falling into the hands of the Romans or making an end to their own lives. Then Joseph had a vision which revealed to him the meaning of the 'ambiguous' Book of Daniel and the future of Rome, and which summoned him to declare his new wisdom in the name of God to the Roman general. So for the sake of this divine mission he had to save his precious life, and he proposed that each should die by the hand of another. The order would be determined by lot, and 'divine providence ordained' that Joseph was the last survivor. He straightway abandoned his doomed men, and went to Vespasian, to whom (as he later asserted) he spoke these prophetic words: 'Vespasian, you think that in Joseph you have merely a prisoner. But I come as the messenger of a greater future. For if God had not sent me to you, I should have known what the law of my fathers commands, and how it befits a commander to die. Vespasian, you will become Caesar and Imperator, you and your son who is present here.' Perhaps Joseph's prophetic words were not quite so precise as he later framed them. At any rate, the fluent Joseph related many things to the Roman commander of the mysterious prophecies of his people, of his own learning and divine illumination, of the divinely ordained succession of empires and of the Iron—that is, on Joseph's view the imperishable Roman Empire; he was careful to say

·nothing of the goal of all prophetic thought—the promise of the kingdom of God.

The prophet Daniel, speaking of the Iron kingdom, mentions the little horn which comes from 'great speech'. Perhaps Joseph felt called to realize this prophecy. However that may be, what we see is a bankrupt scribe, a bankrupt hero and a bankrupt candidate for the role of Messiah, who led his nation and his troops to ruin through his vain exegeses, then left them in the lurch in order to lengthen, perhaps to save, his wretched life as a Roman prophet with the Bible of his fathers in his hand. He might even, with luck, have a successful career —an exegetical speculator with nothing to lose and everything to gain.

Joseph does not reveal in his autobiographical account what he said and what he did not say to Vespasian at that time. He recounts the matter in his analysis of Daniel which he edited later for the *usum Delphini*. Joseph's misrepresentations of the Book of Daniel may be summarized as follows. In Dan. 2.40 the fourth kingdom is called 'iron' because (in the manner of ancient beliefs) it 'breaks in pieces and crushes all things'. According to Joseph, however, it is called iron because it will rule 'for ever'. Second, Dan. 2.45f. speaks of the mysterious stone which smashes the four kingdoms, including the kingdom of iron. Joseph, however, has a simple explanation: 'Daniel also revealed something about the stone, but I do not consider it right to enter upon that matter, for I have to show what is past and not what is to come.'

Vespasian was no exegete, nor was he inclined to trust the torrent of prophecy, but had the divine messenger taken into custody. This happened on July 1 of the year 67. Exactly two years later Vespasian was proclaimed Caesar by the Roman prefect in Alexandria—who, remarkably enough, was also a renegade Jew. On July 3 the Syrian legions joined him. Joseph had made the right wager. He was released, and made himself useful as a court prophet and agitator, making propaganda speeches for the Romans from the walls of the beleaguered city of Jerusalem, glorifying the new emperor as the promised ruler 'from Judaea', and extolling the wonders

10. THE MOTHER OF NERO

11. SENECA

which accompanied the mere appearance of Titus, the heir to the throne, and witnessed to his divine destiny and nature. But his wretched compatriots answered him with stones. One well-aimed stone caught him on the mouth, stirring a veritable tumult of joy in the city, and even giving his old mother bitter satisfaction. Stoning is the traditional Jewish punishment for the apostate. The Jews looked on him as a traitor to God and his people, who had sold his birthright for a mess of pottage.

Titus maintained the siege of Jerusalem. Vespasian went to Alexandria, where he exhibited his divine powers by healing the blind and the lame. The very waters of the Nile flowed unusually high as a welcome to the divine emperor. In September, 70, Titus entered the conquered city. In October his father made a ceremonial entry into Rome. Joseph was not present but he described the scene later, and no Old Testament prophet could have described the coming of the Son of Man more enthusiastically. The advent pilgrims went out in their thousands to lead in the imperial saviour and giver of grace, welcoming him with the liturgical formula: 'Thou alone art worthy to receive the *imperium*.' With this advent day there began a new period of blessing for Rome, which had been so plundered in the past. Some months later Titus, too, entered the capital, and father and son were honoured by that splendid triumphal procession to which the arch of Titus to this day bears witness.

Joseph ben Matthia came to Rome in Titus's following. He was now called Flavius Josephus, and enjoyed a fine sinecure as well as the friendship of the ladies of the court. Eusebius even writes of a statue of Josephus which was erected in the capital. There is a Roman bust of the first century depicting a Jew or Syrian which Eisler thinks might derive from that statue of Josephus. For the rest, Josephus wrote book after book glorifying his people, his own glorious life, and the career of his master whom he, Josephus, was the first to recognize as the Promised One from the east, the saviour-emperor, him who was to come.

But there was at least one man who never believed seriously in the divine nature or saving power of the emperor—and

that was the emperor himself. Vespasian had a strong, even
a metaphysical, sense of his calling. But he had no desire to
be accounted superhuman. It seemed better to him to be
simply a good emperor. The man who had once fallen asleep
during one of Nero's self-exhibitions was no Nero. He kept
his court prophet at a distance, and turned the incense of
praise aside with a soldier's joke. The 'miracle of healing' which
took place among the Alexandrians was suspect as well as dis-
pleasing to him. The triumphal procession in Rome bored
him. The genealogies which showed his descent from the
heroes of old excited his ridicule. And the certain prospect
of being granted divine honours after his death roused him
to sarcasm. 'I think I'm about to become a god,' he cried out,
as his last fatal illness came upon him. But when his last hour
came, he supported himself on the shoulders of his friends
and stood up, saying, 'An emperor must die on his feet.' So
he died—not a divine emperor, but an emperor by divine grace.

XI

DOMITIAN AND JOHN

ON August 23, 79, just two months after the death of Vespasian, the top of Mount Vesuvius flew into the air with a great detonation. The earth shook and thundered, the sea raged, and the air was filled with a deafening roar. Accounts of eye-witnesses have survived. Thick clouds of smoke rose from the mountain. A hail of stones, which hid the sun, fell upon the towns and villages of the gulf of Naples. People rushed hither and thither like madmen. Many fled from the towns, others sought refuge in the houses. Giant figures were seen in the air, great trumpet blasts were heard. People cried that the god of heaven had torn up the mountain and was swinging it to smash the world. The demons of the abyss had burst their chains and were streaming up to the earth. The sun was falling from heaven and the world was going up in flames. Chaos was breaking upon the world, and would swallow up everything. It was probably a devout Jew who scratched on the wall of a house in Pompeii the words 'Sodom and Gomorrha', which were uncovered two generations ago. And only a few years ago, in a house in Herculaneum, there were discovered the marks left by a simple wooden cross which had been fixed on the wall and hastily torn out—the oldest sign of the cross of which we have record. Perhaps a Christian householder had gathered his people round the cross on the outbreak of the catastrophe, and then taken it with him like a palladium into the raging inferno.

In the night sheets of flame shot from the torn-off crater, and many people were killed in the rain of fire and sulphurous smoke. The next morning a cloud of ashes rose up from the volcano and spread across the sky like a black mushroom. The earth grew dark, 'as in a windowless room when the light

has gone out.' The darkness was broken momentarily by lightning flashes from the midst of the cloud. Then a rain of ashes,
white hot, fell upon the earth, slaying men and beasts, the
birds in the air and the fish in the sea. The earth shook again
and again. In their agony men called on death to relieve them.
Many prayed aloud, but most cried that the gods were dead
and the last eternal night had come.

It was not till August 27 that it became light once more.
The proud cities of Herculaneum and Pompeii were buried
beneath a mass of ashes, and with them thousands of people.
Within the last two hundred years they have been dug out
again. They lay as they had been overcome in flight, asphyxiated
or burnt or buried by ashes. Above the immense field of ashes,
as the ancient accounts tell us, 'the mountain smoked like a
great censer'. The ashes were carried as far as Rome, and the
north-west wind even carried them to Africa, Egypt and
Syria. And still the earthquakes did not cease. Terrible prophecies went from mouth to mouth, depriving the terrified
populace of its last shreds of reason, so that they even mocked
at their own and others' misfortune.

Not far from Pompeii lay the legendary grotto of the sibyls
of Cuma. Soon a sibylline oracle was to be heard throughout
the Roman world. It is recounted in Plutarch and others, and
is most fully preserved in the Jewish account.

First the oracle speaks of terrible deeds of violence which
took place in the temple at Jerusalem, and of God's vengeance,
the destruction of the holy city by Vespasian, then of Nero's
mysterious disappearance, fleeing eastwards to Parthia. Then
the divine punishment will fall upon those who destroy God's
people and plunder Asia. Fire rises to heaven from the Italian
earthquake, destroying men and cities. Black ashes fill the air,
and fiery rain falls from heaven—a clear reference to the
eruption of Vesuvius.

This will be the signal for the return of Nero, to accomplish
the revenge of the East upon Rome, with the united forces of
Asia. At the same time plagues will lay Syria waste, and
drought and famine will destroy Asia Minor. God will hide
His face in His wrath.

Repent, cries the sibyl, so that God may not destroy all mankind in universal fire. And these shall be the last signs of the end—a flashing of swords in the air, a roaring and rumbling and sound of trumpets. And when the world has been reduced to ashes, then God will appear for the Last Judgment, and will cast the evil into hell, while the elect will be gathered around Him in a world renewed.

Meanwhile catastrophe followed catastrophe in Italy. In the year 80 there was a fire in Rome which raged for three days and three nights, destroying the Capitol and many temples and public buildings. No one doubted the wrath of the gods. Apollo himself, the god of the sibyls, was calling for propitiation. Titus arranged for a ceremonial atonement, in which the central object, according to the evidence of the coins, was the empty throne of Jupiter with the symbolic lightning flashes. But the gods seemed to have resolved on the fall of Rome and of all things. In the same year there broke out the worst plague which Rome had ever known, and this raged till the year 81. Here demonic forces were at work, said one ancient historian, here the catastrophes of the future were being proclaimed.

At this apocalyptic time Titus died, and his brother Domitian who, it was whispered, had had a hand in his brother's death, became the master of the world. Titus had helped where he could. But Domitian soon seemed to the people of the empire to be the last plague and outpouring of wrath which had been foretold by heaven in all previous visitations of evil. Suetonius called Titus the favourite of mankind. Pliny called Domitian the beast from hell, sitting in its den and licking blood. And John describes him in the picture of the beast from the abyss who blasphemes heaven and bespatters the earth with the blood of the saints (Rev. 13). How did Domitian come to earn this unanimous hatred?

Domitian was the first emperor to have himself officially entitled in Rome 'God the Lord'. It was a battle-gage thrown down before the spirit of ancient Rome, and Rome was quick to take it up. The court poets, Martial and Statius, accompanied the imperial self-revelations with a steady stream of praise. In the circus, man and beast paid him homage. His Olympian features were celebrated by sculptors in gold and silver, in marble and precious stones. The imperial coins carried his divine image to every part of the world, proclaiming his glory to all nations. So we are provided with enough original data to study the development of Domitian's imperial dogma till it overreached itself and was destroyed. Several important discoveries have been made in recent decades which have still to be properly assessed.

Domitian was also the first emperor to wage a proper campaign against Christ; and the Church answered the attack under the leadership of Christ's last apostle, John of the Apocalypse. Nero had Paul and Peter destroyed, but he looked upon them as seditious Jews. Domitian was the first emperor to understand that behind the Christian 'movement' there stood an enigmatic figure who threatened the glory of the emperors. He was the first to declare war on this figure, and the first also to lose the war—a foretaste of things to come.

I

Domitian had a solid peasant's head set on a thick neck, and the face of a hangman. That is how he is represented on the coins of his early years, with the untroubled realism of the old Roman art of portraiture. But after a few years there is a twofold change. The real Domitian became bald and short-sighted, with a heavy paunch and spindly legs—the secret model later used in Christendom for the picture of the Antichrist. The official pictures of the emperor, however, became more and more majestic, merging into the more-than-human lord with Jupiter's divine emblems. In the early pictures Domitian looks with wide-open eyes into the distance. In the later portraits his eyelids are usually disdainfully lowered, like a god looking down upon the lowly race of men.

This change in the coin-type was noted thirty years ago, and assessed in the history of ideas, by the English numismatist, E. A. Sydenham. A German archaeologist, Friedrich Matz, has recently drawn attention to a sardonyx in the possession

of Minden Cathedral, which may be said to contain in itself,
the whole story of the portraits of Domitian. It is a profile
of the emperor with an oak-wreath. The stone comes from
the first years of Domitian's reign. This is proved by the wide-
open eyes and the traces of the original parting in his hair.
But some years later the precious work was worked over in
keeping with the new ruling. The eyes could not be touched.
But the hair, the mouth and the chin show traces of the
touching up. The oak-wreath was left as it was. But it was
given a new meaning. Originally intended as a simple citizen's
crown, it now became the pretentious emblem of the supreme
god on the Olympic brow of the *Imperator*. 'It is the face of
Heaven, it is Jupiter's serene features', said Martial as he
gazed upon a 'bust of the lord'.

Domitian wished to be considered not only Jupiter's son,
heir and agent of his will, but also the earthly manifestation
of the king of heaven. He had his own portrait-bust set upon
the statue of Jupiter on the Capitol. His palace was a holy
place. He himself called his throne a seat of the gods, and he
adorned it with the emblems of Jupiter's throne. He even
insisted that in his absence his empty throne should be treated
as reverently as a high altar.

The wealth of honours and hopes, however, were concentrated on his son, born to the empress Domitia in 73—
the child of heaven who was to fulfil the hopes of the ages.
The young heir to the throne was apparently proclaimed as
the fulfiller of Virgil's advent eclogue. In 83 the lad died.
The emperor immediately had him proclaimed a god, and his
mother the mother of god. A special issue of gold, silver and
copper coins carried the new evangel throughout the world.
The coin-type shows the empress as the mother of the gods
(Ceres, Demeter, Cybele), either enthroned on the divine
throne or standing with the sceptre and diadem of the queen
of heaven, with the inscription, 'Mother of the Divine Caesar'.
Another coin shows the mother of the god seated on the
throne of Olympus with the glorified child before her, in his
left hand the sceptre of world dominion and with his right
hand blessing the world.

The apotheosis of the advent child reached its climax in a gold coin of the year 83. The dead prince is sitting on the globe of heaven, playing with the stars. The legend runs DIVUS CAESAR IMP DOMITIANI F—the divine Caesar, son of the Emperor Domitian. The seven stars indicate the seven planets, a symbol of heavenly dominion over the world. We may see them from early imperial times on provincial coins from Crete. Crete is the home of the myth of Zeus. There Zeus was born, there he lies buried. So the seven planets appear on Cretan coins, now with the Zeus child at play on the heavenly globe, now with the heavenly king with his sceptre, and occasionally, too, along with the deified Augustus. This symbol of the planets was taken over for the imperial child and signifies that after a short life on earth the heavenly child has been raised to heaven's throne and from there rules the cosmos, mightier than any earthly ruler, more glorious than the highest expectations of the nations or the most audacious hopes of his parents could have foreseen.

Our interpretation is confirmed by a coin which has only recently been discovered and has not yet been sufficiently noticed. Its obverse is as usual—the head of the divine mother Domitia in the latest hair fashion—but the reverse shows not the heavenly child but the moon and the other six planets— a connexion of symbols which has from ancient times been an emblem of the golden age. In the context of Domitian's whole coinage this means that the imperial Zeus child, who has been exalted to be lord of the stars, ushers in the age of universal salvation which is to come.

The court poets entered with a will into the spirit of the imperial fantasies of Christmas and Ascension. Martial took the occasion of a circus which was held in snowy weather to glorify the dead prince in a gracious epigram, which begins with a word from Virgil's advent poem—*aspice*—and ends with a poetic picture: the prince moves through the air, play-ing with the seven stars, and bombarding his father with snowflakes. Statius brings himself to relate how the exalted child descends by night from heaven, along with the other divine figures of the house of Flavius, and dances the dance of the stars around the equestrian statue of Domitian in the forum. And even the reserved epic poet, Silius Italicus, joins in the courtly mythology and writes of the son of the stars with the crown of light, who has preceded his father to the heavenly throne of the exalted Flavians.

No one was really serious about these ideas. After as before the death of the divine crown prince, Domitian lived in constant strife with Domitia, and in liaison with his beautiful niece Julia, who finally died a painful death after an abortion to which he forced her. Now Domitian turned to his Juno again, and soon there was news of a new heir to the throne. Statius was already celebrating the emperor as father of gods, *genitor deorum*. Martial hastened to implore the aid of the divine Julia for the empress, and to invite the child of promise to his epiphany, in an epigram whose chief impulse is again the advent poem of Virgil:

> Come to the world, thou who wert promised
>   to our fathers from of old,
> True scion of the gods,
>   come, exalted child,
> To whom thy father, after centuries,
>   will hand the eternal sceptre,
> That thou mayst reign to remote ages
>   along with him.

But the heavenly Julia was ungracious, and the new child of promise never appeared. The emperor adopted two small sons of his cousin, Titus Flavius Clemens, whose mother, Flavia Domitilla, was a granddaughter of Vespasian. They were given the names of Vespasian and Domitian, were named as heirs to the throne, and presented to the peoples of the empire on fresh coins. The court poets applauded the rising stars with exemplary enthusiasm. We shall hear later of their noiseless and unsung end.

Domitian had a passion for public spectacles. He had himself proclaimed as *Imperator* twenty-two times. He was consul seventeen times, and each year of office was inaugurated with a ceremonial procession, a great race-meeting, and similar shows. Four times he held a triumphal procession, without having won a single clear victory, and the accompanying games were extravagantly organized. As an eternal memorial of these triumphs an enormous equestrian statue of the emperor, *equus maximus*, was erected on the forum, and triumphal arches were set up in every part of the city, and dedicated with due magnificence.

The traditional festivals of the seasons, processions, spectacles, games and shows were celebrated with unheard-of extravagance. Domitian completed the Flavian amphitheatre (with about forty thousand seats), and built an odeum, a naumache, and on Mars hill a stadium for thirty thousand spectators, whose grandiose remains have recently been thoroughly investigated. The emperor's chief pride was the exotic beasts with which he surprised the people at the games. A special coin was issued for the admiration of the world, on which was represented a rhinoceros which he had brought to Rome for the amazement of the people. The Secular Games, which really fell due one hundred and ten years after the advent festival of 17 B.C., were celebrated in the year 88 with great lavishness, and marked also by a special issue of coins.

Horace's *Carmen Seculare*, which Domitian brought into fashion again, speaks in apocalyptic style of the Roman prophets and sibyls, who love the seven hills. Vespasian, in the early years of his reign, had issued a bronze coin, which proudly depicts the goddess of the city, Roma, enthroned on the seven hills, with the Tiber and the she-wolf. His son Domitian made it his care to revive the national festival of the seven hills. For many years to come men remembered the enormous banquet with which he brought the festival to a close.

In addition to all this, he established all kinds of new festivals. We know of a festival of Athena, whom Domitian specially honoured as his 'virgin mother', and depicted on innumerable coins. We hear most, however, of the Capitoline Games, which were established by Domitian and were continued throughout the time of ancient Rome. Suetonius mentions the number of victors' wreaths which Domitian distributed at these games.

The emperor was the centre of all these festivities. When

he returned from battle, he was greeted like a returning god.
We know from the time of Vespasian of the splendour with
which these advent festivals were celebrated, and we learn
from Martial's epigrams of the honour and glory paid by the
court poets to the apocalyptic return of the emperor. When
Domitian appeared in the circus, and took his seat beneath
the sacred canopy, in order to conduct the Capitoline Games,
there sat on his right hand the high priest of Jupiter, and on
his left the high priest of the divine imperial house. Both
priests wore wreaths with the emperor's picture on their brow.
Between them Domitian was enthroned, a golden wreath on
his head, emperor and Jupiter in one. The spectators had to
appear clad in white. The populace was in a fury of excitement when the emperor appeared. Martial tells enthusiastically
how the sound of many voices and languages changed to a
single united cry which surged up to the *Imperator* like a
hurricane—the acclamation of the emperor.

Domitian loved to hear, at the State banquet of the festival
of the seven hills, the cry of 'Hail to the Lord!' So Suetonius
relates. Other forms of acclamation are mentioned by court
poets and historians, and others by later writers which probably also go back to the time of Domitian. Among them were
the following: Hail, Victory, Lord of the earth, Invincible,
Power, Glory, Honour, Peace, Security, Holy, Blessed, Great,
Unequalled, Thou Alone, Worthy art Thou, Worthy is he to
inherit the Kingdom, Come, come, do not delay, Come again.
There was a perfect store of formulas, which were handed
down through the generations. An ingenious organization,
whose essential elements were established in the reign of Nero,
ensured that these spontaneous acclamations took on a rhythmic quality, which was given emphasis and order by liturgical
gestures of every kind. So the circus became a temple, the
people's festival became worship of the emperor, and the
festival meal became the Holy Meal of the lord.

It was the court poets who ate the most, shouted the loudest,
and sang the most piously. To see the emperor face to face
at the festival meal filled them with bliss: 'May I gaze upon
thee, Hope of mankind and Favourite of the gods.' They

sing praises to the emperor's servant, who is permitted to touch his divine hand, the most exalted experience for mortals. The entry of the divine lord is an epiphany:

> See, there is God,
>> there he is established with supreme power
> By the Father in heaven,
>> to rule the fortunate earth.

He inaugurated a new day, a new era. The golden age was not to be compared with the overflowing blessings of Domitian's Saturnalia. The world needed no more light from heaven when it had the emperor. When he rode past in his triumph, his countenance shone like the sun, and his eyes flashed like flaming stars. Then the poets cried to him, '*Princeps principum, summe ducum*, Lord of lords, highest of the high, Lord of the earth, god of all things!'

Even the beasts in the arena paid homage to the emperor's divine majesty, Martial assures us. The ancient themes of God and man and the animal world came alive. The animals bowed down before the new lord of creation and bore witness by signs and wonders to the return of Arcadian simplicity. The elephant recognized its master and worshipped him. Hares played in the jaw of the lion, who had learned from its master the supreme virtue of mercy. The hunted antelope fled for protection to the emperor. The very trees grew as never before. The birds perched on the branches and called '*Ave Caesar*'— but they were the imperial parrots who had been taught to say this.

When Vespasian entered Alexandria, shortly after being proclaimed emperor, his epiphany in the Nile delta produced a record harvest. But this divine bringer of blessing soon made himself very unpopular by his pedantic taxation methods, and the Alexandrians scornfully described him as the 'penny beggar' and the 'petty tax-gatherer'. Domitian wanted to excel his father. He made a serious effort to relieve the financial troubles and the currency inflation in the empire, and to restore the old silver content to the *denarius*, which had been much debased. To strengthen public confidence he issued a series of coins showing the *Moneta Augusti*, the patron goddess of the imperial coinage, offering her scales and horn of plenty to the sceptical merchants and farmers. But at the same time he undid the effects of this by economic experiments which he forced upon the people, and he undermined the currency by his enormous expenditure on triumphal arches and rhinoceri. The parrots cried '*Ave Caesar*', but paradise was still to come, despite the banquets. Statius sorrowfully admits that the emperor had no power over the clouds, the air and the winds, so that Africa was still too dry, India still too hot, and Germany still too cold. In brief, the emperor was not the promised king of paradise who would renew heaven and earth.

The whole imperial philosophy reached its climax in the idea of eternal rule. By the time of Vespasian the old belief in eternal Rome was finding its way on to coin-inscriptions. A coin of Domitian of the year 85 pays homage (following an older model) to the eternity of the worshipful emperor— AETERNITATI AUGUSTI. The obverse shows Domitian with the radiate crown of the sun god and with the aegis of Jupiter. The reverse-type shows AETERNITAS facing the eternal fire and grasping the sun and the moon—the ancient Egyptian symbols of eternity. In the year 90 Domitian had his equestrian statue erected as guardian of the *imperium aeternum*. On an Alexandrian coin of the same period the emperor is seated on a horse in the form of a snake—that is, as the god Aion, who embodies and ushers in and dominates the new aeon. The acclamations of the people reach their climax in the cries of 'Lord for ever, Lord from eternity to eternity, Lord in all aeons'.

The court poets faithfully did their best. Martial briefly and simply wishes that the emperor may survive the *seculum*. Statius calls Domitian the supreme renewer of the unending age, who established the new age along with Janus, the god of every beginning. The enthusiastic poet even introduces the sibyl in person, to promise the emperor eternal life. It is the same sibyl as Virgil once summoned as crown witness for the great Augustus, and now she speaks in Virgil's words: 'The great series of the ages awaits thee.'

Not even in the consideration of death are these court poets reduced to silence. Fate is merciless. But the emperor is the father of mercy, who hears the prayers of the troubled and heavy-laden. If all power were in reality given to him in heaven and on earth, then death would groan for a longer time, shut up in the dark abyss (*caeco gemeret Mors clusa barathro longius*); the inexorable Fates would let their hands rest, and lay aside their spinning-wheel. So Statius writes. But here the court poets overreach themselves. For this mythological and imaginary *Credo* can in the end only uncover the naked fact that the power of death is still unbroken, despite Domitian. The emperor is called Lord, God, and Saviour for eternity. But he does not possess the keys of death and hell.

Domitian only made himself ridiculous by this mythological self-exaltation. He made himself hated by his autocratic ways and his rule of terror.

The great Augustus once explicitly forbade his fellow-citizens to address him with the title 'Lord'. He did not want to be the master of slaves, but the first citizen of the empire. Nero had other ideas. One hymn of Nero was officially called the Song of the Lord, *canticum dominicum*. Vespasian loathed the new courtly style. But for his son Domitian it was the perfect vehicle for that arrogant scorn of the little man, and indeed of everything human, which is clearly written in his later portraits.

Suetonius tells us that the imperial missives dictated by Domitian himself began with the words 'The Lord our God commands'. Martial quotes a proclamation of Domitian which begins in almost the same words, 'Edict of the Lord our God'. A wooden tablet has survived with the beginning of an imperial order in the official style of Oriental despots: 'The words of the emperor, son of the God Vespasian, Domitian the worshipful.' A comparison with the letters of Darius in Herodotus, or with the royal inscriptions of the Achaemenidae in Behistun, shows that this Roman speaks like an Oriental emperor whose claims for his own majesty far outreach the claims made for themselves by the great Achaemenidae. He did not wish to be a citizen among his fellow citizens, but a superhuman being playing his sacrilegious game with human destiny. Domitian had a predilection for cruel forms of execution. He had a Roman knight whipped to death in the forum, without any proof of guilt. He liked to preface his condemnations with the words, 'It has pleased the Lord our God in his grace . . .'

Martial finds it possible to praise his rule. 'Under what master have we had so much freedom?' Josephus the court prophet also finds the atmosphere agreeable, and placidly dedicates his books *ad majorem gloriam* of the emperor and his house. But the men who are to be taken seriously hated him with all their heart, especially the senators of the old style, but not only the senators. At this time the three friends were growing up, the senators Tacitus and Pliny, and the knight Suetonius, who later dedicated their lives to the literary struggle against absolutism and imperial madness.

'We no longer need now, as earlier, to sing loud songs of devotion to the emperor. For neither do we, as earlier, speak about him in secret.' So spoke Pliny in his classic speech upon the senatorial emperor Trajan. His descriptions provide the clearest picture we have of the 'secret' talk about the beast with the blood-lust who kept friend and foe alike in suspense with his rule of terror (*plurimo terrore*), and of the public asseverations of loyalty which averted informers and denunciation. 'I look on the mere discussion of an imperial judgment as sacrilege,' was Pliny's reply to a loaded question. We can see how the secret fury and scorn of the imperial comedy found an outlet in savage jokes: the street to the capitol is too narrow for the oxen which are driven up to be sacrificed before the emperor's image; 'he' wants to sacrifice an ox for every man he has butchered. And the loyal populace, which cried itself hoarse during the day with acclamations, scratched by night on the triumphal arches (*arcus*) ARKEI ('It is enough'). Fists were secretly clenched, tracts were written about the human sacrifices demanded by imperial absolutism, conspiracies were formed—but Domitian had his spies everywhere, and delighted in having a senator brought to death for some little witticism he may have uttered. In Judaea there were uprisings

—but Domitian strengthened the occupying forces and nipped the rising in the bud.

But when he introduced, in 86, the description of himself as 'God the Lord', resistance took more serious forms. In 87 the emperor came upon traces of a widespread conspiracy in the senate. The sequel was a wave of executions and a public thanksgiving for the uncovering of the criminal plot.

But the opposition became more serious. In 88 an anti-emperor arose in Mainz, who found his support in the legions of upper Germany and the Germanic auxiliaries, and had also a large following among the senators. Domitian struck swiftly, and with the help of the loyal legions defeated the rebels, exposing the head of the would-be emperor in the forum in Rome. The rebellious divisions and senators suffered terrible punishment, and the secret threads of the resistance movement were traced as far as Ephesus, where none less than the governor of the province of Asia, a very deserving officer and a famous fighter in the Jewish War, was executed for conspiracy and replaced by an imperial procurator of the type of Pilate.

The priestly college of the Arval Brothers, to which Domitian himself belonged, had from the beginning of the revolt prayed unceasingly for the emperor's safety. Now the college arranged a public festival of thanksgiving. The Senate gave thanks to the gods with incense and sacrifices for the merciful deliverance of the emperor, and once more issued coins with the altar of thanksgiving and the inscription, 'For the deliverance of him who is worthy of all adoration', and others depicting Jupiter and Victoriola with the words JUPPITER CUSTOS, the emperor's protector. In November of the same year (89), Domitian celebrated a double triumph over the Germanic tribes. In the year 91 the bronze statue of the *Equus maximus* was completed, with the emperor gazing with proud gratitude to heaven which had given him the victory over all his foes, both at home and abroad. In the same year, perhaps during the games connected with the dedication of the statue, Domitian compelled the consul Acilius Glabrio to fight a lion with his bare hands—probably not from mere wantonness, but because he sensed in him a secret opponent. Acilius came out of the arena alive, but he was not forgiven. In the meantime the new coins with the inscriptions about the emperor's deliverance were carrying the news to the people of the East, not least to the cowed opposition in Ephesus, that the tyrant had survived the great crisis and was as firmly in the saddle as ever.

While the emperor was playing the strong man within the empire, and was celebrating one victory after the other in the north, he was watching the East with increasing uneasiness. Tacitus and Suetonius relate how the ancient prophecy of the revival of the East and of the world-ruler from Judaea had kept the Roman world uneasy from the time of Nero. We have already heard how Josephus had connected this prophecy with the hopes described in the Book of Daniel, and had related it to Vespasian. But even Vespasian did not really believe the court prophet, and the last of the Flavians was always suspicious of the unpredictable East, where the Parthians were a constant threat, along with the tribes of the Danube, and where a false Nero from Asia Minor lived at the Parthian court, claiming on the basis of an ancient oracle the kingdom of Jerusalem and the empire of the East. The situation was rendered the more serious by the fact that this anti-emperor of the East was in secret touch with the rebels in Ephesus and Mainz. If the conspirators could stir up opposition within the empire simultaneously with risings of the old enemies along the Rhine, the Danube and the Euphrates, then not only the emperor but the *Imperium Romanum* itself would be lost. The emperor was preparing for a general mobilization when he succeeded, in the years 88-89, in compelling the hard-pressed Parthian king to deliver up the pseudo-Nero. Domitian certainly had good reason to thank the gods for the miracle of his deliverance from this serious crisis.

But the Jewish Messianic hopes, and their output of oracles, were livelier than ever after the destruction of Jerusalem. At the beginning of the nineties these combined with an increasing hatred of Domitian. He built a triumphal arch in memory of his father's conquest of Jerusalem; he diverted the temple tax, which the Jews of the whole world had paid for the temple on Mount Zion, to the temple of Jupiter on the Capitol, exacting it by the most hateful methods and threats: he apparently even introduced a tax to relieve the cost of the countless statues and portraits of himself in Egypt and elsewhere. This was the time when Rabbi Akiba ben Joseph, the last great apostle of political Messianism in Jewish history, acquired his momentous views. The Jewish sibyl appeared in many places with old and new prophecies, of the false miracles of the Antichrist, of the impending catastrophe of insolent Rome, of Gog and Magog, of war, famine, plague and earthquakes, of the king of peace from the East and of the future glory of Jerusalem. And a Jewish book of the prophets revived the promises of Isa. 11, and wrote of the approaching age of Paradise: 'The wild beasts will come out of the forests and serve men. The adders and dragons will crawl out of their dens and little children will play with them.'

At this time, too, the Fourth Book of Ezra was written— the most splendid and profound piece of apocalyptic writing since the Book of Daniel. The prophet has a vision of the fourth kingdom of Daniel in the form of the Roman eagle, whose wings are spread out over the whole earth, which is more terrible than all the royal beasts that have preceded it. It reigns until the *Imperium* reaches, under the third of the Flavians, the climax of oppression and deceit, and its evils cry to heaven. Then a roaring lion bursts from the forest. It is the Messiah from the house of David, who will conquer and destroy the last emperor. The inhabitants are 'mightily astonished' (4 Ezra 11ff.). The *civitas Dei* appears, first in the picture of a superhuman woman, flashing like the lightning, then in the form of the heavenly city (10.25ff.). Finally the Son of Man comes on the clouds of heaven, destroys the mighty army of the *civitas diaboli* by his fiery breath, and gathers the people of God, to the accompaniment of signs and wonders, in the new Jerusalem (13.1ff.). Such are the prophetic words which stirred the peoples of the East in the years after the destruction of the Parthian Nero and the anti-emperor of Mainz and which were probably to be heard in Rome itself.

It is not difficult to imagine their effect on the irritable emperor.

In the nineties, so Suetonius tells us, Domitian in his obsession turned more and more to political persecution. Now it was Christianity which was the object of his fury: for it came from the suspect East, it proclaimed a world ruler from Judaea, and it refused to worship the emperor in his own capital. It was probably the gossip Josephus who brought suspicion on Christianity by his tendentious remarks and reports, and at the same time diverted the mistrustful emperor's hatred of the Jews to hatred of the Christians and their Christ.

Josephus's second historical work, *Jewish Antiquities*, appeared in the year 94. In Book 18.3 he gives an account of Pontius Pilate and a whole series of Jewish uprisings which the procurator in Judaea had to contend with—according to Josephus these were all forerunners of the great Jewish rebellion so gloriously suppressed by the Flavians. The first account is of the Jewish demonstration against the Roman standards with the emperor's image, the second is of the inviolability of the Temple treasure, the third is of the Christian movement, which Josephus doubtless represented as the rebellion of a political Messiah. (The account was later worked up by a Christian redactor into a confession of Christian belief.)

Josephus's account of the beginnings of Christianity reaches its climax in a note justifying the sentence of Pilate and closes with the alarming remark that nevertheless the Christians have not died out, but unfortunately are active to this day.

Towards the end of his book Josephus speaks of the stoning of some Christians shortly before the destruction of Jerusalem, and explicitly names James the brother of Jesus, the so-called Christ. This is apparently quite an incidental passage, but it is sufficient to make a mistrustful spirit attentive to the fact that the anointed revolutionary hero of the most restless nation of the East still had activist relations. It is easy to imagine the questions and answers which would be attached to such a passage.

But there was not much need to stir up suspicion in an artificial way. For Christianity offered in fact the only open resistance in the whole empire to the cult of the emperor.

This resistance movement became more and more dangerous through its alliance in the capital itself with the senators of the old school, and through its penetration of the ruling classes, of the court itself, and even of the imperial family.

Domitian acted as decisively as in the critical years 88-89. In the year 95 a conspiracy of the senatorial opposition was brought to light. The same Acilius Glabrio was sent into exile, and then executed in exile as a conspirator. *Molitor rerum novarum*, says Suetonius; one who attempts new things. It is the same formula as was used by the imperial office concerning the revolutionaries of 88-89, of the anti-emperor of Mainz, and of the Ephesian governor. It was therefore the official charge against a State conspirator which was here used against Glabrio. His family burying-place has been discovered in the catacomb of Priscilla, and in it a plaque with the Christian inscription, 'Acilius Rufinus, may you live in God'.

The same year (95), and for the same reason, Domitian took action against Clemens and Domitilla, the parents of his own adopted sons and heirs. Clemens, who had been fellow-consul with Domitian from the beginning of the year, was executed immediately after he had relinquished his office. Domitilla and a niece of the same name were banished to the islands of Pandataria and Pontia. The charge against them was of a tendency towards Jewish customs, towards atheism and high treason, that is, to a refusal to practise emperor worship. Tradition relates that Clemens was the third bishop of Rome, and may have been the author of the First Epistle of Clement, which speaks of the manifold temptations, persecutions and martyrdoms in the Rome of Domitian. The two women were buried in the catacomb of Domitilla, along with other Christians of the Flavian family and confessors of the Domitian persecution.

The two boys, Vespasian and Domitian, do not appear to have survived the catastrophe which overtook their parents. They disappear from history without a trace. Presumably Domitian had them quietly disposed of—and thus deliberately destroyed the exciting possibility of a Christian monarchy two centuries before Constantine.

Two Christian soldiers, called Nereus and Achilleus, were also executed in the reign of Domitian, and buried in the catacomb of Domitilla. A basilica was later erected in their honour, and two pillars to right and left of the sanctuary (cf. Rev. 3.12) were adorned with their names and a simple relief of their martyrdom. Above the dying martyrs rose the triumphant sign of the cross, with the heavenly crown. An old inscription whose remnants were discovered seventy years ago in the catacomb of Domitilla relates how the two soldiers cast away the imperial honours with the picture of the emperor and joyfully accepted the mark of the Cross (Rev. 7.3, 13.16):

> They turn round and leave
> The Emperor's godless camp,
> They cast away their shields,
> their medals and bloody weapons,
> Confess the Lord, and joyfully
> bear His sign of victory.

The church historian, Eusebius, describes Domitian as the heir of Nero's enmity to God and his theomachy. Here, however, the theomachy becomes deliberate Christomachy, which reached its climax in the year 96. At the beginning of that year the mistrustful emperor cited some members of the house of David from among the relations of Jesus to appear before his judgment stool. 'For he feared the advent of the Messiah as once king Herod did', added the ancient report (Hegesippus, quoted in Eusebius). Domitian at first intended to have them executed, and cross-examined them, asking about their activities and their political Messianic views. But when he saw their gnarled hands and heard about the kingdom of Christ, which is not of this world, he preferred to make their Christian faith sound ridiculous, and therefore harmless.

But the Galilean was stronger than the emperor. The same year the emperor's course—or rather, his running amok—came to an end.

'By this deed especially he hastened his end', wrote Suetonius after the death of Clemens. From that time the friends of the consul and martyr only awaited a suitable opportunity. Finally, the empress herself, having discovered her own name on the black list of her lord and master, made common cause with the conspirators. An old retainer of Domitilla, Stephanus by name, assumed the responsibility for the assassination. On September 17, 96, Domitian prophesied to his immediate *entourage* a tremendous happening for the following day. The whole world, he said, would speak of it, and the moon would turn the colour of blood. That night he was racked by fearful dreams of pursuit. In the morning he was busy with apocalyptic oracles. At eleven o'clock Stephanus made his way into his presence on some pretext, and with the terrifying cry, 'Clemens is not dead,' he stabbed him.

The Senate passed a resolution of *damnatio memoriae*, the ceremonial execration of his memory, the removal of his name from all inscriptions, and the destruction of his pillars, altars and statues. The mint-masters erased the hated name from his coins. The people took hammers and pickaxes to the sacred 'Pictures of the Lord' with the 'arrogant face' (Pliny, *Panegyricus* 52). Martial changed over as well as he could. Statius had just died. Josephus disappeared silently into obscurity. Pliny, Tacitus and Suetonius took up the tale, and completed Domitian's *damnatio memoriae* for all time.

II

Domitian's assumption of the imperial power was celebrated in Ephesus as in all provincial capitals of the empire by the pompous introduction of the new imperial image. Fanfares announced the holy advent. A ceremonial procession with the wonder-working imperial image moved from the harbour up to the city. Another procession of the priestly and civic dignitaries of the metropolis of Asia Minor came out from the city gate to meet them, received the image of the imperial lord and god with the usual spontaneous acclamations and ushered it into the city in a mass procession with torches and incense and hymns.

'What man is there who does not know that the city of Ephesus guards the temple of the great Artemis and the

heavenly image?' So spoke the Asiatic 'town clerk' in the days
of Paul. But Demetrius, the silversmith and temple agent, was
mistrustfully watching the activities of the apostle of Christ,
and prophesied the decay of the ancient cult of Artemis. 'The
temple of the great goddess Diana is made of no account, and
she will even be deposed from her magnificence, whom all
Asia and the world worships' (Acts 19.27, 35).

In fact the cult of the great goddess seems to have suffered
noticeably through the activities of Paul and his successors.
For at the beginning of the eighties the leading men of the
city and the province looked round for an attractive substitute, and found one in the establishment of a provincial
sanctuary for the worship of Domitian in Ephesus, which
was graciously sanctioned by the divine emperor. The remains
of this temple, of the high altar and the smashed image of
the emperor, were discovered some years ago during the
Austrian excavations, and together with many relevant inscriptions found at other times are now for the most part in the
museum at Smyrna.

Roman coins are extant with the cult image of Domitian
sitting in the holy of holies on the throne of the gods, flanked
by two servant angels (*Victoriae*). There are other types of
the emperor with lights and candelabra, altars and statues of
every kind. In the new imperial temple at Ephesus the marble
statue of Domitian, more than four times life size, was enthroned amid candelabra, altars, statues and inscriptions of
homage from the loyal cities of the province of Asia Minor—
Synaos, Tmolos, Stratonikeia, Aphrodisias, Aizanoi, Silandos
and so on. The head of the colossal statue shows in the style
of the hair and other details the type of the early Domitian,
with an Asiatic interpretation as the young Zeus. The left
forearm has also survived—the length of a fully grown man.
The hand is slightly clenched, and probably grasped the usual
sceptre, while the right hand would hold the thunderbolt.

The head of the Ephesian cult of the emperor was the
'high priest of Asia', who changed each year, and was also
president of the government of Asia, with the title of 'Asiarch'.
He was the supreme native dignitary of Asia, and was always

one of the most eminent and wealthy of the great families of the commercial cities in Asia Minor. He therefore considered it fitting to perpetuate the memory of his year of office by brilliant festivals, public buildings and endowments.

In the course of the last fifty years the Austrians have excavated not only a wealth of inscriptions but also numerous marble statues of imperial high priests. In the theatre of Ephesus a head was discovered with the typical adornment of a high priest, the image of the emperor on the brow, like that in the gold wreath of the Roman imperial priest. The protruding head of the tiny bust of the emperor has been broken off, but the bust itself has survived, half uncovered in the style usual in representations of Zeus. A statue which came to light at the same time as the head from the great Domitian statue, which stood originally in the sports stadium at Ephesus, shows the imperial priest wearing a diadem of ikons, with a whole wreath of images of the emperor, and with his hand on his breast, so disposed as to show the great signet ring, which must have been one of the signs of his office, probably with an imperial picture and inscription.

The significance of this new cult of Domitian for the city and the province cannot be easily overestimated.

The old city of Diana thenceforward bore the proud title of Imperial Guardian of the Temple, and was called on inscriptions 'the city loyal to the emperor'. Its dignitaries received the permanent appellation of 'loyal to the emperor'. The inscriptions from Domitian's time speak of imperial letters of grace, imperial mysteries, and sacrificial festivals. For more than a thousand years Ephesus had been an outstanding religious centre, in the Roman era it was the capital of the province of Asia, during the reign of the Flavians it was the most populous city of the Roman East after Alexandria, and its magnificent public buildings made it one of the proudest cities of the empire. Under Domitian a fresh impulse was given to its building activities. The great library was begun, and the new amphitheatre was completed.

In such a city the cult of Domitian was bound to have a powerful effect, not only on the religion but also on the

politics and the psychology of the masses. For the high priest
of Domitian was not only the religious head of all the priests
of Asia Minor, but also the political confidant of the imperial
government, as well as the chief propagator of the imperial
philosophy in the province. The new temple of Domitian,
where he officiated, was also the new seat of the government
meeting under his direction, which had formerly met in the
Templum Romae et Augusti. It was a matter of course that the
new image of the emperor should be the centre of the whole
ritual of government.

Both before and after their sessions the governing officials
were to be found in their seats of honour in the amphitheatre,
the gymnasium, the Odeion, the Stadion, the Hippodrome,
to take their part in the liturgical festivals arranged by the
high priest and Asiarch in the name of the whole province
of Asia in honour of their imperial lord and god. The modest
parliamentary rights of the Asiarch and his government were
counterbalanced by the splendour of their cultic activity. For
when the political unity of the empire was to be represented
and established by the common adoration of the emperor, the
political loyalty and activity of the province was bound to be
shown chiefly in the holy games in honour of the emperor.

The celebrations were opened by a splendid imperial sacrifice. The high priest celebrated in full splendour, prostrating
himself, with all his officials, before the emperor's image.
Individual deputies, in priestly attire and decked with wreaths,
cast ears of corn into the flaming censers, and approached the
altars of their cities with the sacrificial bowls. Intoxicating
music from flutes and harps overwhelmed the senses. The
image of the emperor was lost in the smoke which filled the
temple. This was the favoured moment for all kinds of trickery.
Voices were heard, and strange movements glimpsed. To
interpret these was part of the high priest's prophetic function.
In the holy hour miracles could be experienced before the
image of the lord. For the emperor's image had to be wonder-
working, if it were to be accepted as an authentic divine
image. This was a belief which was particularly strong in
Asia Minor. About one hundred and thirty miles north of

Ephesus lay the town of Alexandria. A short time before this, it had erected a statue to the imperial governor of the last years of Nero's reign, which was famed as an oracle, and even cured the sick (Athenagoras, *Supplicatio* 26, 2). Ephesus, and its imperial image, could not lag behind Alexandria.

After the sacrifice to the emperor there followed a grand procession through the decorated and crowded streets to the place where the festival games were held. Now the ritual became a truly public affair. For those who joined in it had streamed together not only from the city, but from all Asia and the whole world. As the waves thunder on the shore, writes an author of that time, so do the assembled masses thunder and toss expectantly in the sports ground.

A herald opened the games with a liturgical preamble. There followed the proclamation of imperial messages and parliamentary decisions. Honorary decrees were read, and honorary decorations distributed. Then a fanfare led in the games themselves.

First, poets, singers and choirs stood forth, to sing hymns and odes to God the Lord in Rome, now singly, now antiphonally, now to the accompaniment of flutes and harps. The assembled populace of the province of Asia joined in with acclamations.

Then a new fanfare ushered in the horse-racing, which was the very unliturgical climax for most of the participants in the holy games. The noise of the chariots filled the air 'like the rattling of many teams of horses rushing into battle'. Bowmen on horseback, swordsmen and torch-bearers raced past. The horses raced in four teams and four colours. (For a time Domitian had favoured six colours in Rome, but this had scarcely penetrated to Ephesus.) The spectators, too, were divided among the four parties and their colours, and followed the race with cries of joy and sorrow.

Another fanfare, and the gladiators and fighters with wild beasts entered the arena, and addressed the image of the emperor with the familiar acclamation: *Ave Imperator, morituri te salutant*—and entered on their last battle. Then came processions, plays, contests and gymnastic exhibitions, dances and wedding pantomimes and beauty parades with the triumphal procession of the great goddess, interspersed with fanfares, proclamations by the heralds, acclamations, liturgical interludes and cavalcades. Executions, too, and tortures, could be incorporated into the proceedings. There followed the announcement of the prize-winners. Garlands and wreaths, palm-leaves and other prizes were distributed. On a Hellenistic relief from Ephesus, which was published in 1937, may be seen a victorious *agōn*, with a palm branch in his right hand, crowned with a wreath; a trumpeter is blowing beside him. One may suppose that the honours paid to the victors at the end of the imperial games were similar. The conclusion was a holy meal in great style, which in the land of Dionysus, and the city of the great goddess, may be presumed to have developed into all manner of orgies in honour of the imperial libertine.

The religious ceremonies and games, then, which were regularly arranged by the Ephesian imperial priest, were of some such kind. In the intervals of these regular festivals, in Ephesus as in Rome, there were all manner of special festivals. The tumultuous history of Domitian, and his philosophical revelations, provided plenty of opportunities.

It is likely that the apotheosis of the young crown prince was celebrated in Ephesus, too, by a special liturgical festival, with doxologies and probably the setting up of a little cult statue with altars and dedicatory reliefs and inscriptions.

When the priests and senators celebrated in Rome, in 89, the merciful deliverance of the emperor with thanksgiving and joy, the high priest in Ephesus would certainly not be behindhand in protestations of loyalty. For the imperial procurator who took over control in Ephesus, after the calamity which befell the senatorial governor, was without doubt a good overseer. And the high-priestly Asiarch was the obvious man to stage unparalleled liturgical demonstrations of the immovable loyalty of the province and horror at the senatorial conspiracy.

At that critical moment the imperial liturgy was perhaps enriched by motifs from the cult of Sandon or some other of the myths of dying and rising gods of Asia Minor. All kinds of miracles took place *ad maiorem Domini et Dei gloriam*. It was said that on the day of the decisive victory over the revolutionary emperor a monstrous eagle appeared over Rome, which encircled the statue of Domitian with its wings and uttered loud cries of joy. One may be assured that the image of the emperor in Ephesus did not disappoint the happy and miracle-hungry populace at the great thanksgiving festival.

The cult of the emperor in Ephesus had every chance of becoming popular. Those who did not go near the temple were commanded to appear at the spontaneous mass proclamations, or sent into the circus. Those who avoided the holy games could not avoid, as they went through the streets, the processions with the holy images and songs of the lord, nor could they help hearing beneath their windows by day the hymns of the devout, and by night the Bacchic bawling of the crowds. . . .

The emperor had still another way to reach the hearts of the people, that of the currency, which at that time in Ephesus was the responsibility of the high priest and Asiarch.

The temple of Diana in Ephesus had for centuries possessed a temple bank, which presumably served as the greatest source of credit for ancient times. Perhaps the imperial high priest competed in this point too with the temple of Diana, by establishing an imperial bank in connexion with the imperial temple, as it were a branch of the Roman imperial bank, with all the privileges and monopolies of the currency in this rich commercial capital and the province.

From this bank, first of all, the imperial coins of western provenance were issued which here, as in all the imperial provinces, were standard (cf. Rev. 6.6). These consisted of, first, the *denarii* with the type of the mother of god or her son, now ascended to heaven, second, the coins struck by the senate to commemorate Domitian's deliverance, then the coins with the type of the goddess of money, Annona, and innumerable coins representing the victor over the Germani on horseback, a precursor of the *equus maximus* in Rome, and for remote provincials a substitute for the sight of that bronze marvel.

But Ephesus was also permitted by the central authority in

Rome to strike imperial coins of its own, as, for example, a silver thaler with a Latin inscription and the temple of Roma and Augustus. The Asiarch, too, had the right, in his capacity of leader of the holy games, to strike medallions which were chiefly used as prizes for the victors and for distribution among the guests of honour. Lastly, the provincial government in Ephesus issued the coins which were specifically intended for circulation in the province. All these coins have the type of Domitian on the obverse, usually with Zeus-like features, and the inscription, 'The august emperor Domitian'. The reverse glorifies such events as the emperor's Germanic victories, or the building of the temple of Domitian in Ephesus, or the emperor himself portrayed as Zeus.

There is no need to dwell upon the fact that the political and cultic propaganda of these coins affected every single man in the city and province, even the most determined opponent. To refuse to handle the money which carried the emblems of emperor worship meant automatic exclusion from the economic life of the time, and therefore starvation.

The repercussions of this propaganda are unmistakable. In Smyrna coins were struck with Domitian as father of the gods, Domitia as mother, and bronze coins acclaiming Vespasian, the heir to the throne, as the hope of the nations. Similarly in Pergamon, Thyatira, Sardes and Philadelphia. From Priene comes an inscription describing Domitian as the august emperor, the invincible god, the creator (second founder) of the city. Laodicea struck coins with types of Domitian or of Zeus or the emperor's temple, and others with the double portrait of the imperial pair, given in Olympic proportions; the reverse type a temple of victory with the emperor and empress as Zeus and Hera. An inscription from Laodicea glorifies the incarnate Jupiter in the doxology: 'To Zeus the Supreme, the Saviour, the Emperor Domitian.'

The enthusiasm of the grateful province knew no bounds. It became a raging fury against the Christians during the trials of Glabrio, Clemens and their comrades for high treason in 95. In Ephesus, Smyrna, Pergamon and elsewhere there were severe anti-Christian riots and executions, and there are several

CHRIST AND THE CAESARS

witnesses to the part played by the Jews of Asia Minor, which was similar to that of Josephus in Rome.

But the secret resistance to the emperor was not halted, and in the autumn of 96 the official comedy of loyalty was played out, in Asia as well, to the usual end. On September 18, about noon, as is unanimously related by the ancient writers, the Pythagorean wandering preacher, Apollonius of Tyana, who knew the emperor intimately, was suddenly seized by a visionary ecstasy in Ephesus, and cried: 'Splendid, Stephanus! That's right, Stephanus, strike him dead, the blood-hound! Well struck! Blood! Dead!' Then he turned to the people who had gathered round him, and said: 'Be comforted, for the tyrant has been slain today. You will receive the news in due course from Rome. Let the thankofferings be postponed till then. But I am going now to offer thanks to the gods for what I have seen.' The city of the imperial temple was in a state of suspense until the runner arrived with the evangel (*Euangelion*: see Isa. 52.7) of the tyrant's assassination and the execration of his memory (Dio Cassius 67.18, Philostratus, *Vita Apollonii*, 8.26f.). The delighted people lost no time in going up to the temple, where they smashed the great statue of the lord their god, and hurled the marble fragments from the temple terrace. There they lay until they were used for building walls or removed to the rubbish dumps. The name of Domitian was erased from the inscriptions in all loyal cities, and his father's name and titles substituted. The temple in Ephesus became the temple of Vespasian—the worship of the emperor, which meant so much for Ephesus, had to continue as far as possible undisturbed.

But the damage had been done. Fifteen years later Pliny, the military governor, complained about the isolation of the temple and the holy games in Asia Minor, and blamed the Christians, who refused to worship the emperor, and instead sang antiphonal hymns to Christ as a god.

III

From the time of the apostle Paul Ephesus had been the centre of the church of Asia Minor. After the destruction of

Jerusalem the last surviving disciple of Jesus, the apostle John, the head of the church of the east, lived in Ephesus.

The old Ephesian tradition calls him the high priest with the plate on his forehead, thereby indicating his leading position in the rule as well as the worship of the church. The plate on the forehead of the Jewish high priest was originally a fillet with a golden plate in the centre, with the name of Jahveh engraved upon it (Ex. 28.36ff.). This was the Jewish equivalent of the ancient priestly diadems with the emblem or image of the god on a gold centre-piece, many of which have been discovered in recent times. We may suppose that the high-priestly plate of the apostle John bore the Christo-gram—the Christian equivalent of the bust of Domitian on the diadem of the imperial high priest.

John was present in Ephesus when the worship of Domitian was introduced, and opposed it at once as bitterly as ever the old 'thunderer' (Mark 3.17) had opposed Jewish and Gnostic propaganda. He became willy-nilly the great opponent of the imperial high priest and Asiarch, and must have been the man most hated by the officials of Ephesus.

In the year 95 Domitian, who at that time was persecuting every 'dangerous' confessor of Christ, even in Palestine, heard of a certain 'Hebrew' in Ephesus, who was prophesying the imminent end of the Roman emperor and the rise of a new world ruler of Jewish origin. He had the high priest of the young church of the East summoned to Rome, and there examined and tortured, as we learn from the account of Ter-tullian and the tradition of a hundred years later. There is no reason to doubt the truth of the account, corresponding as it does to our knowledge of Domitian's character, of the facts of the persecution in that year, and of John's exposed position. In consequence, John was banished to the convict island of Patmos in the Aegean Sea 'for the word of God and the testimony of Jesus' (Rev. 1.9).

There on the Lord's day he received that unique revelation, which is nothing less than the answer of the heavenly Christ to the proclamation of war made by Domitian, and the con-fession of faith of His disciple John—a message to the church of Asia Minor from the true *princeps regum terrae*, the ruler of the kings of the earth, who has made His people a nation of priests of God and the ruling people of the future, 'to him be the glory and dominion for ever and ever' (Rev. 1.6). The whole content of the revelation is to be found in this opening doxology—*gloria et imperium in secula seculorum.*

We may read the Book of Revelation with new understanding when we see it as the apostolic reply to the declaration of war by the divine emperor in Rome. And when we realize the perilous political situation in which the book was both written and 'published' (22.10), we understand the reason for its mysterious and veiled pictorial language and its preference for words and pseudonyms from the Old Testament. The Apocalyptist 'indicates more than he expresses his unpatriotic hopes', writes Mommsen with true insight. The book was intended to be enigmatic to outsiders, to the enemies of Christ and the emperor's censors, and at the same time a revelation to those who partook of the affliction of Christ and His kingdom. 'He that hath an ear, let him hear' (2.7).

We are not concerned here to unfold the apocalyptic picture of history, of heaven and earth, past and future, the city of God and the kingdom of hell, the worship of the angels and the Sabbath. We shall confine our attention to the book as a weapon against Domitian's myth of the emperor. Nor can we exhaust even this theme. We can only touch upon much that is now common knowledge as a result of the investigations of writers like Richard Delbrueck, Andreas Alföldi, André Grabar and Erik Peterson. Nor do we intend to discuss the supra-historical interpretation suggested by Ernst Lohmeyer; though to anyone who has once grasped the situation and the language of the Book of Revelation many antithetical analogies between the Roman and the heavenly *Imperator* will be clear without express reference to them. And the historical and theological standpoint of Revelation shows clearly where the real battle-ground between Christ and the false Christ lies.

We begin with the twelfth chapter. There the eternal city of God appears in heaven in the form of the woman of the

12. DOMITIAN

13. JULIA DOMNA

sun, arrayed with all the signs of eternity and heavenly majesty. Her feet are on the crescent moon, and on her head is the crown of the twelve stars. She is the mother of the divine child, which appears only for a cosmic moment, and then returns to the region of the stars, raised to the throne of God.

This is the eternal evangel, the answer to the transitory evangel of the glorified son of the emperor, playing in the heavenly throne-room. The exalted child of the Book of Revelation carries a sceptre just as the consecrated son of the empress, the mother of God. This sceptre is not an ornament from Olympus, but an apocalyptic sign that the child of the *ecclesia eterna* will come again to rule the nations with a rod of iron. This child of the Apocalypse, like the emperor's son, passes through death. But his death is innocent and painful, a slaughter for the saving of many. The saints in heaven know this, and sing with a great voice a song which surpasses all the court poetry of Rome and the Ephesian cult: *Nunc facta est salus et virtus et regnum Dei nostri et potestas Christi eius* (12.10).

But the Christ child has an enemy, the great dragon. He that hath an ear, let him hear how the great acclamation of the courtly verse is here filled with demonic potency. It is the old serpent called the devil and Satan, God's enemy from the beginning, and now the mortal enemy of God's Son. The theomachy becomes a Christomachy. In vain the serpent tries to prevent the birth, and then the victorious ascension of the Christ, in vain he tries to prevent his own fall from heaven. The blood of the Crucified is stronger than Satan's power. The old serpent is given only a short time more, a last span in which to exert its power and its cunning on those who confess Christ. The Christomachy becomes an ecclesiomachy. It is in this apocalyptic framework that John sets the history of the Roman empire and of Domitian's religious policy.

Satan stood upon the seashore and called to the false Christ. He came up out of the sea, a monster with ten diadems, uniting in himself, and surpassing, all the horrors of Daniel's royal beasts. Are we meant to think of the arrival of the imperial image in the harbour at Ephesus? The beast was mortally wounded, but the wound was healed again—this is the pseudo-messianic perversion of the mystery of Good Friday. This seems to refer clearly enough, though in veiled terms, to the abortive conspiracy of 88-89, in which, as we know, the city of Ephesus played a special part. And now the political monster makes his entry with all the pomp of an imperial advent. The whole earth wondered after him, and fell down before him. And they cried, 'Who is like him?' The imperial false Christ is the complete revelation of political omnipotence in its demonic self-glorification. His history is a unique theomachy. His words are sheer blasphemy.

The spontaneous acclamation of the masses has a subdued appendix, which sounds like the capitulation of the Ephesian resistance movement—'Who is able to war with him?' The false Christ is the very embodiment of aggression. Power was given to him over all peoples, and victory over the saints of God. He was all-powerful. Resistance was folly, and meant suicide. So the whole earth worshipped him.

But power loves deceit. The beast from the sea was joined by the beast from the earth. The Roman false Christ was joined by the native false prophet, who is described exactly as the imperial high priest and Asiarch—revealing the whole lying nature of the political myth. He wore the garments of a priest, but he spoke with political authority. He was the propaganda chief of the imperial cult, whose aim was to have all Asia worship the image of the emperor.

His favourite theme was the Good Friday gospel of the mortal wound, and the overcoming of death by the false Christ. His show piece was the liturgical thanksgiving for the wonderful deliverance of the emperor. The false prophet was the deceitful perversion of the prophet Elijah, who caused fire to fall from heaven before the eyes of the priests of Baal, and would come again to prepare the way of Christ. He celebrated the political liturgy of Good Friday before the colossal statue of Domitian, and caused fire to fall upon the altar before the eyes of the assembled populace, who saw with devout amazement how at the climax of the celebration the miraculous image of the emperor moved its lips and spoke.

When eyes refused to be dazzled, terror was called in to help. Those who would not worship the imperial image were condemned to death. The false prophet and high priest wore the imperial image on the golden circlet on his brow and on his signet ring. He sealed the worshippers with the sign of the emperor on his brow and his hand—both great and small, rich and poor, freemen and slaves. For all are equal before the Lord god in Rome. The false prophet and Asiarch circulated among the people the coins with the mythological pictures and titles of the emperor—and those who wished to have nothing to do with this could neither buy nor sell. 'Here is wisdom', said the apocalyptic writer (Rev. 13.18). 'He that hath understanding, let him count the number of the beast; for it is the number of a man: and his number is Six hundred and sixty and six.'

In these chapters we see described, in apocalyptic language, yet with historical and theological clarity, first the birth and death of Christ, His exaltation and worship, and then, in eschatological concentration, the false imperial Christ and his false political prophet, that is, the myth of Domitian, the crisis of the years 88-89, and finally the cultic propaganda, the religious policy and persecution of the Christians by the high-priestly Asiarch, who demanded of all the mark of the official imperial name—A*utokrator* KAI*sar* DOMET*ianos* SEB*astos* GE*rmanikos*. This is the name concealed in the cipher 666, which has for 1800 years caused so much fruitless racking of brains.[1]

But where in all this tumult of a false Messiah is the Christ who has overcome Satan, and is to rule the peoples of this world with an iron rod? 'Behold, he cometh with the clouds; and every eye shall see him, and they which pierced him; and all the tribes of the earth shall mourn over him. Even so, Amen' (Rev. 1.7).

In the first chapter of the Book of Revelation we see the Son of Man, Imperator and Pontifex Maximus, in the heavenly

---

[1] See the present writer's article '666' in *Coniectana Neotestamentica*, XI (Lund, 1947), pp. 237ff. The abbreviation A for Autokrator might seem dubious, but can be proved from a study of coins. The other abbreviations are fully attested.

courts, clothed in a priestly gown, and wearing the golden girdle and the 'Persian' brocade shoes of the *triumphator*. His countenance shone like the sun. His eyes were as a flame of fire. In His right hand He held the symbol of omnipotence, the seven stars. Round about Him arose out of seven candlesticks the incense given by the seven churches of Asia Minor. This was the true *Dominus et Deus*. The apostle, who had not bowed the knee to any image of the emperor, fell on his face, and heard the self-revelation of the heavenly *princeps regum terrae*: 'I was dead, and behold, I am alive for evermore, and I have the keys of death and of Hades.' This is more than an antithesis. It is the overcoming of the dogma of the emperor at the point where the myth of Domitian had obviously failed, and where every political messianism must fail—at death. This is the answer to the question about our eternal destiny.

The Son of Man appeared at the opening of the Messianic games.

There began the last game to be played on earth, a game unlike any other played by any emperor, holy, immense, bloody, and derisive. In the Book of Job we read how God the Lord played with leviathan (Job 41.25ff.), and in Psalm 2 how God had in derision the mighty of the earth: 'He that sitteth in the heavens shall laugh: the Lord shall have them in derision.' In Psalm 37 we find the threatening prophecy— *Dominus autem irridebit eum; quoniam prospicit quod veniet dies eius*: 'The Lord shall laugh at him: for he seeth that his day is coming.' In such a way Christ mocked the emperor and all his display and boasting, in a wrathful murderous parody, and the kings and mighty ones fled, and all the nations of the earth howled aloud. So He made game of the dragon, and every creature joined in this apocalyptic game, whose arena is the universe.[1]

The Messianic games began, just like the imperial games at Ephesus, with the proclamation of the imperial decrees. The heavenly Imperator proclaims seven messages, addressed

---

[1] Similarly Paul and his school: the world still has its game with the saints of God (I Cor. 4.9ff., 15.22; Heb. 10.32f.); but the Messianic triumphal games have already begun (Col. 2.15).

to his seven messengers in the seven churches of Asia Minor. In a Latin Apocalypse from the time of Jesus, Moses is called the great *Nuntius* of God (*Ascension of Moses*, 11.17). In the second Epistle to the Corinthians Paul calls himself the ambassador of Christ (5.20: *pro Christo ergo legatione fungimur*). And in the Epistle to the Ephesians there is an echo of the phrase in 6.20—*pro quo legatione fungor in catena*, 'for which I am an ambassador in chains'. So the heavenly emperor of the Apocalypse has His messengers in the seven cities.

The preamble of the seven decrees is in unmistakable contrast to the opening words of the edicts of Domitian: 'So speaks he who holds the seven stars in his right hand.' Also the negative continuation with the threat of punishment (2.5, 16) is in the same style as the usual imperial announcements. For example, in a decree which has survived from the early years of the Empire, the formula runs, 'If anyone . . . him will I . . . but if not, then . . .'

We may also refer once more to Herodotus 5.24 and the style of the ancient Asiatic royal proclamations. A messenger of king Darius proclaims to the 'loyal' Histiaeus: 'King Darius says, Behold, I look and see none more loyal to me and the kingdom than you, and I have found you so not in words but in deeds. Therefore now, for I purpose to accomplish great things, hasten and come to me, that I may take counsel about them with you.' Histiaeus hastens and the king addresses him personally to the same effect, ending with the words: 'I bear witness to your friendly disposition towards me and the kingdom. Now, therefore, that you have done well to come in haste, here is my proposal. Leave Miletus and come up to me here in Susa, share all that I have, sit with me at my table and in my council.' How many monarchs in the six hundred years from Darius to Domitian may have appealed in such a fashion to the loyalty of the Greek cities of Asia Minor!

In the messianic messages of Revelation, too, the loyalty or disloyalty of the seven cities is the general theme. For particular themes we hear of persecutions in Ephesus, of Jewish calumnies in Smyrna, of the first martyrdom in

Pergamon, of the imperial temple and the throne of Satan, of sacrificial meals and erotic orgies. Finally the seven prizes are announced for the victors in the final battles: the 'public banquet', the crown of life, the white stone with the new name of the victor on it, citizenship in the kingdom, the white festival garments, an honourable place in the temple of God, and, greatest prize of all, the right to sit in the heavenly throne. 'He that overcometh, I will give to him to sit down with me in my throne, as I also overcame, and sat down with my Father in his throne.'

The apocalyptic games continue in the correct style with doxologies and antiphonies to the Lord and His Anointed. The heavenly throne-room is opened. The Ancient of days on the throne of God dazzles the eye with His glistening jewels. Over Him shimmer the seven-coloured bow, the triumphal arch of the heavenly ciborium. Before Him the seven eternal lamps are burning, reflected in the crystal floor. Round about Him the four and twenty elders are sitting on their thrones, arrayed in the white garments of senators, and on their heads crowns of gold, assembled for heavenly counsel and worship at the same time. The four living creatures round about the throne of God are singing the *trisagion* of eternal worship. The elders fall down before Him and cast their crowns before the throne, and sing, *Dignus es, Domine Deus noster*—'Worthy art thou, our Lord and our God' (4.11).

In the course of the year twenty-four priestly orders had to execute the priest's office in the temple at Jerusalem (I Chron. 24; Luke 1.8). On great feast-days all had to appear together in the sanctuary, led by their twenty-four elders. This must be remembered in Rev. 4. The elders of twenty-four priestly orders of heaven have assembled, a great festival liturgy is about to begin, a feast-day for all history.

'And I saw in the right hand of him that sat on the throne a book written within and on the back, close sealed with seven seals' (5.1). It is the letters of investiture, with the eschatological supreme authority. Such heavily sealed rolls have been found undamaged in the Egyptian desert. We know that a legal Roman will had to be sealed at least seven times, and

that Augustus as well as Vespasian left such wills for their
successors. A bronze statue of Hadrian shows the emperor
with his letters patent in his hand, while the eagle of Jupiter
sweeps down to him with the heavenly sceptre. The emperor,
triumphator or leader of the games, carrying a parchment roll,
is commonly to be found on Roman statues from the time of
Augustus.

In the year 390 Theodosius erected a victory obelisk in the
racecourse at Constantinople with the inscription, 'The whole
world is subject to Theodosius.' The reliefs on the socle show,
first, the emperor appearing in the imperial box, carrying the
wreath of victory in his right hand, to the acclamations of
the people, which were supported and given rhythmic liturgical form by instruments and singers. Secondly, the emperor
is shown enthroned in the imperial box, holding the roll, with
the conquered barbarians prostrate before him with their offerings, once more accompanied by the victory hymns of the
assembled masses. The other reliefs show the emperor motionless on his divine throne, the hand with the roll resting in
his lap, and below his throne the masters of the ceremonies
(*Silentarii*), who give the signal for the games with their
changing scenes to begin. The last relief shows the arena with
the white, red, blue and green horses starting the first race.
The representation is late, but the traditional forms of the
games which it depicts go back, as we know, to Flavian times.
The centre of these imperial games is the emperor with the
written roll in his hand.

The herald angel steps forward and calls, 'Who is worthy
to open the book, and to loose its seals?' No one is worthy,
no power in heaven or hell, and no emperor on earth. This
is the sentence of doom upon all political messianism. Shall
the secrets of creation then be unresolved, shall history remain
without goal or meaning—shall the fury of the dragon and
the cries of the martyrs, the self-glorification of the world and
blasphemy against God, never cease? The whole creation waits
fearfully, and the seer weeps.

In the midst of the throne-room stands the Lamb with the
wound, silent. He does not answer when the herald cries,

'Who is worthy?' He says nothing about the mortal wound, about which His demonic caricature in Rome spoke so much. He does not draw attention to Himself in loud-sounding self-assertions. He neither cries out nor calls, nor causes His voice to be heard in the streets. The Saviour has come. He has fulfilled His great work. But He waits in silence, till the excited world notices Him.

Then one of God's counsellors whispers to the weeping seer, 'Behold, the Lion that is of the tribe of Judah, the Root of David, hath overcome, hath overcome.' These are the words of destiny about the Strong One of God from the land of Judaea and the house of David, the offence for Josephus, the nightmare of Domitian. But for the seer and the waiting creation it is the joyful news of the victory of victories.

Now the quiet conqueror comes to the steps of the throne, and from the hand of the Ancient of days He takes the book with the apocalyptic authority, the divine cession of the triumphal rights, the divine investiture to the emperor of the empire of a thousand years. An immense excitement stirred the cosmos (5.8ff.). The heavenly assembly falls down before the Lamb with the mortal wound, and worships Him with incense and the music of harps, interrupting the eternal liturgy with a new song: 'Worthy art thou, Lord . . .' And the hosts of heaven join in: 'Worthy is the Lamb . . .' And every created thing sings with one voice the doxology, 'Glory and dominion for ever and ever.' And the four living creatures said, 'Amen.' So the worship of Christ triumphed over the comic worship of the false Christ with his tame parrots and elephants and senators.

The Victor opens the seals. The messianic games begin with the usual race in four colours. But it is not the usual race, it is the apocalyptic death-race, a frightful game in which the heavenly Imperator mocks the defiant and fearful heart of the Roman false Christ. All hopes and promises of the imperial rule are shattered, all the fears of the Roman world are realized. The Parthian races up with his bow and wreath of victory, and there is no one to withstand him. The anti-Caesar rides his red horse, swinging the sword of civil war, that mankind may bleed to death. Then there comes prancing one with a balance in his hand, so beloved by the imperial politician, but he brings not the cornucopiae but a reign of regulation and confiscation. Then Death himself rides upon a pale horse, and smites mankind with famine and plague.

When the cruel fights in the amphitheatre were over, the executioners appeared in the mask of the gods of Hades and removed the twitching bodies through the 'door of the goddess of death' into the cellar for the dead. Behind the last horseman of the Apocalypse, 'Hades' appears in person on the field of death and clears it.

The apocalyptic games go on. The most horrible omens and sayings of the sibyls are fulfilled. Nature is in rebellion, worse than in the terrible days of the year 79, when Herculaneum and Pompeii disappeared in mud and ashes. Where is the Arcadian peace of which the court poets had raved? All that is beastly in creation arises and falls upon men. The sun becomes black, the moon becomes as blood, the stars fall from heaven, the earth quakes. The mighty of the earth knew that the great day had come, that the apocalyptic judgment of the heavenly emperor had become the cosmic judgment day.

The first sequence is closed with a liturgical interlude. The procession of the hundred and forty-four thousand passes across, along with the countless multitude of the Saints of God, arrayed in white robes, on their brows the seal of deliverance, and victory palms in their hands. They are passing to the daily service in the sanctuary, and they greet God and the Lamb with the cry of salvation. It is not the cry of the condemned, but the cry of those who have been pardoned and brought to eternal life: *Salus Deo nostro et Agno*—'Salvation to our God and to the Lamb' (7.10).

When the Lamb opened the seventh seal, there followed a silence about the space of half an hour (8.1). It is the silence which was proper to the ceremonial of the triumphal games. A new sequence of scenes is being prepared in this silence. 'And I saw the seven angels which stand before God; and there given unto them seven trumpets. And another angel came and stood over the altar. . . .' Towards the end of the night the priest in the temple at Jerusalem went to the altar and with a silver shovel turned over the coals until they burned bright. Then he threw the shovel on the stone floor, and the sound of the rattling shovel echoed through the stillness of the night 'as far as Jericho', announcing the new day and the resumption of the temple liturgy after the night's pause. The Ephesian Silentiarius opened a new series of games by throwing down the *mappa*, or purple signal-cloth, or emptying a sacrificial bowl. In the museum at Smyrna there is a statue of an Ephesian dignitary with a *mappa*, which was found in Ephesus. And from late classical times we possess innumerable ivory tablets, which were issued by the imperial high priests or consuls on the occasion of their entry into office and the games associated with it. There one may see the giver of the games seated in the raised box, beneath the image of the emperor, raising the *mappa* in his right hand or emptying the bowl, while below in the arena the fight of the beasts or some other terrible scene begins. In the Book of Revelation, Chapter 8, however, something different happens, something terrible—an act combining and loading with eschatological significance both the temple worship of Jerusalem and the ritual of the games at Ephesus. The heavenly Silentiarius approaches the altar, from which the dying prayers of the martyrs ascend like incense, day and night. He stands over the altar with a golden censer, and he fills it with the fire of the altar, and casts it upon the earth, so that the earth shakes with thunder and voices and lightnings. The trickery of the false prophet with his miracles of fire and voices was transformed into uncanny reality.

This was the apocalyptic starting signal for the new sequence of scenes, which race by in a frightening *prestissimo*. The first trumpet sounds—and each fresh trumpet blast is the signal for a new catastrophe on earth. Hail and fire consume trees and grass. A burning mountain is cast into the sea, destroying sailors and creatures of the sea. A flaming star falls from heaven. The sun is darkened. The abyss is opened, and there goes up a smoke out of it, like the smoke of a great furnace. The demons of the storm are set free, and the air is filled with the rattling of weapons and the rush of chariots, with fire and smoke and sulphurous fumes. But men curse God and do not repent or cease from evil and murder. It is like the reports of the terror which came upon Herculaneum and Pompeii.

The sound of the sixth trumpet is over. The two martyr prophets bleed to death in the struggle with the beast of the abyss—and rise up to heaven before all eyes. When the seventh angel sounds, the heavenly hosts sing, 'The kingdom of the world is become the kingdom of our Lord, and of his Christ: and he shall reign for ever and ever' (11.15). And again the four and twenty elders fall down and worship. And as they give thanks, the curtain before the holiest of holies is opened, high above them, and the ark of the covenant is visible. Pliny and Suetonius speak with scorn of the cult attached to the divine throne of the emperor Domitian. This throne stood in the circus in a raised tabernacle, exalted above the common life and withdrawn from the vulgar gaze. In the provinces the empty throne symbolizes the emperor himself, a sign of his invisible presence at the holy games, and the centre of the circus liturgy. On a gold coin of Domitian the thunderbolts of Jupiter are shown above the empty throne—a simple but significant representation. Like the heavenly counterdemonstration to all this empty parade of glory, the ark of the covenant is seen above the clouds in Rev. 11, the ancient throne of the invisible God. The lightning motif is also present: 'and there followed lightnings and thunders'.

We pass now to Chapter 14. Below in the arena the worshippers of the false Christ are tormented in fire and brimstone. The smoke of their torment ascends to the heavenly seat, where the Son of Man appears in the midst of His holy angels, with the golden wreath of victory on His brow, and in His right hand, instead of the Olympic thunderbolt, the apocalyptic sickle (14.9ff.). Once again seven angels go forth from the heavenly temple, and pour out the seven bowls of the wrath of God upon the earth. One thinks of the imperial official in the emperor's box, pouring out the bowl over the arena. But God is inexorable, and His temple remains

187

inaccessible, until the seven plagues of the seven angels are finished (15.1, 8).

The old Thunderer had always been a great hater (see Luke 9.54). The writer of Revelation was not a mild old man, but a hater like the Psalmist who wrote, 'Do not I hate them, O Lord, that hate thee?' But he had also something of that divine scorn in his heart which is described in Ps. 2. He was a pitiless parodist, like the prophet in Isa. 14 who sang the song of scorn over the king of Babylon. He had something of the destructive irony of Christ. This breaks out in a remarkable way in the hate and scorn with which he treats self-glorified Rome.

A carnival procession sways past, the beauty parade of the great harlot sitting upon many waters, committing fornication with the kings of the earth, making the peoples of the earth drunk with the wine of her fornication, drunk with the blood of the saints (17.1ff.). She sits upon a scarlet-coloured beast, arrayed in purple and decked with gold and precious stone and pearls, having in her hand a golden cup full of abominations and unclean things, and upon her forehead the mysterious name, Babylon the Great, the Mother of the Harlots and of the Abominations of the Earth.

Who is Babylon the Great? One thinks involuntarily of Cleopatra, sitting upon many waters and committing fornication with the kings of the earth, of her description of herself as 'Queen of kings and kings' sons', of her mythological processions in Ephesus and elsewhere, of her portrait-bust on the late coins, as the ageing goddess of love, laden with jewels. One thinks of the intense hatred with which the Jews followed her career, dragging her memory in the dust into the time of Domitian and the writings of Josephus. Everything fits with the description in Rev. 17. So the picture of the whore of Babylon is probably a traditional piece of Jewish polemic, an apocalyptic picture of the hated Cleopatra, which has been scornfully transferred by John to Cleopatra's conqueror, the new Babylon of the West, the woman sitting on seven mountains (17.9).

It is hated Rome which is described—we need only recall

the Flavian coin depicting the goddess on the seven hills. It is the *civitas magna quae habet regnum super reges terrae*, the great city that rules over the kings of the earth. It leads the history of the world in its Christomachy, which is now in full course. It creates the united front of the false messiah for its struggle against Christ and His saints.

But this is a false unity, sunk in lies like the whole world of the false messiah. For the kings of the earth hate the great harlot, who makes kings her servants, and they wait for the day of her destruction (17.12ff.).

When after the destruction of Jerusalem Rabbi Akiba journeyed as an ambassador to the imperial court, and from afar off heard the tumult of the great city and saw the sea of lights, he became an apocalyptist, and prophesied the destruction of *Roma aeterna* and the future glory of the city of God. So the Haggada relates. In the time of Akiba, according to the tradition of the early Church, the apostle John was taken to Rome, and the scenes he saw then were reproduced in an apocalyptic *Inferno*. The herald angel cries, 'Fallen, fallen is Babylon.' With the fall of the great city the whole order of the old world breaks up. Kings and merchants and mariners stand afar off, crying, Woe, woe. Artists leave the places of desolation, the voice of harpers and minstrels and flute-players and trumpeters are silent. The city becomes the dwelling-place of demons and jackals, of owls and bats. For the blood of the saints was found in it (18.24).

But the smoke of the ruined city rises up to heaven like incense. And the four-and-twenty elders fell down again and worshipped. And a sound went through heaven like the voice of a great multitude, like the voice of many waters, like the voice of mighty thunders, saying, Hallelujah: for the Lord our God, the Almighty, reigneth (19.6). For the marriage of the Lamb is come, and his wife has made herself ready—the wife who knows only *one* man. The scarlet whore had played her part, her luxurious banquets have been swept away. The heavenly bride in white linen awaits the holy marriage, the guests await the Messianic marriage-feast, the eschatological *Coena dominica*.

Then heaven opens, and the King of kings and Lord of lords rides forth on a white victory horse. His eyes are a flame of fire, upon His head are many diadems, about His shoulders hangs the toga, red with blood, and the armies of His saints rode after Him (19.11ff.). Did John have in mind the popular coin showing the victorious emperor riding past? Or did he see in Rome the great statue of the *Equus maximus*, to which he was now opposing this picture of the *Dominus dominantium*?

The Christ was riding to His final victory—to the last struggle with the false Christ who had declared war on Him. He conquered him and threw him into the lake of fire along with the false prophet. The time of signs is over. When the master has been brought down, then his sorcerer falls too. Once more it is made clear that the secret of the worship was terror (19.20).

'And I saw an angel coming down out of heaven, having the key of the abyss' (20.1). He had received it from the Son of Man, to lock up Satan in the abyss. The idea with which the court poet in Rome had played has become a reality. The demon of the world groans in the pit—not just for a generation, but for a millennium. Then he breaks out again, and once more stamps out an army from the earth, the last great army of the East, before whom the nations tremble from one generation to the next. But it is only like the last ghost of the night before the dawn. The *Civitas Dei* is triumphant over West and East, it has conquered the Babylon of the West, and now it conquers Gog and Magog in the East. Satan disappears in fire and brimstone, and his hangmen, death and Hades, follow him (20.10, 14).

The Messianic triumphal games have ended. The historical task of the Son of Man is accomplished. Now the last prophecy of prophets and sibyls is fulfilled, which political messianism can only promise but never achieve. He who sits upon the throne says, Behold, I make all things new. The city of God comes down to earth, the new capital of a new world, and through its twelve gates there streams in the new people, from the four corners of the earth. In their midst is the double

throne of God and the Lamb. And they see His Face, and
carry His name on their foreheads and serve Him for ever.
And they need neither sun nor moon. For the glory of the
Lord shines upon them, and their light is the Lamb. And the
nations shall walk in their light. The kings of the earth shall
bring their glories into the holy city. The new kingdom will
be made perfect in a new creation. The river of paradise will
flow, and the tree of life will flourish on its banks and yield
many kinds of fruits. And God will wipe away all tears; and
death shall be no more; neither shall there be mourning, nor
crying, nor pain, any more (21.1ff.). These closing scenes pass
before us like ecstatic visions.

Here too every word is a rejection of the imperial myth.
The Book of Revelation is a polemical book to the very end.

'The morning-star shines bright, but brighter shines the
Caesar', sings Statius of his emperor. And many before and
after him have written in similar strains. But the Son of Man
ends His self-revelation in Rev. 22.16 with the words, 'I am
the bright, the morning star.'

> Morning star, bring on the day.
> Come soon, and let us not be fearful.
> Rome begs that Caesar
> May soon appear.

So prays Martial in the name of the *Civitas Roma* for the
return of Domitian from the north. In the Book of Revelation the bride, the holy city, says, 'Come!' And he who hears,
let him also say, Come. And the heavenly emperor answers,
Yes, I come quickly. The apocalyptist sets his seal to the
words with 'Amen: come, Lord Jesus.'

The Book of Revelation began with an imperial acclamation: *Ipsi gloria et imperium*: To him be the glory and the
dominion. It ends with an imperial advent cry: *Veni, Domine*:
Come, Lord Jesus.

XII

PAUL AND AKIBA

A GENERATION ago there appeared two Jewish books
which set the Jewish question in the light of Jewish history.
They are Franz Werfel's *Paul among the Jews*, and the play by
Moritz Heimann, *The Woman of Akiba*. They are neither
psychological studies nor biographies. But they are books
about the destiny of the Jewish people, about the great question of Jewish history, the question of the Messiah. The
writers turn unerringly to the two great apostles of the
Messiah and guides for Judaism, to Paul and Akiba. In fact,
the historical achievement of these two men has determined
the destiny of the Jewish people. Hence every consideration
of the future of the Jews must go back to that destiny-laden
time, when the question about the historical course of the
Jewish people was being asked with elemental power. The
question had two answers, which till this day have not been
surpassed, the answer of salvation and the answer of tragedy.
Let us look at these two men again, and hear their answers.

I

What kind of man was Paul, that he had such far-reaching
significance for the Jewish question? He was a patriot, sprung
from one of those old families of the Hebrews who proudly
preserved the name and the inheritance of the race to which
they belonged. He was of the tribe of Benjamin, and bore the
name of the great king from his tribe, Saul. But he was no
warrior hero. He was a believer who clung with unshakable
loyalty to the old God, and was zealous for His law. Towards
the end of his life he was still able to confess, 'I was blameless

before the law' (Phil. 36). For him, his nation and his faith
were not two separate things, but closely interwoven. Paul
was a religious patriot, one of the greatest in history. This
determined the course of his life from Tarsus to Damascus.

Paul grew up in a home where the old faith was practised,
where the honourable customs, the holy times and prayers,
day by day and week by week, were observed with reverence
and loyalty. He was a stranger in Greek Tarsus, and to the
end of his life he remained a stranger in that world of street
philosophers and comedians, of dancers and boxers. He was
at home in the synagogue of the orthodox community, which
was like an island in a sea of foreign culture. There with his
fellow-believers he celebrated the Sabbath, and the great festivals which quickened the memory of God's mighty deeds
among His people, every festival a memorial of the loyalty
between God and His people. There from his childhood he
heard the holy words of the Torah, which God had given
His people: the commandments which shut off the people in
dispersion like a fence, and made them a united whole; the
promises which gave them strength and seriousness in times
of need and temptation; the songs of praise which filled the
heart of the despised people with gladness when they remembered the glory of their God.

Paul's parents must have been deeply concerned about the
religion of their fathers. For they took their son, who could
scarcely have been more than a child, to Jerusalem to attend
the Torah school.

A new world was opened to the young Paul: Jerusalem,
the city of David, the city of hope. The temple, the place of
God among men, the goal of desire for every Jew. The school
of Gamaliel the elder, the intellectual centre of the Jewish
world. The students in that school experienced the first great
upsurge of a new learning. It was the time of the great scribes,
on whose spiritual and intellectual inheritance Judaism still
lives. Hillel had just established Jewish understanding of the
Scriptures on a solid foundation, and his son-in-law, Rabbi
Gamaliel the first, was continuing the work he had begun.
They were men who worked conscientiously, and with all the

force of their intellect, to create on the basis of Scripture and tradition a firm order for life. What the Jew did and did not do was to be regulated down to the smallest detail. Every step, every stirring of the will, was to be placed under the will of God. No doubt many petty regulations and hair-splitting questions were discussed in the school. Nevertheless, the education which Paul received at the feet of Gamaliel meant a disciplined training of his intellect and his will. It was a unique school of obedience and of reverence for the will of God as revealed in Scripture. Nor was it a self-sufficient or tired pedantry which was practised there. Gamaliel's own son was famous for his motto: 'Not study but action is the chief thing.' Above all, Paul himself was a fiery man of action. He entered the order of the Pharisees, the order of those who were determined to deal with God's statutes seriously, without any reservation or deduction. They regarded themselves as picked troops of God's people, who were preparing the way for the kingdom of God. If only *one* Sabbath were kept without failure or blame, then the Messiah would come. That was the passionate desire and fervent hope, the patriotic belief, which filled the young Paul. Soon enough he was to find a field of action.

The great national party of the scribes and Pharisees had a modest yet dangerous enemy, the young Christian community. Jesus, the young Galilean, not a scribe, had come forward with an arbitrary exposition of the Writings and the Law and had dared to attack the sacred authority of the great teachers. He had promised the Kingdom to tax-gatherers and sinners, and thereby undermined the Pharisees' work of educating the people. He had imperilled the purity of the people of God, and He had called in question the Messianic hope. As if that were not enough, He had declared that He Himself was the Messiah, without stirring a finger on behalf of the cause of national liberation, and thus He had brought into doubt the belief in the national future of His people. Now He was dead, but His community was not yet dead. It was already reaching out to the rest of the world, and there was a danger that the Law and the prophets and the whole unique inheritance of the people of God would be handed over to the hated heathen, and that the impure would throng into the holy circle of the chosen people. What did these doubtful efforts mean but high treason to the Jewish people and their national future? They must be suppressed by every possible means. The national movement was fortunate to be able to put forward to the Jewish central authorities a man who was created for the post of a grand inquisitor—Paul. He was clever enough and educated enough to succeed in any position and in any circumstances. He was theologically immensely superior to the little Christian apostles of the Messiah, and their Bible students. He was fanatically nationalist, he knew how serious the situation was, and he would give the heretics short shrift. We know of the zeal with which Paul devoted himself to the extirpation of the Christian community.

We know too how Paul, on an official mission to Damascus, finally met Him who was mightier than he, who stepped in his way in order to take him into a new service. Paul learned that Jesus was not a teacher whose teaching can be despised, or a leader whose movement could be suppressed, but the Messiah of God who proclaimed God's will with authority, who had been set by God over all things, all destinies and plans of this world. He called. Paul followed.

It is surprising how immediately from the day of his call Paul's life followed one great line. The Law was set aside, and Christ alone was the measure and goal and content of his life, the living Christ, whose command sent him from city to city, from country to country, from one part of the earth to another: Ephesus, Corinth, Rome, Spain. In great leaps history pressed forward to its goal. He must reach the end of the world before the world's time ran out. In his speeches and letters his thoughts tumbled over one another like a river in spate, thoughts whose fullness and depth surpassed his hearers' capacity. It is even related how a hearer once fell exhausted from the window-seat while Paul spoke on. During the night he worked to keep himself, during the day he worked for his Lord, he fought with sickness and with obstacles of every kind, he was persecuted, arrested, three times he suffered shipwreck—he was invincible. Behind him, dark and threatening, lay his memory of the time when he had persecuted the Christian community, while before him lay the glory and the freedom, the work to which he had been called of grace— the new people of God that knew no other law or bond than Christ alone.

Not only Paul's work but also his thought is characterized by this great line. Everything petty and narrow and pedantic fell away from him, a new desire and thought took their place, a creative shaping of a picture of God and the world and history. He got to know the God who causes all things to work together for good to them that love Him. He felt himself caught up into paradise, and he saw the secrets of the other world. He surveyed the course of history: the promising beginnings of creation, the period of the Law and its end in Christ, the new people of God which embraced all generations and all nations, the epoch of the Cross and the coming age of glory.

It cannot be disputed that the Jew Paul, in becoming a Christian, grew out of narrowness into openness. Did he therefore pass from loyalty to disloyalty? No; for Paul remained a Jew for the Jews. He recognized Jerusalem as the base and centre for the world Church. In other cities he always began his work in the synagogue. His gospel was for the Jews first, and then for the Greeks. Paul never abandoned his belief in the unique mission of his people. Rather, this belief too grew, under the sign of the Cross, out of narrowness into openness. The apostle of the Gentiles could not deceive himself into imagining that Palestine was the place for the development of a powerful national life. The imperialist hope of a Jewish messianic kingdom was utopian. A new picture of the future emerged in his mind from the collapse of the old hope. Israel was called to be the ancestral people for the new people of God, which was to gather round the Messiah throughout the world. But here too Paul's thought did not come to a stop. With keen and deep insight he recognized that this world itself is not the place for the unfolding of the dominion and the glory of God. The Cross outside the gates of Jerusalem was the symbol of a world whose form was dissolving; it pointed to a new age without sin or suffering or death. The apostle Paul was the ambassador of the kingdom of Christ, which is not of this world. He waited for his people to accept and sustain the coming world of God. Israel, the apostolic nation among the other nations—that was the new way on which the passionate patriot and theological realist wanted to lead his people.

It was his own way, the way from narrowness to openness, transposed and magnified. Certainly, it was a way which led across a terrible break: Israel was expected to sacrifice its national hopes to its future task for the kingdom of God. Nevertheless, and in virtue of this sacrifice, it was a way of deliverance. A new future appeared, in which the hopeless tragedy of its national struggle for existence was overcome, and a world task was laid upon it, in which its assurance of election and its hopes were realistically grasped, and imperceptibly but gloriously fulfilled.

Israel refused to take this course. The Jewish people could not abandon the dream of being a nation like other nations. First Jesus, and then Paul, discovered this. 'Ye did not wish it.' From that time the people of Israel has borne a secret wound, which lets them neither live nor die—a wound like King Amfortas', the guardian of the Holy Grail, which could not be healed by any human means.

Paul saw this, and offered his own eternal destiny in exchange for the salvation of his beloved people. 'For I could wish that I myself were anathema from Christ for my brethren's sake, my kinsmen according to the flesh: who are Israelites.' He wrestled faithfully with this problem, and won afresh the certainty that God was faithful to His people, in spite of everything; he was able to glimpse the mysterious ways of God. Israel remained the ancestral tribe of the new people of God, and Israel's very rejection of the Gospel forced the Gospel out among the nations. And if Paul was tempted for a moment (Rom. 9.6ff.) to dispute his people's assurance of election, he ended by being all the more certain: for God is faithful, and His promises are true, and His mercy is mightier than Israel's resistance. The hour of deliverance for the whole house of Israel will come. 'For if the casting away of them is the reconciling of the world, what shall the receiving of them be, but life from the dead?'

Paul wrote these words just before his last journey to Jerusalem, and in view of his world-wide missionary plans. It was given to him to seal his faithfulness at home, and on this way of faithfulness to conquer the far places of the world. He went to Jerusalem and was received by his fellow-countrymen as a heretic and enemy of the people. Then he turned to his last recourse. He took over a work of sanctification in the temple, following an ancient custom such as only the strictest and most pious members of the Jewish community took upon themselves. But the mob were incited to raise a great clamour at the intruder and his pollution of the temple, he was arrested by the Roman police, and was two years in prison in Caesarea. He was taken as a prisoner to Rome, and there, despite his fetters, he continued his work for the gospel. According to one tradition, he even succeeded in carrying out his mission to Spain. Then his life of passion and sacrifice and fulfilment reached its end. His death was like his life. He died by the sword, outside the walls of Rome, far from his beloved country, but faithful and near to his Master.

II

What became of the people which had delivered its most faithful member to the sword of the heathen?

In Palestine the movement for independence continued to grow, extreme groups won supremacy, and in the same year as Paul died a martyr's death in Rome there broke out in Judaea a furious rebellion against the alien Roman rule. It ended in the destruction of the Holy City and reprisals of unparalleled savagery. Israel's strength was broken, its hope destroyed. It was then that the Christian community recorded the strange words which Jesus had spoken before His death, concerning the brief period of decision for Israel and the threatened end. Now the decision had been made and sealed in the most frightful way. The seers of Israel appeared before God to lament the cruel fate of the city of God. 'Our holy place is laid waste, our heroes are weak, our harp has been cast into the dust.' Then, too, Akiba ben Joseph appeared in Palestine, the man who was to make the last real effort to avert the tragic fate of his people. We shall briefly sketch the picture of this man which has been handed down in the Jewish literary tradition.

He was a man without a background, a 'wild man of the fields'. He was one of the worthless people of the land so hated by the Pharisees for their ignorance of the Law and their indifference to the teachings of the rabbis. Akiba was a man of natural powers who abhorred book-learning and the petty cliques and busyness of the students of the Law. 'Give me a scholar, that I may bite him like an ass,' he said once. Later these words troubled him deeply, and he did not weary of thanking God for His mercy in leading him to His Law.

For Akiba became a scholar himself, in the prime of his life. We have no clear account of how this came about. But so much seems certain, that the decisive impulse came from his marriage. His wife was the daughter of an ancient Jewish family who broke with her people for his sake, abandoning everything in order to share his poor and despised life. It seems that he learned from her what the Law could mean for a people which had lost everything. So he became convinced that the Law was not a matter merely of learning, but of national significance, the palladium of Jewish unity and power and hope. With glowing heart he entered upon his calling as a student of the Law for his people's sake.

He determined to enter the house of a great rabbi in which the same tradition of learning was practised as that in which Paul had grown up one or two generations before him. His wife willingly remained behind, even sacrificing for his studies her last possession, her costly hair. He promised her a golden head-dress when he had reached his high goal. Twelve years later he returned, followed by twelve thousand students. The people of the district streamed in to pay homage to the unknown teacher. A woman in shabby clothes tried to approach him, but his pupils indignantly repulsed her. Then Akiba turned and said, 'All that we know and have we owe to her.' It was his wife. But once again he set off, his zeal for the Law giving him no rest. When he returned after another twelve years with a host of twenty-four thousand pupils, she was an old woman. But she had been unswervingly loyal for the sake of his people and his mission. The time had come for him to fulfil the promise of his poverty. He gave her a golden diadem adorned with the pinnacles of the Holy City which now lay in ignominious ruin. So runs the legend, a profound expression of the passionate mourning which filled and joined the hearts of these two people.

The man who had won his way to the Law through such sacrifices became the greatest teacher of the Law among the Jews. He was great as a guardian and collector of the sacred traditions. He was greater as a systematizer, arranging the mass of traditional material, and strictly sifting its authority in Scripture. He was a thinker who said nothing that was not soundly based. But he was greatest of all as a teacher, who not only taught as long as the pupil could understand, but also was himself the living embodiment of the spirit of the Law. He extolled the law of love to one's neighbour as the chief element in the Torah, and he himself was accustomed to read the *shema'* with special fervour: 'Hear, O Israel: the Lord our God is one Lord: And thou shalt love the Lord thy God with all thine heart, and with all thy soul, and with all thy might.' But he was tormented by the thought whether he would have the strength to love God in deed and truth to his last breath.

We feel that with Akiba we have to do with more than one learned in the Law. He was in truth a creative theologian, who, like Paul, faced reality, and followed the ways of God in the destiny of men and nations.

The most precious theological inheritance which he had from his own teacher was the saying, 'Everything is for good'. He developed this into an all-embracing recognition of the work of God in history. All things and all happenings in this world must serve the will of God and the salvation of His

elect—even the sufferings and misfortunes, even the evil,
everything in the end is turned by God to good. Nor can the
freedom which God has given to man destroy God's plan
and providence; God's goodness has the last word in the
judgment. The audacity of Akiba's theology often frightened
his contemporaries. He dared as no other teacher had done
to speak of certainty of salvation. In prayer, he taught, man
is certain of the divine favour. He dared, too, to press into
the mysteries of the other world. Rabbi Akiba is the only
man, according to an old saying, who has gazed upon paradise
without suffering in body or soul.

His thoughts continually circled round the fate of Israel.
He gave all his strength to encouraging his people's spirits
and faithfulness and hope in their time of affliction. When
Israel took with them the treasures of Egypt, their condition
was evil, and all the prophets cried woe. But the poverty of
the daughter Israel was as lovely as a red bridle on the head
of a white horse. Akiba had deep understanding of the pessi-
mism of the preacher Solomon, he loved Job and once made
the noble utterance, in the spirit of the Book of Job: 'The
heathen curse their gods in times of affliction. But we praise
our God in good fortune and bad, and cry, Praised be the
Judge of truth.'

Akiba loved above all The Song of Songs, honouring it as
a hymn to the defiant and faithful love between God and His
afflicted people. It was Israel's office to proclaim the honour
of God among the nations. For the heathen said, 'How is
your Friend to be exalted above other friends, that you so
swear by Him? What is there to him, that you let yourself
be slain for Him? You are fine and brave people; come and
mingle with us!' But Israel replied: 'Do you not know Him?
We will tell you of some of His glory. Our Friend is bright
and glittering, and surpasses ten thousand. His lips are like
roses, and His whole Being is delight.' Then the nations said:
'Where is your Friend gone? We will seek Him with you.'
But Israel replied: 'You have no share in Him. We belong to
our Friend, and our Friend to us.'

A terrible time of testing had come upon Israel. No festival was as serious or as holy as the day of the destruction of Jerusalem. But blessed is the people which even now bears the punishment for its sins. It will emerge unscathed from the great judgment day. For God punishes the guilt of His people daily. But the guilt of the godless He will settle in one stroke at the end of this age. Therefore blessed is the people which the Lord visits with His severity. He will deliver it for His name's sake. For God delivers Himself when He delivers Israel.

We can understand that this rabbi, who could speak in this way to the hearts of his people, was a man of the people and a rare leader. The masses loved him, and even the bandits let his pupils pass in peace, for he was a man of the people who neither forgot nor concealed his humble origin. He had a warm heart for the rights of the poor, and an open hand for their need. No service was too lowly for him. But when he sat in the judgment-seat the contestants bowed reverently before his words, 'You are not standing before Akiba ben Joseph, but before Him whose voice called the world into being.' Politicians sought his friendship, for he was a far-travelled man, who knew the languages and customs of the nations and how to deal with them. We read of how he once suffered shipwreck, of many religious conversations with educated pagans, and of a delegation to the imperial court in Rome. There is a touching description of how the mission saw the heathen city in its wanton splendour, and broke out in laments at the thought of the ruins of the holy city on Mount Zion. But Akiba joyfully encouraged them with the words, 'If God gives the heathen so much glory, how much more glorious will be the glory of Jerusalem in the day of its exaltation.' The verses of the Passover prayer are Akiba's work:

> So may the Eternal, our God
>   and our fathers' God,
> Let us attain to the festival days and seasons
>   which lie before us,
> In joy at the building again of the city,
>   in delight at the temple service,
> That we enjoy alike
>   from the Passover sacrifice and the sacrificial gifts.

His confident faith was destined to endure a frightful trial.

Unrest continued to ferment in the people, until finally, in the year 132, a century after Paul's call on the Damascus road, a new rebellion broke out. An enthusiastic national hero led the people. Akiba was exultant: 'There shall come forth a star out of Jacob, and a sceptre shall rise out of Israel' (Num. 24.17). Bar Kochba was this son of the stars, the Messiah. It was like a rushing spring storm around the messianic liberator and his venerable apostle. The troops of Bar Kochba conquered Jerusalem. The war lasted three and a half years. The rebels were finally shut up in a mountain fortress, and the Messiah fell. Then the Jewish people collapsed like a man mortally sick after a last feverish flicker. The end had come.

In these years the figure of the old Rabbi Akiba grew to tragic and almost superhuman proportions. His people had lost their home. He made them a new home in the Law. The Romans saw the new danger and forbade the teaching of the Law under penalty of death. Akiba taught on. The Romans cast him into prison in Caesarea, in all likelihood the same prison in which Paul had lain for two years. Secretly, Akiba issued prophecies and rallying-cries. A friend warned him and besought him to preserve his life. Akiba replied, 'Can a Jew leave the Law? Can a fish live without water?' The hangmen brought him to the judgment-place. Akiba counted himself blessed to be allowed to love God with his whole soul. It was the hour for the reading of the *shema*'. While the iron combs were rending his body, Akiba spoke the words of the call to prayer: 'Hear, O Israel, the Lord thy God is one . . .', and died.

There is a legend that when Moses ascended the heights of Sinai he gazed in spirit through the centuries and saw Rabbi Akiba sitting in the house of learning, expounding the Torah to his pupils. Moses himself sat humbly amongst them in the eighth row. And when he enquired about the end of this chosen teacher, he saw another image—Akiba in the midst of the iron combs.

Can we look down on this people and its destiny as the figure of the Church on Strasbourg Cathedral looks down on the Synagogue with its broken staff? Paul warns us against such wicked pride. We cannot cease to bring this people the gospel, not in arrogant importunity but in the assurance that it is the power of God to salvation, for the Jew first, and then for the Greek. Paul did not cease to do it. And still Akiba stands above the centuries, looking out, motionless and questioning, beyond us into the future. Can we abandon the belief that the day will come when Israel will find the way of deliverance which leads it beyond the hopeless tragedy of these centuries? Paul believed in that day, and worked for its coming.

May none of us have to remain behind when Paul steps up to his brother Akiba, in the name of Jesus Christ the Crucified, and calls out to the hosts of the Jews who surround their teacher: 'Lift up your heads, for the hour of salvation has come.'

XIII

LIES AND TRUTH

ONE of the most remarkable facts of history is the victory
of Christianity over the combined religious, cultural and political powers of the Roman Empire. Why did the early Christian
faith triumph in this struggle of spirits and powers?

The unreflecting answer of the Christian to this question
is that Christianity triumphed because the witness of the New
Testament was the witness of truth in the midst of a world
full of confusion and semblances and self-deceit. That is an
expression of faith about which there can be no discussion.
Church historians have tried to find a scientific reason. Thus
a generation ago Karl Holl, the Berlin expert in Luther studies,
delivered a famous speech in which he defended the thesis
that Christianity conquered the religions of the Roman Empire
by its message of a merciful God condescending to the sinner
—the same message, that is to say, as triumphed at the Reformation over the spiritual powers of the Middle Ages. But Holl
neglected the fact that in the days of the first struggle of the
Church scarcely anyone understood the gospel of the merciful
God. This message was first understood by Augustine and
later pre-eminently by Luther. On this fact Holl's theory
comes to grief. For an idea which was not understood can
scarcely conquer a whole civilization. Later Erich Seeberg,
Holl's successor in Berlin, attempted a different answer to the
question. In his *History of Christianity* he writes: 'The message
of Christ triumphed because the gospel was the message of
the Incarnation of God, the proclamation of the God-Man in
whom the world of heaven and the world of earth, time and
eternity, myth and history, meet one another.' This was the
great new idea with which Christianity conquered the ancient

world and defeated its religions in open battle. But Seeberg himself knew that the idea of the God-Man was not the exclusive property of Christianity. Rather, it was to be found in many forms in the religions of the ancient world, and at the very time that Christian faith was rising to prominence this idea enjoyed its most powerful and brilliant expression in the emperor cult. Why then did the Christian faith triumph over faith in the emperor? That is the question which must be answered, but to which Seeberg gave no satisfactory reply.

We must therefore first look at the pagan religious world of the Principate, then at the world of Christianity, and finally at the conflict between the two worlds, if we are to find the proper answer to our question. We have already mentioned the answer of faith, that Christianity was the witness of truth in the midst of a lying world, and for that reason triumphed over the old pagan religions. Perhaps this affirmation of faith will receive surprising historical corroboration from our scientific investigation. Perhaps the struggle of historical revelation as a struggle between truth and lies, which is visible only to faith, may come to light as an intellectual and historical phenomenon patient of scientific investigation.

I

In late classical times belief in the old gods had ceased to have any power. I shall illustrate this by two examples.

In the second century B.C. a ruler in the Greek East found himself without any money to pay his troops. To relieve his necessity he requisitioned the property of the neighbouring temple of Zeus, plundering its treasury of the solid gold image of Victoria, which he melted down into gold coins. He wittily added that Zeus gave him Victoria, and perpetuated his pun on the coins themselves with the image of Zeus holding out the figure of Victoria. In the Principate, it is true, the old belief in the gods was encouraged by Augustus and his successors on political grounds. But the philosophers shrugged their shoulders at the superstition of the people, who worshipped the grave of Zeus in Crete, or recounted tales of heroes playing dice with the gods in the underworld, and bringing back a golden towel as a souvenir. And when the Christians were offended by such stories of the gods the philosopher Celsus smilingly explained that nobody really believed these things any more, and for that very reason people should not be asked to believe their stories about Christ. . . . It was the end of the old religion of the gods, which ceased to be taken seriously.

Other religions took its place, above all the so-called mystery religions, secret initiations which were supposed to mediate to man the knowledge of higher worlds, sinlessness, and eternal life. The history of religion of the past generation has made a great deal, doubtless too much, of these mystery religions. For they did not give man real support. Here too I give two illustrations. A satire of the second century A.D. tells the story of a dissipated youth who was metamorphosed into an ass, and after many adventures invoked the goddess Isis, a favourite figure of the mysteries. On her command, at the next Isis procession, he ate up the holy wreath of roses, regained his human form, and had himself initiated into all the secrets of the Isis mysteries. One does not write in this fashion of a religion from which one expects salvation. From other sources we know that even believers in the mysteries were not always very sure of their salvation. Many were initiated into several of these religions, like a mistrustful capitalist who spreads his investments over as many ventures as possible, hoping in this way to rescue at least something in the next financial crisis. This was the secret sickness of the mystery religions. Their adherents believed, and yet they did not believe.

That early Christianity should triumph over religions of this type goes without saying. But there was one religion in the Roman world with which Christianity had to fight a mortal battle, and that was emperor worship. In this there was concentrated once more the ancient longing that lived on in all nations and religions of the East, the longing for the appearance of God on earth. In worship of the emperor this longing was united with the ancient Roman idea of the divine revelation in history and politics. In this worship the fulfilment of the Eastern longing and the realization of the Roman idea were proclaimed. This proclamation was accompanied by the clatter of the legions' weapons and by the hymns of the court poets. It was celebrated in the Senate and in the circus, it was repeated in ever new forms, and was hammered into the mind of the meanest subject by the imperial coins, which dominated not only the international market but also international propaganda.

What did emperor worship really mean? In 44 B.C. Caesar was assassinated in the Roman Senate House. Not long afterwards the same Senate issued an official decree declaring the deification of Caesar. His adoptive son and successor Octavian received the name of *Divi Filius*, in Greek Huios Theou, in English 'Son of God'. In 27 B.C. Octavian received the honorary title of Augustus, in Greek Sebastos, 'worthy of honour'. These two names, Son of God and Augustus, belonged thenceforth to the regular stock of imperial titles. For example, they are to be found together on the tribute money which Jesus handled in the last years of His life. New names and formulas were added later. The emperor was addressed as 'Lord our God', on one coin he was called 'God and Lord from birth', he was celebrated as the Bringer of Salvation, he who was to come, the divine King of Salvation for whom all ages had waited. Hercules and other supermen of prehistoric times were reincarnate in him. The emperor was even the human manifestation of Zeus, king of heaven, or Helios the sun-god.

If the emperor was a god, then his whole life must be like the earthly course of a heavenly being. His birth was surrounded by wonders and mysteries. The intimation of his birth was described, in the official language of the court, as a 'joyous message', in Greek *euangelion*, in Latin *evangelium*. His assumption of power signified the beginning of a golden age. His entry into the capital city, even his arrival in provincial cities, was described in official language as the imperial advent. Much could be told of the extravagant cries of jubilation, the prayers, the sacrifices and divine honours with which the emperor was received on such ceremonial entries. Happy the land that is trodden on by the imperial saviour! The sick are made well, the trees flourish, the fountains flow, the rivers water the thirsty land as never before. Heaven gives the quickening rain again which had been withheld for seven years. The climax of this wonder-working course was the ascension to heaven of the imperial son of god. Out of the flames of the pyre which consumed the mortal remains of the deified emperor there arose an eagle which carried the soul of the imperial god and lord to heaven in the sight of all people. On the coins which were struck in those days even the most remote peoples of the empire could see with their own eyes the bodily ascension of the emperor, carried by the divine bird, to his heavenly throne.

The outward expression of the emperor's divinity was his dress on official occasions or on the official coins. He carried the sceptre of the king of heaven, he wore the radiate crown of the sun-god, and he sat on the divine throne. His throne room was a temple, and when he appeared from behind the curtain the congregation welcomed the sight of 'the most holy emperor' as a manifestation from another world. When he raised his voice to speak, he was heard as though it were a voice from heaven. The business agenda of the Senate became a divine service. A regular parliamentary liturgy grew up. Every utterance of the emperor was received with devout jubilation, every speech was interrupted by rhythmic acclamations, and it appears that in late Roman times the number and distribution of these spontaneous outbreaks of enthusiasm were set down in the agenda of the liturgy. That is how laws were made in Rome at that time. And when an imperial decree was proclaimed in the provinces there was an official preamble, 'The divine word of destiny of our august lord has determined . . .', or 'The heavenly prescriptions of the august law demand . . .', or 'The divine mercy of the most holy emperor commands . . .'. The imperial governors spoke of the 'divine commandments' of the 'eternally august majesty'. And in one report of a trial there come the words: 'The most merciful rulers have commanded either that people offer sacrifice or be given to the torture.'

The culmination of this whole tendency was in the divine

honours paid to the emperor. Oaths were taken on the divine spirit of the emperor. His image was publicly adored. In all the large cities of the empire imperial temples were erected with statues of the emperor, with altars for sacrifices and incense. In the barracks and camps the image of the emperor occupied the centre of the sanctuary of the standards, and was surrounded by the emblems of the empire. Worship of this image was a regular military duty.

The Roman authorities were fundamentally tolerant in religious matters. Every people of the empire could have its own beliefs, and every individual could strive for salvation in his own way. No religious community was suppressed so long as it fell in with public order. Only the worship of the emperor was obligatory on all, for it was grounded on imperial law, and the Roman authorities permitted no laxity in matters of law. The worship of the emperor was therefore not fundamentally a matter of belief, but one of public order and discipline, a duty for civilians and soldiers alike, an obligation of honour which every loyal subject strove eagerly to fulfil. It was clear that anyone who refused to fulfil this obligation had no place at the imperial court. He could not be an official. He had no prospect of promotion in the army. He received no commissions from the State, and came under an economic boycott. It was likewise clear that anyone who was pre-eminent in the fulfilment of this obligation had the very best prospects in trade, in the army, in the civil service, and above all at the court. Thus it came about that without pressure from the emperor or compulsion from the authorities, worship of the emperor spread spontaneously, penetrating and dominating the whole of public life, and became what the great Augustus in the time of Jesus had desired—the spiritual bond which united and held together the innumerable people and religions of the empire. One empire and one faith throughout the world! That was the splendid picture of the *imperium Romanum* which was historically realized in the third century of our era—and prophetically foreseen in the thirteenth chapter of the Book of Revelation.

Before attempting to describe the other picture, of the

Christian world, we must note one further detail, without which the picture of Roman beliefs would be incomplete. The emperor himself did not believe in any of this emperor religion. When Augustus listened to the pious outpourings of the Eastern court poets, he burst out laughing. Vespasian on his death-bed mocked at himself and the whole imperial myth of ascension, in the grim words, 'Ah, I believe I am becoming a god.' It is true there were also emperors who seriously believed they were divine, men like Caligula, Nero, Domitian, Commodus. But it was they who after their death were declared not divine but mad. So long as they lived and had power, they were overwhelmed with divine honours. But there was no sincerity in this adulation. For perhaps the rumour had just arisen that the mad emperor had killed his young pregnant wife by a kick. The result was that the court too did not believe in the imperial mythology. As for the army, the legions had no illusions. It was they who in times of crisis made and unmade emperors—that is, made and un-made gods. In the year 270 the legions summoned General Aurelian to be emperor. He was fifty-seven, and had seen the rise and fall of about thirty emperors. Nevertheless, he had the above-mentioned coin struck in 275, which celebrated him as god and lord from his birth. What may his officers and troops have thought, when they received this coin among their pay? We know very well what they thought, for that same year they assassinated him. As for the people, we have already mentioned the divine eagle which carried the soul of the emperor from the funeral pyre to his heavenly throne. Everyone in Rome knew that the eagle had been captured in the mountains and was bound to the pyre by an ingenious shackle which was burnt through by the flames, allowing the bird to soar free. Everyone knew this, but it was expedient to greet the miracle with pious jubilation. The princes of this world exercise authority, says Jesus, and are called dispensers of blessing. The peoples hate the beast, says the Book of Revelation, but they worship it.

Such, then, was the inner state of the people of the Roman world. What was the truth? Reasons of state must decide

what was valid and invalid, what was to be said and not said.
What was faith? Everyone had ceased to believe in the gods,
or the mysteries. All that was left was belief in the emperor.
Nor was even that taken seriously, in the end. No one believed
in anything. The veneer of piety masked an absence of all
belief. Was the Christian far wrong when he said that the
Gospel in the Roman world was the witness to the truth in
a world full of semblance and lies and self-deceit? To speak
of deceit was no cheap Christian reproach, but deceit was in
fact the fatal sickness of the worship of the emperor, known
by all, acknowledged by none. It was the state of affairs
described by Hans Christian Andersen in his story of the
emperor's new clothes. The emperor passed through the streets
with his great entourage. He was stark naked. But it was proclaimed that he was wearing the new State clothes which
could be seen only by loyal subjects. Those who could not
see the marvellous clothes were unfit for their calling. And
behold, everyone saw the marvellous clothes and praised them
aloud. Everyone saw, but no one believed.

II

Such, then, was the state of affairs in the Roman empire
when the apostles and their successors were summoned to
proclaim their message.

This message was not a political programme. 'Nothing is
more foreign to us than politics', wrote Tertullian to the
emperor. Early Christianity scorned all political means to
power and all political means of fighting. It avoided all political provocation, and even renounced any form of political
protest. 'God loves the confessors', said the martyr-bishop
Cyprian, 'and not demonstrators.' The Christians could be
attacked, persecuted, tortured to death without uttering a
word that could be called political polemics. They did not
need to fear anything more, for death was certain. But no
revolutionary words came even from the dying. There can
be only one reason for this: the hearts of these men were free
of all thoughts of hostility to the State.

Rather, the hearts of these men were filled with loyalty to the empire and its head. We know of the decisiveness with which Jesus based His attitude to the tax for Caesar on the political facts, declaring His allegiance to the Roman empire and emperor. The same declaration of loyalty is found in Paul. And the early Church developed from this loyalty a whole *Philosophia Imperii*, which could almost be translated as a theology of the empire, a historical and theological picture of the universal mission of the Roman empire.

The heart of this theology was the idea of God's grace. There is no authority apart from God. God Himself has established the reigning emperor. God Himself leaves him in power, in spite of all his weaknesses and even crimes, so long as it pleases Him to do so, in His inexhaustible grace and incomprehensible historical plan. Therefore God demands of His Church to give to Caesar what is Caesar's. Loyalty and obedience are therefore not only the duty of a Roman citizen, they are also the duty of the Christian conscience.

But more than that, the Church also prays for the emperor. If the heathen who basked in the brightness of the imperial favour brought sacrifices and vows to their altars for the welfare of their imperial lord, the Christians who stood in the shadow of the imperial disfavour were not behindhand in praying at God's altar for the emperor and his task. They were indefatigable, and were not turned aside or embittered by anything. For they were convinced that God wished to have it so. They knew that the prosperity of the empire and the future of its peoples depended on the person of the emperor. And they were convinced that their highest service of him was in the intercessions which the Church offered on his behalf.

The Church refused only one thing to the emperor—worship. The Church would not take the oath by the holy spirit of the emperor, it would not recognize him as divine, or worship his image; its refusal was quiet, steady and consistent. In the year 250 a representative of the Church said: 'What man is more concerned about the emperor than we are? Who loves him more honestly than we? For we pray incessantly for him, that he may be granted long life, that he may rule the nations with a just sword and know an age of peace in his empire. Then we pray for the welfare of the army and for the blessing of mankind and the world. But we cannot sacrifice to the emperor in the temple. For who may pay divine honours to a man of flesh and blood?' No one is more concerned about the emperor than we are: the Church of Christ considered that even its refusal to pay the emperor divine honours was a service, a thankless service which no one in the Roman empire wished to undertake. For the Church was certain, from its study of Scripture and history, that God casts into the abyss and strikes with madness and destruction the man who exalts himself to heaven. If it prayed God with upright heart for the welfare of the emperor and the empire, then it had also to do what it could to save him from that fate. But what if its prayers, and its refusal to worship the emperor, were in vain? *Animam salvavit* (Ezek. 33). When the emperor's fate was sealed, and his murderers rejoiced like the regicides in *Richard III*—'The day is ours, the bloody dog is dead'—then the Church mourned, 'How art thou fallen from heaven, O day star, son of the morning!'

But in the midst of the kaleidoscope of worship and assassination, the tumult of the dance of death and the pious farces, the Church continued to proclaim the message of Jesus Christ, the gospel of the heavenly emperor. He was the Saviour of the world, the Son of God, God and Lord from His birth. He had truly come down from heaven, He inaugurated the New Age, to the accompaniment of miracles and signs of the coming creation, He had truly ascended into heaven and sat on the right hand of the Throne, from whence He would come to establish the last Kingdom, the age of eternal peace. The divine sceptre and crown were His; His sceptre the Cross, His diadem the crown of thorns. To Him alone, the Crucified and Resurrected, was worship to be rendered. So the apostle John, the prisoner of Patmos, had seen and proclaimed Christ, the Emperor on His heavenly throne. And soon theology and worship, poetry and sculpture, were united in a single chorus of praise to the glory of His divine Majesty.

This was the Christian faith which was opposed by the ancient Church to emperor worship. Each believed in the God-man, the mediator between heaven and earth. Even the forms of the two beliefs are similar. But the opposition was absolute. On the one hand the divine emperor with a sword; on the other hand the heavenly Emperor with a Cross. On the one hand a confusing twilight, blurring the lines between God and man, religion and politics, on the other hand everything soberly and clearly thought out, cleanly separated and ordered. On the one hand the imperial government, with its lies and deceit about religion and politics, stumbling in both spheres; on the other hand a Church with a clear, open and consistent attitude to the emperor and the empire. They were two different worlds: in the empire the sham freedom of emperor worship for one's own advantage; in the Church the true freedom of Christ worship even at the cost of one's life. And this, I think, is the decisive contrast: emperor worship did not take itself seriously; but the worshipper worshipped with his fist clenched in his pocket, or an involuntary smile on his lips. But those who confessed Christ were serious about their faith.

III

These, then, were the two opposed worlds. We must now study the collision between them. This took place on two fronts: that of the Christian mission and that of Christian persecution. We shall concentrate here on the persecutions, for it was here that the decisive factor lay. Fundamental though the work of the early Christian mission was, in the end it was not the drive of the missionaries but the endurance of the martyrs which won the victory in the battle between emperor worship and Christ worship. So we turn to the documents themselves, the files of the trials of the martyrs.

Like a sign of things to come, established by God Himself, the trial in the praetorium at Jerusalem stands at the threshold of the time of persecution. 'Yes, I am a King', says the Son of God. 'To this end have I been born, and to this end am

I come into the world, that I should bear witness unto the truth. Every one that is of the truth heareth my voice.' Pilate asked him, 'What is truth?' The imperial politician shrugged his shoulders when he heard of truth. The Roman man of the world smiled imperceptibly, and was disappointed when Jesus did not respond. Pilate did not grasp what was happening, that divine truth confronted political truth, absolute truth confronted relative truth, genuine and full truth confronted a debased and spurious truth.

In February of the year 156 the president of police said to the aged Bishop Polycarp of Smyrna, whom he wanted to save, as Pilate had wanted to save Jesus: 'What is there after all in calling upon the lord emperor, sacrificing to him, and all the rest?' In the same spirit of unbelieving faith the governor himself sought to persuade him: 'Think of your grey hair,. swear by the divine spirit of the emperor . . . and I shall set you free; only curse Christ.' And Polycarp answered, 'Eighty-six years I have served Him, and He has never done me any wrong. How can I bring myself to blaspheme my King, who has saved me?'

A generation later the weak-minded Commodus reigned in Rome, who had himself officially recognized as the Hercules Romanus. A whole group of confessors of Christ were summoned to appear before the governor in Carthage. They declared, 'We are not criminals, but servants of our emperor Jesus Christ.' The governor replied, 'We too are believing men, and our belief is simple: we swear by the divine spirit of our lord and emperor and offer sacrifices for his well-being; and this you should also do.' The martyrs answered, 'We know our Lord, He is the King of kings and the Emperor over all peoples.'

During these same years the Christian Apollonius had to answer for himself in Rome. 'Think well,' said the governor to him. 'Swear by the divine spirit of the lord our emperor Commodus, sacrifice to his gods and to his image.' Apollonius replied, 'We Christians worship no man, though indeed we honour the emperor as the earthly image of the heavenly King, established by divine Providence to rule over the earth.'

A popular philosopher intervened in the trial, claiming to give an expert opinion. Then Apollonius spoke out clearly: 'In the hypocrite's mouth the truth itself becomes mere phrases and blasphemy.'

Sixty years later a casual worker, a Christian called Conon, was brought from a remote estate before the governor. In a reply which is very significant for the complete elimination of the Christians from all public life at that time, he said, 'Why does the governor ask about me, who am a foreigner and a Christian? Let him summon his own kind, and not a labourer.' In court the official questions were read out to him. 'He was found to be a true friend of the gods, obedient to the laws and to the Great King' (as the emperor was often described in the East). Conon interrupted: 'Not so. For the Great King whom I obey is Jesus Christ.' The governor, who liked the man, wanted to adopt the principle of both-and. 'If you call upon your Christ, call upon our gods too. I don't ask you to offer sacrifices and the like. Here, just take this little bit of incense and the wine and the olive-branch and say, "Supreme Zeus, save this people." That's all you need to say, and from henceforth you will be completely unmolested.' But the old man stood firm. 'May God grant that I continually sing praises to Him, the God and Saviour of the whole world, together with all who call upon His Name, and that I speak no word of denial.'

In the last and most severe persecution, in the time of Diocletian, the veteran Julius was arrested in his farmhouse. The governor wanted to save him. 'What is there to it? You scatter a little incense, and go home.' Julius replied, 'I am an old soldier, and in twenty-seven years of service I was never accused of any fault, not even a quarrel. I went through seven campaigns and was never found wanting. The emperor discharged me with honour. And now do you want me, who was faithful in the least, to be unfaithful in the greatest thing of all? I have always feared God and now I am ready for my last service. . . . I pray you, honoured governor, in the name of your emperor, to pronounce the judgment which you must, that my oath may be fulfilled.' 'Your emperor', said the old soldier. We must grasp what a profound alienation existed between the emperor and his faithful veteran, and glimpse the incomprehensible tragedy of these persecutions, in which Rome raged against her most faithful and most fearless children, those who were most ready to be sacrificed, and displayed the best character of all, those who were quiet in the land, who had shared in the emperor's wars. How long was such madness to continue?

At that same time Bishop Phileas was brought before the governor. The hearing was like a final encounter between the spirit of Pontius Pilate and the spirit of Jesus Christ. The governor treated the bishop as an equal. 'I have sworn. Do you swear also.' That is the very spirit of Pilate—I have had my own thoughts about it, and so may you. Thought is free. But the bishop refused. 'Just sacrifice,' said the governor, nodding to him. The bishop refused. The governor gave it up. 'So you wish to die for no reason?' Then the bishop replied, 'Not for no reason, but for God and the truth.' That is the very spirit of Christ.

This state of war lasted for three hundred years, a war not between State and Church, but between emperor-worship and the worship of Christ. Finally the emperor gave in. Three hundred years after the Crucifixion of Jesus Christ the emperor Constantine the Great made peace with the Christians, and established the new Roman empire under the sign of the Cross in Constantinople—the only empire which has endured for a thousand years. Only once after Constantine did the heathen world raise its head again—under Julian the Apostate. His efforts broke down in the cross-fire of public laughter, and tradition relates that the emperor died with the words 'Thou hast conquered, O Galilean' on his lips.

Why did Christianity win in this spiritual struggle? This was the question with which we began, and now we are in a position to give it a sharper edge: why did the Roman emperor, the mightiest man in the world, capitulate to the Christian confession? Was it because he was attracted by the Christian world of ideas, the message of the gracious God, or the dogma of the God-man? No; for to the end of his days

Constantine had little understanding of the Christian world of thought; he was not a great theologian, but a great statesman. Nor was he the only Roman politician of his day who stretched out the hand of peace to Christianity. We know now that his two most dangerous opponents as claimants for the empire had already decided, before Constantine, to follow the same policy of peace. Did he then yield to the Christians because they were in the majority? No; the Christians in the time of Constantine were a tiny minority without power or influence in the enormous Roman empire. Constantine capitulated because Christianity could not be exterminated, because in the last great persecution, which Constantine as well as his two rivals had seen at work, it had proved incapable of extermination.

But why was this so? Modern historical investigation has not been able to provide the answer. The Roman judges acknowledged that they faced an enigma. The accused Christians were excellent people, the emperor's best men and women. But in the matter of Christ the most peaceable and intelligent people were remarkably thick-headed and hopelessly wrong-headed. No one could understand it. When the accused, the martyrs themselves, were asked, they replied, 'We have met the truth.'

We have met the truth, and the truth has compelled us, and the truth has made us free. So we stick to the truth and can do nothing else. That is why we are in such dead earnest about our faith. Kill us. We cannot change. God help us. Do not suppose that we hold life cheap, or that we do not see the glory of the creation, so the martyrs expressly declared. Do not suppose that we do not love the light of this world. But another light has dawned upon us, the true light. We have met *the* truth, so the confessors of Christ bore witness, not *a* truth, like Socrates, but *the* truth. *The* truth is not of this world. So the witness to the divine truth is a wonder in this deceitful world, a riddle at which one shrugs one's shoulders, a danger which one fights. So the divine truth is hated and persecuted in this world. But the divine truth is mightier than the lies of the world, and carries the victory over the might and cunning of the devil. Kill us. You cannot kill the truth.

But the martyrs witnessed to more. He who bears witness to the truth is not alone. He is surrounded by a cloud of witnesses, encompassed by their prayers. 'All martyrs unto blood stand by me with their prayers,' said an unknown soldier of Christ before a Roman judge. 'All who have stood fast to death in this battle.' We can now see why Christianity could not be rooted out. The persecutors of the feeble witnesses of Christ in the Roman empire were not fighting against flesh and blood, but against an invisible army, the great army of Christ, the army of the hundred and forty-four thousand which grew larger and more powerful with every confessor who sealed his confession with his blood.

Finally, the Roman martyrs bore witness to the fact that they were not alone, but the crucified Christ was with them. No one can read without emotion these witnesses to a community with the crucified Christ, which is known only by him who bears the Cross.

So the crucified Lord speaks to the prisoner of Patmos: 'Fear not, I am the first and the last, and the Living one; and I was dead, and behold, I am alive for evermore, and I have the keys of death and of Hades' (Rev. 1.17f.).

'Your tortures cannot touch me. I have a God who makes me strong', said the martyr Conon as he made the sign of the Cross and died. The martyr Crispina said, 'He Himself is with me and helps me and strengthens me in all need, so that I do no evil.' Felicitas said, 'When I go to my death Another will be alive in me and will carry my cross, because I carry His Cross.' The martyr Euplius prayed, 'Christ, preserve me, Christ, come to my help.' And Agathonike called in her deepest need, 'Lord, Lord, Lord, hasten to help me, for with Thee is my refuge.'

The Crucified and Risen Lord heard the prayers of His martyrs. Julian was right: the Victor, to whom the Roman emperor capitulated, was the Galilean Himself.

Why was the witness to the divine truth, silenced a hundred times, not utterly destroyed? Because it was the self-witness of Jesus Christ, who was dead and is alive for evermore. Why could the Christian witness not be extirpated? Because the Crucified and Risen Lord is not an idea, but a reality, and a power which is not of this world, and which cannot be driven from the world by any power of man or subtlety of the devil.

A martyr of the time of the Reformation fittingly ends this discussion: 'The divine truth cannot be slain. Even though it may be mocked and crucified and buried, it will rise victoriously on the third day and reign in triumph through all eternity.'

XIV

THE LAST STRUGGLE

THE struggle between Christ and the Caesars had three phases. First, there was Domitian's attack, and the counter-attack of Revelation. Then there followed almost a hundred years of static warfare in the age of the senatorial emperors. Finally, in the time of Commodus, there began the last struggle which culminated in several great battles, ending with the victory of the Cross in the year 312. This last struggle is the subject of the present chapter.

I

In the year A.D. 180 the philosopher-emperor Marcus Aurelius died of the plague while on a campaign in Germany. His eighteen-year-old son Commodus, who showed a tendency to mental infirmity, became sole ruler. Three years later a group of conspirators from the circles of the imperial family and the court plotted his assassination. The attempt failed, and brought in its trail a wave of reprisals. The emperor thanked the gods for his merciful deliverance and assumed the name of the 'blessed Commodus'. The cities of the East showed their delight at the outcome by striking a coin with the inscription: 'Under the sceptre of Commodus the world experiences an age of blessing.' Gold coins with this inscription appeared in different regions. The words were probably inspired by Rome, and taken over by the Greek cities in the usual rivalry in courtly flattery—presumably first by those cities with the most uneasy conscience.

Meanwhile in Rome there were new conspiracies, murders, executions. The emperor thanked his heavenly guardian with a coin showing Jupiter holding his thunderbolt and his mantle in protection over the emperor, who is depicted in every trait as the earthly image of the heavenly king. In the imperial house death raged. The emperor took the name of 'Blessed of fortune'. PF, Pius Felix, the Blessed and Fortunate, was henceforth to be the official double title of the Caesars—as though to mock the age of emperor-assassination and deadly strife which began with Commodus.

Finally, this mental defective discovered that he was Her-cules *redivivus*, the strong man sent from heaven and armed with superhuman powers to set the poor world free from the powers of destruction. As a sign of this he ranged the streets of Rome with a cudgel and lion-skin, and had himself depicted on the official statues and coins in this heroic masquerade, which did not conceal his weak-minded features. For two years this ghastly show went on. Then the beautiful and pious Marcia (who was also well-disposed to Christianity), the favourite wife, for many years, of the imperial weakling, who maintained a double harem of three hundred women and three hundred boys, took matters in hand. The emperor sought to take her life, and she anticipated him with the same resolution as had saved Domitia from the murderous inten-tions of Domitian. On January 1, 193 the blessed and fortunate Commodus, who in sport, too, doggedly trained to be a Hercules, was strangled by his trainer at his morning exercises. The Senate resolved that his name should be execrated.

The father of Commodus, in the early years of his reign, had condemned the Christian philosopher Justin to death. In Marcus Aurelius's last years Bishop Melito of Sardes wrote a defence of Christianity, in which he described Christian teaching as the philosophy of the empire. For, as he said, in the spirit of the Christmas story in the Gospel, Augustus and Christ were contemporaries. The empire and the Church had grown up together and therefore belonged together. There-fore the Roman emperor was the appointed protector of the Roman church. It was the Church's duty to provide the historical and theological interpretation of the imperial office.

But all efforts at philosophical defence were vain. The very first year of Commodus's reign saw persecutions and martyrdoms. The Christian Donata in Carthage was asked to swear by the spirit of the emperor, and sealed her refusal with her blood.

Some years later the highly educated Apollonius appeared before the Roman judge. He was summoned to pay sacrifice to the imperial image, and to swear by the spirit of the emperor. He refused, and said: 'Our sacrifice is the prayer we offer for the living image of God, who is established as master of the earth. So we pray daily, in accordance with true divine command, to the God who dwells in heaven, on behalf of Commodus, who bears the sceptre in this world. We know that he has been established as lord of the earth by none other than our unconquerable God in accordance with His divine decree.'

Imitatio Dei, God's decree, and intercessions to Him—all this is good Christian and good Roman practice, and entirely in accord with second-century ideas. Apollonius deliberately made use of the formal language of the imperial coins and of the apologetes. We only need to think of the coin with Jupiter protecting the emperor and to refer to the seventeenth chapter of Justin's *Apology*, on the Church's prayers for the divinely instituted emperor.

But once again the State demanded more than the Christian was able to give, and this time with unparalleled severity. The governor asked not only for affirmation of loyalty to the State, and prayers, but also for worship of the emperor. The conflict was hopeless. Then Apollonius presented an impressive picture of the fight which the brutal world at all times wages against the just and the wise. In his own words, 'the just cause discomfort to the unjust. So in the Bible they utter the evil words, "we want to bind the just man, for we hate him". And a Greek writer [Plato] says, as is well known, that "the just man is whipped, tortured, fettered, blinded, and at the end of his suffering brought to the stake". As then the denouncers of Athens bore false witness against Socrates and brought the people over to their side—in the same way some cunning schemers put our Lord and Saviour-King in bonds, and bore false witness against Him.'

But the son of the philosopher-emperor had no room in the empire for philosophers of Apollonius's sort, and the pupil of the martyr apologist Justin died the death of a Christian believer.

II

After the assassination of Commodus, on the first day of the year 193, the imperial guards proclaimed the city governor, Pertinax, emperor. He was the son of a freed slave, whose father had made money in the manufacture of felts. The son was therefore able to promise every member of the guards an honorarium of twelve thousand *sestertii* (about £250) when he ascended the throne. That was the secret of his rise. The coins with which he fulfilled his obligations admittedly represented his career in somewhat more poetic terms. On the obverse was the crowned head of Pertinax, on the reverse divine Providence, crowned, her hand outstretched to receive a star which is gliding down from heaven to earth, with the inscription, 'Through the Providence of the gods'. Providence, which rules over all historical powers, had brought down Pertinax from the stars of heaven and made him lord of the earth. It was left to the fancy of the guards whether they regarded this heavenly self-disclosure as referring to the birth of their master, or to his ascension of the throne. But the star did not shine for long. The soldiers soon spent their *sestertii*, and despatched their emperor, after eighty-seven days of rule, by means of a dagger-thrust, back to the world of stars.

Two new candidates for the throne emerged, and the guards auctioned the mastery of the world to the highest bidder. General Didius Julianus, with the highest bid of twenty-five thousand *sestertii* per head, won the auction. The new emperor was not quite so romantic as his predecessor, and the coins with which he paid his soldiers no longer spoke of Providence, but proclaimed in the style of daily orders, 'Through unanimous resolution of the army (chosen emperor)'. The new agreement, however, lasted only sixty-five days. In spite of a 100 per cent. increase in the price he paid, his time was 25 per cent. less than that of Pertinax. Then the first flush of love was past, and Didius Julianus was assassinated by a soldier on June 1, 193.

His successor, Septimius Severus, restored the almost forgotten Pertinax to honour. By a resolution of the Senate, he had him raised to the circle of the gods of Olympus—as incidentally he also arranged later for the blessed Commodus. He also endowed a temple for Pertinax, with a college of priests, and established holy games for the birthday and the coronation day of the divine emperor. So the myth of the miraculous star was happily made to serve both advents, the emperor's coming to earth and his ascent of the throne.

But the coin with the heavenly star consisted of very earthly material. It was inflationary currency, and marked the beginning of a financial crisis which lasted a whole century, and then ended in a rapid depreciation and rise in prices. The emperors tried to meet the crisis with constant emergency measures, which only made the breakdown of public confidence more complete. The emperor Quintillus, scarcely known today outside the circles of numismatists, issued in the seventeen days of his reign, from the imperial mint alone, more than seventy-five different coin-types, each more boastful than the last. But one only needs to handle a third-century coin to learn the truth. These so-called silver coins are made of the cheapest alloy or of copper with the thinnest of silver-plating, which must have worn off in a few days. No one wanted to accept this money, in spite of the exaggerated inscriptions and their wonderful promises. We can see this clearly from the hoards of coins which have been discovered in the frontier provinces. The German tribes preferred the silver coins of the good old times of the Republic; the Indians preferred the *denarii* of Tiberius as late as the third century. They did not have the romantic images and inscriptions, but they were coins of real value. In the empire itself these had completely disappeared.

226

The emperor who bribed and cheated his soldiers with this base currency was Pertinax, the first soldier-emperor.

III

Septimius Severus had his entry into the capital celebrated by a Senatorial coin, which outdid all the epiphany coins of his predecessors, establishing a new tradition of advent coinage, both in the portrait and the inscription. The emperor is entering the city on horseback, and the inscription proclaims the most blessed advent—ADVENTUI FELICISSIMO. Another coin promised the people serene times, and depicted a gay circus scene—the first of many coins from the age of the dance of death.

The emperor was well-intentioned, and at first exercised great tolerance towards the Christians and the Jews. We learn that he suffered Christians in his own palace, and protected them from the mob in the city. In the struggle for power the Jews had been consistently on the side of Severus, and played an important role, especially in the eastern provinces. The coins of Asia Minor give an astonishing illustration of this.

In Apamea in Phrygia it was the fashion to issue coin-types of popular wall-paintings. Thus there were various coins depicting by name Noah emerging from the Ark. This type —like a still from a film—is without parallel among ancient coins, and recalls the mosaic of the Flood in the synagogue at Gerasa, or the newly-discovered wall-paintings in the synagogue at Dura-Europos, which are fifty years later than our coin. The further fact that the sequence in the type is from right to left supports the view that there was a Jewish model. I am inclined to think that in the town of Apamea, which had many Jews, some prominent Jew was the mint-master, and took the main frieze of the town synagogue as the model for his coins—a motif that was certainly a favourite one with Jews and Greeks alike, on account of its relation to Deucalion, the hero of the flood of Apamea.

This is only one example of the well-meaning policy of the new emperor. Similar responses followed in other places. The coastal town of Chios in Asia Minor acclaimed him on their coins in a formula known to us from the time of Commodus: Beneath the sceptre of Severus the world knows blessed times. And to the old formula the loyal town adds a new benediction: Blessed are the people of Chios.

But the emperor's main concern was dynastic. For he was the first emperor for one hundred and twenty years, since Vespasian, to have two sons when he ascended the throne, to guarantee the prosperity of his house and the empire. Their names were Caracalla and Geta. Severus was tireless in having himself represented, along with the empress Julia Domna and their two sons, in paintings, on jewels, and in other works of art. He was especially assiduous in proclaiming on every possible coin to the peoples of the empire the joyful news of the unique blessedness of the ruling house and of the universal empire.

One of these coins shows the empress as the mother of God with her little son Caracalla in her arms, with the legend, SAECULI FELICITAS—'the happiness of the century'. Another coin-type shows the emperor on the obverse, and on the reverse the two sons with the inscription, AETERNITAS IMPERII—'the eternity of the empire'. A gold coin shows the whole family, the emperor on the obverse, the empress between her two sons on the reverse, and again the emperor's favourite inscription, FELICITAS SAECULI. The age could not be other than a happy one. For what the father had begun, the sons would in due course fulfil.

Soon the two young heirs appear on coins by themselves, with the same basic motifs. Caracalla issued a gold coin with the double portrait of his parents as a divine couple with the emblems of the sun and the moon, and the inscription, CONCORDIAE AETERNAE—'dedicated to eternal concord'. Geta issued a coin with the pious words, 'The son of the blessed and adorable Caesar, who is invincible as the sun'; adding his own portrait as the sun-god blessing the earth.

Family concord and dynastic politics flourished in the young generation as well. Caracalla introduced his young wife Plautilla on several silver coins to the peoples of the empire. The crown

prince and the crown princess are clasping hands, to the words
'To the eternal covenant', or 'The continuance of the monarchy'. Or the crown princess appears, as the empress herself
formerly did, in the likeness of Venus, accompanied by a
little Cupid.

So in the family of the emperor everything was happily
arranged and prepared for the good of the empire—or so it
seemed. But Caracalla was obsessed with a passionate craving
for power, and had no desire to play the lifelong role of the
dutiful son and brother. In January 211 he made an attempt
on the lives of his father and his brother. The attempt failed,
but his ailing father died a few weeks later.

So Caracalla became emperor, along with his brother Geta.
His new coins began with false devotion by celebrating the
dead emperor's reception among the gods, depicting his divine
throne in the conventional style. At the same time a memorial
coin was struck in Asia Minor with the liturgical acclamation, 'Lord in eternity'. Caracalla also celebrated the empress
Julia Domna on a silver coin as the divine mother of the new
emperors, as well as of the Senate and the empire. Finally,
there appeared everywhere in the empire numerous coins with
the double likeness of the two rulers and optimistic inscriptions, such as CONCORDIAE AUGUSTORUM, with the brothers
clasping hands affectionately. In December 211 they made
their ceremonial entry into the capital.

The same month Caracalla made another attempt on his
brother's life, and again without success. The third attempt
was successful. On 27th February 212 Caracalla stabbed Geta
with his own hands while he was in the arms of his mother,
Julia Domna. A little later Caracalla summoned his guards
and disclosed that Geta had long sought to take his life and
that his action had been one of necessary self-defence. A contemporary from the circle of the emperor has preserved the
fine words with which he won the sympathy of his soldiers,
words as old as history: 'Comrades, I come from your midst,
and only wish to live in order to make you rich.'

The conclusion of the whole affair was that all likenesses
and inscriptions of the murdered emperor were removed from

all monuments. In Berlin there is an Egyptian miniature, a family picture of Septimius with his consort and sons: the likeness of Geta has been effaced at a later date. In London and elsewhere are various coins of Asia Minor with the busts of Geta and Caracalla, and again Geta's likeness and name have been effaced.

While the dies of the provincial mints were thus raging against Geta's name, in Rome the dagger was busy, and blood was streaming. Caracalla became the grave-digger of his own family, and he worked with a will. Even the young Plautilla, to whom Caracalla had once offered his hand in eternal covenant, was exiled and then assassinated.

In the same year, 212, Caracalla extended Roman citizenship to all free-born members of the empire, as a popular move which at the same time brought in taxes from the new citizens. But this did not help the crisis in the State finances, and the emperor resolved to issue a completely new coinage. It was credit money, called *Antoninianus* after one of the emperor's many names, and for decades it was the dominant currency. The material was worthless, but the claims made by the coins were all the more exalted. The emperor appeared on all *Antoniniani* with the radiate crown, while the empress appeared on the crescent moon. The bankrupt ruler was the lord of the stars, and the coins assured his empress: 'The sun accompanies you, and the silver moon casts itself at your feet.' One of the first *Antoniniani* issued by Caracalla depicts the important but no longer beautiful empress-mother, Julia Domna, as Venus enthroned, with the shameless inscription, VENUS GENETRIX—that is, Venus the ancestral mother. The coins with the effaced image of Geta were still circulating, recalling the day when brother had slain brother in the arms of the ancestral Venus.

Caracalla spent his last years imitating Alexander the Great, a subject for veiled scorn among contemporary writers. The transformation in his likeness on the coins can only be followed with a sense of humour. Caracalla had brutal and malicious features, and on the earlier coins and statues he is shown with head lowered like a furious beast: a small man, trying

to force history to take his course. In his last years he is shown
with his head cocked heavenwards, with wrinkled brow—
Alexander the political visionary. In 215 he made his ceremonial entry into Alexandria, Alexander's own city. It was
a great affair. The imperial coins made it known in every
land. Egyptian papyri speak of the camels which were requisitioned for this glorious epiphany of the lord our emperor:
epidemia tou kyriou hēmon autokratoros, as the official Greek
language put it. But the Alexandrians, who delighted to mock
such theatrical monarchs, made the most unsuitable jokes
about this Alexander *redivivus*, for which the infuriated emperor's revenge was a gruesome slaughter, wholesale banish-
ment and boycotting. Two years later he was assassinated in
Edessa.

So the hope of a prosperous dynasty and an age of prosperity foundered in unbridled passions, in self-glorification
and deceit, in blood and tears. Only Julia Domna survived,
the much-lauded mother of the camp, the Senate, and the
empire, the unhappy ancestral Venus. She retired to her Syrian
home, and ended her life by means of a hunger-strike.

During the reign of the house of Severus there lived in
Carthage the lawyer Tertullian, son of a Roman soldier, and
one of the most powerful personalities of the ancient Church.
In many books he provides comments on imperial and religious policies, written in lively and controversial Latin.

'Nothing is more indifferent to us than your parties', he
writes, 'nothing more foreign to us than politics' (*Apology*,
38). 'For our citizenship is in heaven.' He quotes these words
of Phil. 3.20 at least four times, as the first and most objective
exegete of a passage which was later to be so often misinter-
preted (*politeuma=municipatus noster in caelis*, *De Corona*, 13;
Against Marcion, 3.24, 5.20; *Ad Martyros*, 3). Yet in Tertullian's
view the Church performed a notable service for the State,
in that it interceded before its God for the emperor. 'A long
life, security for the empire, protection to the imperial house,
a brave army, a faithful Senate, a virtuous people, the world
at peace—whatever, as emperor or as man he might desire, we

pray for from the living God' (*Apology*, 30). When these words are read in the Latin, it may be seen how closely Tertullian sticks to the official sequence of ideas in policy, not least as these are to be found on the coins of Severus: *Vita prolixa, imperium securum, domus tuta, exercitus fortes, senatus fidelis, populus probus, orbis quietus—Vota Caesaris*. Or elsewhere, *Diurnitas Romana, Salus Caesarum, Pro statu saeculi, Pro rerum quiete, Pro mora finis* (*Apology*, 32 and 39). But this also makes clear the double reservation with which Tertullian uses and transforms the imperial philosophy: the reservation about the emperor's divinity and the reservation about the eternity of the empire.

Tertullian first plays off the ancient Roman custom of having the words 'Look behind you, and remember you are but a man' whispered in the emperor's ear while he rode in his triumphal car, against the dogma of the divine emperor. Secondly, reverently and with a fine sense of history, he invokes the *formator imperii*, Augustus, who consistently refused to be called *Dominus* (*Apology*, 33f.). Finally, in his polemic against emperor-worship he again and again quotes Jesus' words about tribute to Caesar, sometimes alone, sometimes in conjunction with Paul's words in Rom. 13.7 (*Scorpiace*, 14; *De Corona*, 12).

The favourite dogma of the house of Severus was the gospel of the *imperium aeternum*, and Tertullian corrects it with lucid seriousness. 'We know', he writes, 'that the Roman empire holds off the final collapse of all things. Therefore the Christian desires the welfare of the emperor and the whole empire. For so long as the empire stands, so long will the world hold together. But if it collapses beneath the assaults of Antichrist, rising out of chaos, then it will drag the world down with itself into the abyss. Then Christ will reveal Himself, and establish the last eternal Kingdom' (*Apology*, 32; *To Scapula*, 2; *De Resurrectione*, 24). The Pauline theology of the State comes alive in these ideas of Tertullian. He is the first and clearest interpreter of the mysterious words about the apocalyptic restraining function of the imperial power, which Paul wrote to the Thessalonians in the days of Claudius (II Thess. 2.3ff.). The romantic idea of the eternal empire was overcome, and the empire of the Caesars received a new and exalted definition as the forerunner of the empire of Christ. The emperor was not the Saviour for whom the ages had waited. But the earthly emperor was the forerunner of the heavenly, and that was both his greatness and his limitation.

Through Tertullian's Cassandra-like words there goes a sound like the echo of distant thunder, which grows louder with each year. The Christians must not grow weary in their intercessions for the world, lest evil get the upper hand, and so that God may still wait with the end of the world and the last judgment. Nor must they grow weary in raising their voice in warning. For the powers of chaos are already storming the empire, and the Antichrist is drawing near (*On Flight in Persecution*, 12). The Book of Revelation also comes to life, and Tertullian writes like an apocalyptist to the governor Scapula, 'We are filled with grief at mankind's error, and we see into the future, of which every day shows threatening signs' (*To Scapula*, 1).

Tertullian was one of the most fearless witnesses to Christ in a time of great violence. Yet he was unmolested to the end. Others were led another way.

In the year 202 we hear of a host of Christians in Carthage, Tertullian's native town, who were condemned, shortly before the birthday of the emperor Geta, to fight with wild beasts in the circus—as a special delight for the birthday celebrations. We have words written by these men and women in the days between sentence and execution, and presumably handed to their brother Tertullian—accounts which are filled with the martyr passion and the very words and pictures of the Book of Revelation. Perpetua, a young mother of twenty-two, writes how in a dream she defeated an athlete in wrestling, and received the prize from a towering figure clad in the imperial purple toga. 'Then I understood I would have to fight not with wild beasts but with the devil. But I knew that Christ would give me the victory.' Saturninus writes of a different vision. The martyrs of Christ had fought their fight and left their earthly bodies far behind. They rose to the heavenly throne, clothed in white raiment, and heard the angels

singing with one voice, 'Holy, holy, holy,' and they saw a figure
sitting on the throne, in form as a man, with snow-white hair
but with the face of a young man, and on his right hand and
his left were the assembly of the elders. 'And we stood and
gave the greeting of peace. And the elders said to us, Go
and play. And I said to Perpetua, You have your heart's desire.
And they said to me, Thanks be to God. Though I was happy
while in the flesh, here I am still happier.'

The same year persecution broke out in Alexandria. The
Christian *Magister*, Leonidas, was arrested and sentenced to
death. He had seven children. His eldest child was called
Origen, and was then seventeen. He wanted to join his father
as a martyr for his Lord. But his mother prevented him by
hiding all his clothes. Then he wrote his father an urgent
letter: 'Endure to the end, father, and do not change your
mind for our sake.' The father was executed. The son kept
the family by giving lessons, by the age of eighteen he was
a gifted teacher, and in the raging persecution a fearless com-
forter of the prisoners and support to the tortured and dying
—the most hated man among the mob. Only after the extreme
terror of the year 215 did he join the trek from his native
town and settle in Palestine. He became the most brilliant of
all the Church Fathers.

IV

From the early twenties of the century a niece of Julia
Domna, the Syrian empress Julia Mamaea, was the dominant
personality at the imperial court. She was a brilliant woman,
filled with the desire to amalgamate all the higher religions.
Eusebius relates how she commanded the great Origen to
attend a religious conference at Antioch, sent him a cavalry
escort, and readily accepted his exposition of the glory of
Christ and the divine Word. In the palace chapel she set up
the figures of Christ and Abraham between the votive images
of Orpheus and Apollonius of Tyana.

The centre of her pantheon, however, was herself, dominating and embracing everything by her brilliance. We can

see this from a bronze medallion, which tells more clearly than many words how the liberal mingling of religions in the third century was used *ad majorem Caesaris gloriam*, and led in the end to self-exaggeration and self-refutation of the *gloria mundi*.

On this medallion the empress appears as the great goddess of her Syrian home, surrounded by serving deities, and provided with the sceptre of the heavenly queen, the half-moon of Diana, the wings of the goddess of victory, the globe of world dominion, the wand of Hermes, the cornucopiae of Mother Earth, and other symbols. They signified that the empress was the incarnation of all the goddesses, the goddess on earth, the guarantor of unceasing felicity and the giver of all good and perfect gifts. All the riches and blessing of heaven and earth were gathered up in her alone.

This gospel of the coins can be illustrated chronologically from the tragic story of the great empress. In the year 222 she had the reigning emperor, her mad nephew Elagabalus, assassinated, in order that her fourteen-year-old son, Alexander Severus, might reign alone. In 227 the Sassanid Ardishir or Artaxerxes founded the neo-Persian empire in Parthian Ctesiphon, and had himself crowned with the mural crown with the globe above it. No Parthian king had ever struck gold coins, but Artaxerxes began at once to issue gold money like the Achaemenian Darius. Once again, as in the days of Darius, the eternal fire burned on the imperial altar of Ahura Mazda. Once again the nations heard with anxiety the old cry of the Persian empire: 'One God, one King, one Empire in all the world.' Was the pre-eminence of Europe to be only an insignificant interlude in the ancient and irresistible succession of Asian empires? The world was larger than the Roman empire, which the Roman empress had just confused with the universe. The first collision between Persia and Rome came quickly, a prelude to coming world wars. Then the Germanic tribes broke through on the Rhine, and the young emperor, accompanied by his mother, went to the northern theatre of war. In March 235 the divine empress and the new Alexander were murdered by some soldiers in Mainz.

In these revolutionary and ominous years Bishop Hippolytus
of Rome was writing his apocalyptic works, a *Commentary on
the Book of Daniel* and a *Tractate on the Anti-Christ*. We read
of Satan at work in politics, but also of the protective function of the empire in the manner of Paul and Tertullian. The
Roman empire with the emperor at its head is the last bulwark
against the Antichrist. The Antichrist is the demonic concentration of power in the last Oriental ruler, whose coming was
foretold for centuries by prophets and sibyls, and who has
now become imminent in the sudden rise of the Persian king.
He will subdue the kings of the East and establish his headquarters in Jerusalem. He will assemble his forces from the
rising to the setting of the sun, so that the plains will be black
with their shields, and the sea white with their sails. Nor will
the Roman empire in the end be able to meet the challenge.
When his empire is fully manifest, the whole political and
creaturely order of the world will collapse in a tumultuous
inferno.

Like the apostle John, Hippolytus had liturgical as well as
apocalyptic interests, and he gave to his Church a liturgy
which combines the most precious elements of the past in a
splendid unity and which is still the unsurpassable model for
all future forms. While the emperors came and went, while
the Persians were attacking in the East and the Germans in
the North, the Church was praying: 'And we beseech Thee,
Lord, for the emperor and for all who have authority, and
for their armies, that they may preserve peace in our world.'
While men were glorifying in the East the succession of the
Persian great kings, from Cyrus to Artaxerxes, and in the
West the European emperors from Alexander the Great to
Alexander Severus, the Church was remembering the history
of the Kingdom of God and its heroes from Adam to Joshua.
'Thou hast called Joshua to be a captain of war, Thou hast
destroyed seven peoples by his hand, Thou hast parted Jordan
and dried up the rivers of Etham, Thou hast caused walls to
fall without battering-rams or the hand of men.' And while
the peoples of the empire worshipped the divine empress, and
the Olympic gods themselves served her, the Church sang,

'The countless hosts of angels and archangels and thrones and dominions and powers and might and eternal forces do worship, and let all people say together, Holy, holy, holy, Lord God of Sabaoth, heaven and earth are full of Thy glory, glory be to Thee for ever and ever Amen.'

V

On a marble sarcophagus from the middle of the third century there is depicted a lion-hunt. One of the beaters has fallen. The hunters ride heedlessly over him. A raging lion rears up before him, with raised claws. The next moment it will throw itself upon him and all will be over. The fallen man knows this. But he can neither defend nor save himself. He is like a man in an air-raid pinned down by ruins, watching a wall about to smash down upon him. The face of the man tells the whole story. It is the face of the third century.

Alongside this picture we may set the portrait of the emperor Decius. It is the same face, only burdened with world power. It is the same situation, magnified to apocalyptic dimensions. The wide open eyes gaze into a world on fire, which no emperor can extinguish.

In the year 248 the capital celebrated its thousandth anniversary. For three days and nights the Romans celebrated the end of their thousand years of glory. The same year Decius, a General from the Danube province of Pannonia, was proclaimed emperor by his legions and announced on his coins a new age, a happy millennium. In 249 Decius conquered and slew his predecessor. The son was strangled. The victor rode into Rome, with the laurel wreath on his brow, the divine sceptre in his left hand, and his right hand raised in the sign of blessing. So he introduced himself to the peoples of the empire in these latest advent coins.

In the year 250 he issued a unique series of coins. Every good emperor—that is, every emperor who had been officially deified after death—was represented in the series, adorned with the radiate crown: Augustus, Vespasian, Titus, Nerva, Trajan, Hadrian, Antoninus, Marcus, Commodus, Septimius and Alexander Severus. Every good spirit was invoked once more for the welfare of the empire. The cities of the East followed the example of Rome and issued similar series. A cloud of witnesses was to surround the emperor, a heavenly guard and council. We are reminded of the angels and heroes and saints of God in the eucharistic liturgy of Hippolytus. But the imperial coins, which carried into all the world the proud assertion of the proudest imperial traditions of a thousand years, were wretched *Antoniniani*, base coins of cheap alloy. This was the state of Rome at the beginning of the new century.

The same year plague broke out in Abyssinia, and for fifteen years raged like the rider on the pale horse of the Apocalypse from one land to another. In the summer of 251 Decius, betrayed by his generals, fell in battle against the Goths.

The next emperor died of the plague four weeks after ascending the throne. His successor struck a touching bronze coin for the propitiation of Apollo, god of sickness and health, with the god standing on a rocky mountain-peak. His terrible bow has been laid aside, as well as his lyre, and he is holding the protective olive branch over the earth, whence men are gazing up to him like the fallen man in the lion-hunt. But no such propitiary rites availed, and the plague raged on.

In 253 General Valerian seized power and introduced himself to the Roman world by a coin with the promising words, 'Restorer of the earth'. He himself at least believed in this promise. The likeness on the coin shows a self-satisfied man, gross, energetic and stupid—the exact opposite of the agitated face of Decius. Valerian at once made his son Gallienus co-emperor. The two men had their hands full. The Franks had pushed through as far as Tarragona on the Spanish Mediterranean coast, the Goths to Greece, and the Scythians to Asia Minor. The Alemanni were moving on Milan with three hundred thousand men. Sapor the Persian king conquered Antioch and sent unrest through all the Mediterranean lands by assuming the title of 'Sapor, god of a divine race, king of kings over Aryans and non-Aryans'. But the two emperors defended themselves with success. The father won a victory over the Persians, and the son defeated the Alemanni decisively. This was in the year 259. It was the most fortunate year in the turbulent reign of the two emperors. The coins of that year tell us better than the spare, dry words of the writers how high hopes were raised at that time. Let a few examples suffice to indicate this.

Valerian issued a victory medal with the inscription VIC-TORIA PARTHICA, and a Roman Victoria with a prisoner bound, similar to the victory monuments of the ancient Eastern Great Kings. (The motif of a bound prisoner can be seen as early as 3500 B.C., in early hieroglyphic form on the oldest monument of Egyptian courtly art, and it enters Roman art in Egyptian reliefs of the early empire; but only in this life-and-death struggle with the East does it begin to appear on Roman coins.) Gallienus struck a medal with the words VICTORIA GERMANICA, with the globe between two prisoners, and above, Victoria with triumphantly raised laurel wreath. At the same time he prepared the way for his son Saloninus, the guarantor of the prosperity of the dynasty and the empire. In the traditional mythology of the heir, the prince is shown as a youthful Zeus on the Cretan goat, and the inscription pays homage 'To the young Jupiter'. On his prancing steed he displays a boyish arrogance, as though he were riding into a future of pure sunshine. The sentiment was echoed in the East. The Greek mint-masters celebrated the year of hope with a goddess of victory, with her foot on a globe, and on her shield the well-proven acclamation, 'Lords in Eternity'.

It was probably at that time that Gallienus issued an enig-matic and much-discussed gold coin, the obverse showing the bearded head of Gallienus with a corn-wreath. The literary tradition describes Romulus with such a wreath. Busts of Augustus and other emperors are extant with the same adorn-ment. But on this coin there is the surprising inscription, GALLIENAE AUGUSTAE, 'To the august Galliena'. In other words, Gallienus is adorned with the wreath of Ceres; he wishes to be worshipped as the goddess of the earth, as he appears similarly on other gems and coins of the time as Minerva. Yet he is wearing his beard. This can only mean that he looked upon himself as the universal god in human form. Even the conflict between the male and the female principle, which separated the gods of Olympus, has been vanquished. All that god and the worship of god meant in heaven and on earth was concentrated in him.

The reverse has the type of Victoria on a *bigae*. Why not the emperor himself, as is so frequently found, in a *quadriga*? Perhaps we may risk the answer that the two steeds of Victoria are riding to the two victories which she has just won, in the persons of the two emperors, in the two most-feared theatres of war, the East and the West. The ancient conflict between East and West has been overcome, and all strife on earth is over. That is the meaning of the high-flown inscription, UBIQUE PAX, 'Peace on Earth'.

This coin, then, proclaims a twofold gospel to the nations, blessing of the earth and world peace. It is the culmination of the imperial philosophy which lies behind this gospel. In the emperor the conflict between heaven and earth, between West and East, between male and female, between power and blessing, has been overcome. In the emperor the fullness of the godhead dwells bodily, and gives life and peace to the universe in the year of salvation.

The young victor looks at the world with self-conscious assurance. Have the demons whom Decius faced been exorcised?

In the summer of 260 Valerian was defeated and taken prisoner by Sapor. He never saw Europe again. The Persian emperor perpetuated this tremendous triumph of the East over the West in every possible way—on precious stones and on an enormous relief, three times life-size, carved on rock above the ancient Persian city of Persepolis. The same year the heir to the throne, Saloninus, died. The legions began to mutiny, the generals revolted, and in every quarter of the empire anti-emperors arose. Ancient authors count thirty such revolutionary emperors, though today we can count only twenty. Their power may be illustrated from the case of Postumus, who reigned for ten years in Cologne, and struck hundreds of thousands of self-adulatory coins, which still come to light in the Rhineland.

14. DECIUS

15. THE FACE OF THE THIRD CENTURY

The isolated Gallienus fought like a lion against the foes within and beyond the empire. In the year 263 he won a breathing-space, and returned to Rome with a great advent ritual. The Senate struck a bronze coin in eternal commemoration of the day of salvation. The divine Gallienus is shown with the mural crown and halo as the tutelary god of the empire, with the words: 'The genius of the Roman people has entered the capital.' But the plague was still raging. The emperor placed himself under the protection of Apollo, the preserver of the divine. But the revolts of the generals and the foreign invasions continued. Peace on earth? In vain the emperor honoured the god of war, holding an olive-branch and summoning to the last of many battles, on the coins he issued to his armies. The coins were not of gold, but of cheap alloy, mere credit tokens. The legions had ceased to believe either in the olive-branch or the *Antoninianus*. They had lost heart. Gallienus had large quantities of wine distributed among them, and issued a coin with the image of the ivy-crowned god of wine and the significant words, 'The Preserver of the Army'. The emperor himself, as coins show, put himself under the protection of Bacchus. But his protector left him in the lurch. On March 4, 268, he was murdered by his generals.

During the reign of Decius and Valerian the two first great battles between Christ and the Caesars were fought.

At the beginning of the year 250 the emperor Decius issued, through Valerian, who was then his minister for home affairs, an edict which required all Christians to recant their faith and to take part in the State sacrifices. The authorities distributed application forms in the official writing on little papyrus rolls, with which everyone had to appear before the official commissions for the cult. Many of these forms, duly signed, have been discovered in the sands of Egypt. One of these, of June 16, 250, now in the State Library of Hamburg, runs as follows: 'To the commission for sacrifices. Application of Aurelia Charis of the village of Theadelpheia. In your presence I have made the required sacrifices of wine and of blood, and have tasted the sacrificial meat, and request that this be attested by your signature.' In another hand is written the attestation of the commission: 'We, the Aurelians Serenos and Hermas, have seen you make sacrifice.' Finally, in large letters (as in Gal. 6.11), the signature of the head of the commission: 'I, Hermas, have signed.'

The issue of this form marks the beginning of the first systematic persecution of Christians. Throughout the Christian communities of the empire there passed a kind of shock, as the seriousness of the situation became apparent.

The aged Origen was the first to speak. 'Look at the wars and triumphs of our Lord and Saviour. For the kings of the earth, the Senate and people and emperor of Rome, have joined together in order to destroy the name of Jesus and His people. They have made laws to put an end to Christianity. Every city, every organization, fights against the name of Christian. But where He leads the fight, His soldiers will always triumph and say, "From Thee, Lord, comes the victory, and I am Thy warrior." '

Origen speaks in the true succession of the Book of Revelation—apocalyptic words, in which the final significance of that violent century is disclosed: the emperor moves to battle against Christ.

Bishop Cyprian of Carthage (Tertullian's native town) writes in the same spirit. Again and again he quotes the words of Revelation, 'Such as worshipped not the beast, neither his image, and received not the mark upon their forehead and upon their hand; and they lived and reigned with Christ a thousand years—that is, those who have not bowed before his bloodthirsty and blasphemous edicts.' 'The Antichrist comes, but above him comes Christ', he wrote to the prisoners, the tortured and the condemned. And again, 'He who rules in you is greater than he who rules in this world. . . . His is the battle. It is He who establishes and strengthens and fills with the Spirit those who fight for Him and confess His Name.'

On the walls of the catacombs they painted the picture of the three men in the furnace who had not bent their knee to the idol. And soon to this picture of these early martyrs was added the votive image of the emperor. This is a clear indication that the point of the struggle was not this or that item of the cult, but, as in the days of the Book of Revelation, emperor worship itself.

Not all the persecuted stood firm. The words of the New Testament about the great falling away, and the necessary divisions of spirits, were fulfilled at that time. One may well believe the ancient Church writers who speak of many who saved themselves by securing an official signature for their papyrus forms. But many, too, chose death.

In May 250 a simple man called Maximus appeared before the governor of Asia Minor. The governor, Optimus, asked, 'Are you a Christian?' Maximus answered, 'Though a sinner, yet I am a Christian.' The proconsul said, 'Do you not know of the new decrees of our invincible Masters?' Maximus asked, 'What decrees?' The governor replied, 'That all Christians should give up their superfluous superstition, acknowledge their true master, to whom all are subject, and worship his gods.' Maximus replied, 'I know the unjust decree of the lord of this world, and that is why I have come forward.' Maximus was tortured, and cried, 'In me is Christ's grace mighty, and will give me eternal salvation through the intercession of all the saints who have fought in this war, overcome your fury, and bequeathed their courage to us as a model.' Then in the name of the all-merciful emperor the governor proclaimed sentence on him, 'The divine mercy commands that for the discouragement of other Christians this man be stoned to death, since he has refused obedience to the holy laws.'

It may be observed that emperor worship had produced a formal style, not only on the coins but also in the courts, which is characterized by mendacity. Maximus replied to it in his own way, on his way to execution, by thanking God for considering him worthy to fight with the devil and to win the victory. The account of the trial strengthens the apocalyptic atmosphere by a final remark which is to be found again and again in the accounts of the martyrs of the third century. 'Maximus the servant of God suffered death in the province of Asia under the emperor Decius and the governor

Optimus, and under the kingship of our Lord Jesus Christ, to whom be the glory for ever. Amen.'

In the autumn of the same year Origen's hour also came, for which he had waited for forty-eight years. He was arrested, tortured, put in the pillory, and in the stocks. He stood firm. The white-haired teacher, once an honoured guest of the imperial court and of philosophical schools, was not sentenced to death. But he died soon afterwards as a result of his treatment.

Still the death-rate from the plague increased enormously, but the persecutions continued. Bishop Cyprian tended the victims of the plague, and wrote a series of wonderful little books, *Concerning the Lord's Prayer, Concerning Dying*—'*Adveniat regnum tuum*: Thy kingdom come. We pray for the coming of the kingdom which God has promised to us and which Christ has won for us by His suffering and death—and pray daily that His Advent may not be postponed.' 'War, famine, earthquakes and pestilence have all been foretold to us by the Lord, preparing us for ever worse afflictions, and leaving with us His words, When all this comes to pass, know that the kingdom of God is near. Dear brothers, God's kingdom is being now proclaimed. . . . See, the world shakes and falls, bearing witness to the coming collapse, not by reason of its age alone, but through the end of all things. So gather beneath the standards of Christ and fight like heroes without fear of death, because you have joined the standard in the time of great affliction. For you know that the fall of this world is the sign of the coming kingdom.' As we read the words of Cyprian, we have in our mind's eye the picture of the sarcophagus with the image of the fallen man, over-whelmed by fear of death. 'So let us face this assault of death and destruction with whole hearts. Let us stand erect among the ruins of the world, and not sink to the earth, like those who have no hope.' *Rectum stare inter ruinas* is the word of the Church in this time of persecution.

Some months before his death Decius called a halt to the persecutions. Christ had won the first battle.

But the breathing-space was short. Only two years later

THE LAST STRUGGLE

Valerian, who hated the Christians, seized power. At first he seemed well-disposed, then in 257 he let loose a new and severe persecution. Now Cyprian had to seal with his own blood the words he had written to the Christian communities. He was summoned to appear before the governor of the province of Africa, who opened the hearing in these words: 'The most holy emperors Valerian and Gallienus have honoured me with a message which commands that all who have hitherto not confessed their loyalty to the Roman religion must in future take part in the Roman services to the gods.' Cyprian replied: 'I am a Christian and a bishop. I know no other God but the one true God who has made heaven and earth, the sea and all that is contained therein. We Christians serve this God, we beseech Him day and night for ourselves and for all men, and for the preservation of the emperors themselves.' The governor threatened him with exile. Cyprian replied, 'Good. I am ready.'

The year 258 brought a new governor, and the situation became more acute. The Christians were deprived of their posts in civilian life, and of their rank in the army. The leaders were executed. Valerian was systematic. He dealt first with the two great churches of the West, in Rome and in Carthage. On August 6 the bishop of Rome was slain in the catacomb of Praetextatus, while celebrating mass. On August 10 his deacon Laurentius was martyred. At the beginning of September Cyprian was recalled to Carthage and brought to trial. The governor declared to him, 'The most holy emperors have decreed that you must make sacrifice.' Cyprian replied, 'I refuse.' The governor concluded, 'Even the blessed and most holy emperors . . . have not been able to move you to accept their religion', and declared sentence of death by the sword. Cyprian said, 'God be thanked.'

Martyrdoms followed in every part of the empire. In the year 259 the Spanish bishop Fructuosus was brought before the judge on these grounds: 'Who is to be listened to, and feared, and prayed to, if the gods are no longer honoured, and devotion is refused to the emperor?' From the same year come the records of the martyr Montanus and his companions, which

say: 'Where the temptation is great, greater is He who overcomes them in us. And where there is battle, there the Lord
fights before us, and triumphs, He who has triumphed in
the Cross.'

The opposing forces are clearly displayed. On the one side
are the shadows of the twilight of the gods. The brightness
of the ancient Olympians has been extinguished. A faint light
from the dying age plays like a will-o'-the-wisp round the
emperor's head. Men cling to their faith in him, only in order
to have a faith at all. On the other side there is the light of
a new morning of creation, streaming from the Face of Christ,
before which the ancient lights grow pale. Those who look
upon His glory know what faith is, and fall down and worship.

A year later Valerian was taken prisoner by the Persians,
and soon afterwards his son suspended the meaningless persecution. The first persecution had lasted seventeen months,
the second, four years. The result was the same. The second
Christomachy of that dark century was a defeat for the emperor.

VI

After the murder of Gallienus, General Aurelius Claudius
was elected emperor by the legions of the Danube, and the
Senate went in a body to the temple of Apollo on the Palatine
to celebrate with acclamations the end of the turmoil and the
beginning of a new age. In fact something like a new and
happy era began with the reign of Claudius. It was no more
than an interlude, which did not last more than fourteen years.
But it was like evening sunshine after a stormy day.

We have spoken of the head of Decius, of his wrinkled
brow and his eyes wide open with fear. The likeness of
Claudius has also been preserved. It may be seen in the
Thermae museum in Rome. He too gazes into the distance,
but his gaze is as it were extinguished. What in Decius was
still a fire is in Claudius ashes. Instead of a reproduction we
give the description of one of the best observers, H. P.
L'Orange: 'The profound care to be seen in every face of
the seventies and eighties of that century has found a moving

expression in this portrait. It has stiffened in a kind of fatal resignation which places the man beyond the influence of events, hardening him and shutting him up against the future, or good fortune, or any change, making him inaccessible to every stirring of passion, of mood, of humour. One feels that here is *the* face of the emperors of that terrible time. An asceticism of inescapable duty . . . is imprinted on the sunken, fleshless cheeks, on the bloodless drooping mouth, expressing both resignation and hardness, and on the heavy, motionless gaze.'

But Claudius was no Hamlet. Without wasting time or words he proceeded to put together the disjointed world. With a strong and fortunate hand he re-established order within the confines of the empire. At the same time he and his cavalry General, Aurelian, threw back the Gothic tribes who had broken in at the delta of the Dniester, three hundred thousand strong, with two thousand ships. Fifty thousand Goths were slain. A year later the emperor met his death in a fresh campaign against the Goths. Ancient writers say that he sought death voluntarily, that he might be an expiation for the victorious future of Rome. His body was never discovered, and a halo has surrounded his death from ancient times. The Senate resolved not only on apotheosis, but also on special honours. Besides the customary coins of consecration with the eagle and the altar, there appeared a solemn memorial coin, which borrowed an honorary title of the great Trajan to describe him as the best of all the emperors, OPTIMUS IMPERATOR. On the obverse the glorified emperor is shown sitting on the heavenly throne with his sceptre, the greatly enlarged right hand raised in blessing over the Roman world. The inscription reads REQUIES OPTIMORUM MERITORUM. One recalls the blessing in Revelation 14.13: *Requiescant a laboribus suis; opera enim illorum sequuntur illos*: 'that they may rest from their labours; for their works do follow them.'

Meanwhile, Aurelian energetically continued the work which Claudius had begun. He introduced a currency reform, and he won decisive victories over the Goths in the north, and over the great Zenobia of Palmyra—the Cleopatra of Arabia

and fairy-queen of the East, who at that time held both
Antioch and Alexandria. The coins which described the emperor's achievements were of truly sacral solemnity. The king
of heaven handed the emperor the globe of the earth. Eternal
Rome gave him the imperial palladium. He himself appeared
as the restorer of the world, raising mankind up again from
the earth; as the sun-god, rising in triumph over the East
and in blessing over the whole world; and finally as god and
lord from his nativity: DEUS ET DOMINUS NATUS is the description given to him by the famous coin of Sofia, which is
now in the *Cabinet des Médailles* in Paris. This is a new peak
in the history of the dogma of the emperor. The self-revelations
of Caligula and Domitian are by contrast very primitive. But
even in this rarefied mythological atmosphere Aurelian is still
the sober soldier, and he is unaffected by the liturgical rivalry
of his mint-masters. He is depicted in the golden garments of
the sun-god, but he is indifferent to the masquerade. He is
surrounded by the sacred court ritual proper to the sun-
emperor, but in his heart and in the manner of his life he is
completely Spartan. The likeness on the coins shows him to
be a man bereft of illusions, never forgetting his beginning
or his end. Soon after the famous silver coin was issued he
was slandered as a murderer by his private secretary and
stabbed by his officers on the public street.

In the year 276, after the usual struggle for power, General
Probus succeeded him. He was an emperor of peace in martial
garb. On a coin announcing his ascension to the throne the
king of heaven is shown handing the sun-emperor the globe
of the world. This traditional scene is accompanied by the
touching and unique inscription, CLEMENTIA TEMPORUM—the
god promises, and the emperor proclaims, times of clemency.
The oldest and most profound idea in the whole philosophy
of the Roman empire is expressed here: clemency is the most
divine attribute of divinity. The emperor should be, and
desires to be, the earthly image of the godhead. Therefore
clemency must be his guide.

With these ideals Probus stood solitary at a post which
demanded a man of utter ruthlessness. He had no illusions

about his task. There is a great head of the emperor in the Capitoline Museum which tells us a great deal. He is no longer a youthful romanticist, but a man who has aged early, and who is waiting for the storms of the time to sweep him and all his aims and achievements away. But till that happens he will persist in the service of that goodness which is not of this world, in the midst of a world which without this goodness will collapse. He will persist in silence, and faithfulness, and without hope, and he will go down without a word.

For five years he had to struggle against foes of all kind, within and beyond the empire. The culmination was his triumphal return to the capital, glorified by innumerable advent coins. At last his hands were freed for the works of peace. The coins proclaimed imperial peace and felicitous times (FELICITAS TEMPORUM, with the cornucopiae and the wand of Hermes). Even Hercules with his lion-skin appeared as a worker and an angel of peace, with his cudgel in his left hand, and in his right hand an olive-branch. It was said that in the intervals between wars the emperor had used his legions to drain the swamps of the Danube and for similar peaceful undertakings. These wild troops were very mistrustful when he spoke, in the style of Virgil's *Eclogue*, of the hope that the trade of war might be abolished from the earth.

His deepest desire, the deepest need of his century, and the deepest hope of antiquity, was expressed in a gold coin of the year 281. It bears the inscription PACATOR ORBIS, 'The Peacemaker of the world'. The emperor of peace, clad in armour, with the victor's laurel on his brow, is standing in the midst of those that labour and are heavy-laden from all nations, thronging round him and kneeling before him with their prayers and pleas, touching his divine sceptre, kissing the hem of his cloak, beseeching a cure and a blessing from his wonder-working hand. This hand, disproportionately large, is in the centre of the picture. It is the hand which has laid aside the sword, after the war to end all wars, in order to heal the wounds from which mankind has bled since prehistoric times. This picture is like a last despairing cry for succour from all the world.

In October 282 Probus was assassinated by his troops.

When Probus issued his gold coin about the peacemaker an anonymous painter in the catacomb of St. Priscilla was painting the splendid fresco with the picture of the prophet Isaiah, pointing to Mary and Jesus and to the star of promise above them. And the church gathered in the crypt to hear the Messianic words from the Book of Isaiah: 'Ecce, virgo concipiet et pariet filium, et vocabitur nomen eius Emmanuel' (7.14). 'Quia omnis violenta praedatio cum tumultu et vestimentum mistum sanguine erit in combustionem et cibus ignis. Parvulus enim natus est nobis, et filius datus est nobis, et factus est principatus super humerum eius, et vocabitur nomen eius admirabilis, consiliarius, Deus fortis, pater futuri seculi, princeps pacis. Multiplicabitur eius imperium, et pacis non erit finis' (9.4ff.). 'Et iudicabit gentes et arguet populos multos, et conflabunt gladios suos in vomeres et lanceas suas in falces; non levabit gens contra gentem gladium, nec exercebuntur ultra ad proelium' (2.4). 'Sed iudicabit in iustitia pauperes, et arguet in aequitate pro mansuetis terrae' (11.4). 'Habitabit lupus cum agno, at pardus cum hoedo accubabit; vitulus et leo et ovis simul morabuntur, et puer parvulus minabit eos' (11.6).

On the forum the epiphany of the sun-emperor was being celebrated with advent hymns, palms of victory and incense. In the catacombs the victory was being exalted which the Christ of God had won in two great battles over the Caesars of this world. They sang the Hosanna and the Benedictus with which the city of God had once welcomed the Prince of peace. They glorified the Messianic King who had been announced by the Advent star and worshipped by the wise men of the East. Tertullian had said that the men who had paid homage to the King of kings with frankincense, myrrh and gold, had been of royal rank (*Against Marcion*, 3.13). He quoted the promises of the prophet Isaiah, and the words of Ps. 72, concerning the kings of the nations who bring their presents to the Anointed of God. Even in Tertullian's time one 'king' was often depicted giving a golden collar to the King of kings, his hands covered as though making a dedicatory offering. Even then certain communities in Alexandria celebrated the feast of the Epiphany of Christ. In the time of Aurelian and Probus this feast spread through the Church, and the homage of the East to the divine Child soon became a favourite theme of Christian art and liturgy. In the cities of the empire triumphal arches and victory reliefs proclaimed the emperor's fame, and the nations of the East paid homage to him with sacrificial gifts. In the pictures in the catacombs the same figures may be seen, in the same garments and the same posture, with the same gifts of homage, hurrying now to worship the Promised One of God. And the multitude of believers sang: 'Iudicabit pauperes populi, et humiliabit calumniatorem. Et permanebit cum sole et ante lunam, in generatione et generationem. Et dominabitur a mari usque ad mare, et a flumine usque ad terminos orbis terrarum. Reges Tharsis insulae munera offerent, reges Arabiae et Saba dona adducent. Et adorabunt eum omnes reges terrae, omnes gentes servient ei. Et adorabunt eum de ipso semper, tota die benedicent ei. Et benedictum nomen Majestatis eius in aeternum, et replebitur Majestati eius omnis terra. Fiat. Fiat' (Ps. 72). One only needs to quote these words in Latin, in the official language of the empire, to see that it is largely the same formal language which is used alike in the Forum for the advent of the emperor and in the catacombs for the celebration of the Epiphany of Christ. Where is the truth? That was the question about which the struggle of the century raged.

At this time Christian painters and sculptors were setting the figure of the Good Shepherd in the centre of waiting creation and praying mankind. On gravestones could be found the lapidary words, *In Pace*. On the ceilings and walls of the catacombs appeared symbols of a better world, in which true peace and joy are to be found. So Christian art developed, in the midst of a world filled with scenes of fear and proclamations of a peace that was no peace, a unique doxology of the glory of Him who loves us and loosed us from our sins by His blood, and has made us to be a kingdom, to be priests unto His God and Father.

When the years of terror under Valerian were succeeded by days of peace, a pupil of Origen, Bishop Dionysius of

Alexandria, wrote, 'Now the Lord is fulfilling His promise to
Isaiah: Behold, I will do a new thing; now shall it spring
forth; shall ye not know it? I will even make a way in the
wilderness, and rivers in the desert. The beasts of the field
shall honour me, the jackals and the ostriches: because I give
waters in the wilderness, and rivers in the desert, to give
drink to my people, my chosen: the people which I formed
for myself, that they might set forth my praise.' It was at this
time, according to a contemporary witness, that the spacious
basilicas, palaces for the glory of the King of kings and Lord
of lords, began to be built in every city of the empire. The
course of the pillars led to the east, to the apse. There, on
a dais like the raised throne of the sun-emperor, beneath the
baldachin and the triumphal arch, stood the altar of Christ.
There the Church glorified Him who is *super omnia Deus benedictus in secula* (Rom. 9.5), in confession and hymns, in doxology
and acclamation, in word and gesture. We quote some of the
forms of that time, which give us an idea of the kyriological
meaning and the Christological content of the liturgy.

'I believe in Jesus Christ, God's begotten Son, our Lord',
says the Creed of the ancient Church in Rome. And its catechism asks, 'Do you believe in His coming (*Adventus*) and in
His kingdom (*Regnum*)?' In a Confession from Caesarea, also
of that time, we read: 'We believe in *one* Lord, in Jesus Christ,
God of God, who proceeded from the Father before all ages,
who became flesh for our salvation, who has ascended to the
Father and sits at His right hand and will come again in glory.'
'And His kingdom will have no end', says the oldest baptismal
confession of the Eastern Church.

In the time of Trajan we have both pagan and Christian
witness that Christians sang hymns to their Christ 'as to a
God'. In the third century a Christian author mentions the
very old psalms and odes about the divinity of Christ. Eusebius
describes the efflorescence of hymns, in honour of the divine
majesty of the Lord Jesus Christ, which took place in the
sixties of the same century. The same tone and spirit are to
be found in the liturgy of the Mass at that time. There you
find the Psalms of the Old Testament, with which the Church

sings the praise of the divine majesty and kingship of Christ; the Christmas doxology of the angels, as contemporary then as ever—*Gloria in excelsis deo et in terra pax*; and the *Trisagion* of the heavenly throne-room. The theologians of that time love to say that all doxologies on earth are but the echo of the eternal song of praise in heaven. From that time comes the exclusive and almost polemic prayer: 'Lord our God, heavenly King, Lord Jesus Christ, only-begotten Son, Thou alone art holy, Thou alone art Lord, Thou alone art worthy to be called the Highest.' Clearer still, if that is possible, is the prayer: 'Almighty God, to Thee be the glory, the honour, the majesty, the adoration and worship, to Thee and Thy Son Jesus Christ, our Lord and God and King.' These are all prayers from the altar liturgy. The congregation joined in with gestures and responses, kneeling or raising their arms and crying or singing: 'It is worthy and meet, Christ is Victor, Christ is King, Christ is Caesar. His is the glory for ever. Amen.'

Here again we may see that many of the same expressions which were used in the imperial court were used to glorify Christ in the basilica. The antithetic significance of these Christian forms becomes clear as a rejection of the imperial cult. Nor can we say that the Christian doxology is always an intensification of the imperial doxology. The exaggerated imperial forms of those decades were hardly capable of further intensification. It is true, however, that even the latest and most exaggerated of the imperial formulas with which the priests and the mint-masters, the senators and creatures of the court sought popularity with their latest master, were bound to sink rapidly to empty phraseology, in the incessant alternation of acclamation and assassination; whereas the formulas of Christian worship were hallowed and sealed by the blood of the martyrs. They were the fruit of grave theological work through the generations. 'Who does not know the books of the Fathers, which proclaim all the divine majesty of Christ?' asks a writer of that time. These descriptions of Christ were worked through and established by severe dogmatic struggles.

In the days of Claudius and Valerian the theologian Paul

of Samosata was at work in the kingdom of the great Zenobia. He was regent of Palmyra and at the same time bishop of Antioch, a prince of the Church who even for ancient times was a remarkable person. But he had certain theological reservations about the eternal divinity of Christ, and was not ready to accord even that honour to the Lord of the Church which every loyal citizen paid to the lord of the empire. He expressly forbade the use of the old liturgical forms about the coming down of the Son of God to earth, and of the new hymns about Christ *Dominus noster*.

This set the whole Church in the East in a turmoil whose effects were felt as far as Rome. The great Synods struggled with the bishop of Antioch about the right Christological confession. They quoted Rom. 9.5, the Pauline confession of Christ 'who is over all, God blessed for ever'. They set up against him a confession which said, 'We confess and proclaim that the Son, from eternity God and Lord of all creation, was sent from heaven to earth and became man in human form. We confess that the fullness of the Godhead dwelt in the Son of the Virgin, and we worship Him in His servant's form.' The Synod uttered a solemn anathema of the bishop's confession, which 'denied his God and Lord', and expelled him from his bishopric. The Roman bishop took the side of the Synod.

Nevertheless, the condemned bishop was able, in virtue of his political powers, to maintain himself for some years longer. But when Zenobia's power came to an end and Aurelian entered Antioch, the emperor himself was called upon to be the judge. He decided in favour of the Roman bishop and the Synod against the regent of Zenobia. Very appropriate, writes a contemporary. Religious and holy (*religiose sancteque*), writes a later historian. Very understandable, we say today. For the sun-emperor decided on political and personal grounds, and paid no heed to the theological significance of the controversy. So we reach the paradoxical position, that the 'god and lord from his nativity' unwittingly supported that confession of the Divinity and Lordship from eternity of the Galilean, which was the very heart of the struggle of the whole century.

VII

In the autumn of 284 Diocletian became the lord of the world.

Diocletian represented the last despairing effort of the pre-Christian world, the last upsurge of its power, the final disclosure of its weakness, a splendid and tragic spectacle. Diocletian had worked his way up from being a slave to being the head of the imperial bodyguard, at an opportune moment had seized supreme power, destroyed his most dangerous rivals with his own hand, and in the year 286 nominated his old comrade-in-arms Maximian (who had had a similar career) to be co-emperor with him.

His first coins announced his programme: (1) the culmination of the imperial religion in a philosophy which combined Roman names with oriental ideas. Diocletian called himself Jupiter, and was worshipped as Father of the gods in human form. Maximian was given the name of Hercules, to be worshipped as the Son of the Father, and the saviour of suffering mankind. Both emperors bore the official title of *Dominus Noster*, Our Lord. Both were surrounded by religious court ceremonial. (2) The reconciliation and combination of East and West in the realm of political ideas. Sometimes the coins depict the *Genius* of the Roman people, sometimes the god of the rising sun. (3) The reorganization of the army to be once more a reliable instrument in the hand of the emperor—reliable not only in a military sense but also in its views. CONCORDIA MILITUM, the old watch-word of the soldier-emperors, received a new meaning in those years—the unanimity of the army. (4) The reform of the empire, to issue in planned regulation of the whole of public and private life. The leading principle of this all-embracing new order is expressed on a coin in the words UTILITAS PUBLICA, the Common Weal. This was the cultural expression of Diocletian's spirit. With sober calculation and unbending will he proceeded to fulfil his programme with the icy passion of the pure doctrinaire.

Written fragments of his list of maximum prices have been found in Greece, Asia Minor and Egypt. Purple silk was not to cost more than 150,000 *denarii* per pound, ordinary beef 8 *denarii*, and Brabant ham 12 *denarii*. To ask for higher prices than these carried the death penalty. The prices were in fact very high. One only needs to compare them with the maximum prices mentioned in Rev. 6.6. However, everything immediately went off the market, and could only be bought on the black market at steeply rising prices.

Nor did Diocletian's state machine function always in political matters as well as it ought. In the north there was chaos. It was there that the ancient advent philosophy reached its culminating exaggeration. A sailor from the Scheldt, called Carausius, had built his own fleet at the emperor's command, which was based on Boulogne and was intended to fight the piracy of the Saxons and Franks in the Channel. But the barbarian joined forces with the barbarians, and when the news leaked out he made himself sea-emperor of the north, and in the year 286 he crossed with the whole imperial fleet to Britain, where he was well received. To celebrate this momentous landing, which was long remembered in the ancient British traditions, a silver coin was struck, showing Britannia with the trident in her right hand welcoming the emperor with the advent words EXPECTATE VENI—an ingenious play on Virgil's words in *Aeneid*, 2.282-3 (disfigured on some coins by spelling mistakes): 'From what shores, O Hector, do you come, expected one, to us? . . . How we wearied ones look to you.' Did Pius Felix Augustus understand the classical allusion? The 'blessed and fortunate and august' seaman from the Scheldt looks like a prize boxer in his laurel-wreath. Maximian built a fleet against the pirate-emperor, but lost half his ships in a storm, and the remainder in an unlucky battle. Nothing daunted, Carausius extended the hand of brotherhood to his colleagues, and struck a coin of peace with the friendly inscription, Carausius and his brothers. In the year 293 Allectus, the chief of his bodyguard, who knew too much, and was scheduled for liquidation, murdered Carausius and had himself made emperor. But the new Caesar appointed by Diocletian for the north, Flavius Constantius Chlorus, a grandson or grand-nephew of the emperor Claudius, was already on his way.

16. CONSTANTINE

17. THEODORA

Constantius conquered Boulogne, crossed the Channel in a fog with two fleets, defeated Allectus, and in the summer of 296 celebrated his advent in London. The Britons received him with awe, as one fallen from heaven (*ut caelo delapsum*), reverently fingering the rudder and sail of the ship which brought his divine person to their shores, and casting themselves before him as he entered the city, that he might ride in over their backs—so a contemporary account relates. In memory of this epiphany, Constantius had a gold medallion struck in Trier, the northern capital, which was found near Arras in 1922. This shows the female representative of London kneeling with hands raised in prayer before the emperor, as he rides up. The holy ship is also shown, a reminiscence, for those who knew their mythology, of the holy vessels with which Apollo came to Greek shores, and Saturn to Italian shores; but chiefly, no doubt, intended as a counter-demonstration to the epiphany of Carausius from 'Far shores'. The inscription is faithful to the emperor's theology, celebrating him as the incarnation of Mithras, Helios and Aion, and his epiphany as the dawn of eternal light on the people that walked in darkness: The Restorer of Eternal Light.

On May 1, 305, the self-styled Jupiter and Hercules abdicated the throne in accordance with their agreement, to be succeeded by Constantius and Galerius. But the intricate mechanism of the State machinery broke down once more. The usual cry arose for the old man. But Diocletian laughed at the embassy which besought him to return, saying, 'You should see the cabbage I am growing in Spalato, then you would give up your efforts to bring me back into politics.' In the year 306 Constantius died, and his son Constantine succeeded him. In 307 the number of rival Augusti rose to six. In 310 Maximian was forced to take his own life. In 313 the sixty-eight-year-old gardener of Spalato committed suicide. So ended the story of the *imperium naturae*.

The Diocletian theory of empire with its absolute claims demanded, 'for the sake of the unity of the empire', the extirpation of Christianity. Diocletian drew this conclusion with the ruthless and self-destructive logic of that doctrinaire and bureaucratic spirit which animated his whole rule.

He began with the purification of the army. In the year 295 every soldier of the empire was commanded to make sacrifice. Violent conflicts were inevitable, as service in the army was by no means voluntary. There is an excellent record from the year 295 of how the veteran Victor was cited to appear before the governor at Carthage, along with his well-grown son Maximilian. The proconsul said, 'Put on the uniform'. While the clothes were being tried on, the young Maximilian said, 'I cannot become a soldier. I cannot commit blasphemy. I am a Christian.' The governor only said, 'Is the size right?' When he had been measured, the N.C.O. said, 'Five foot ten.' The governor gave the order to equip him with the identity token, a lead seal which was hung round his neck, and which, like the imperial coins and portraits on the standards and military decorations, clearly bore the symbol of the imperial religion. Maximilian resisted. The governor said, 'Be a soldier, or you die.' Maximilian said, 'Strike off my head. I am no soldier of this world, but a soldier of God.' The governor addressed him, 'Be a soldier, and accept the token.' Maximilian: 'I will not take this sign, I am already signed with the sign of my God, Jesus Christ.' The governor: 'I shall send you speedily to your Christ.' Maximilian: 'I wish you would do it at once.' The governor turned to the recruiting officer: 'Put on the token.' Maximilian resisted again. 'I will not put on the sign of this world, and if you put it on me, I shall tear it off, for it has no meaning for me. I am a Christian and may not wear this piece of lead, now that the saving sign of my Lord Jesus Christ has come, the Son of the living God, of whom you refuse to hear, who has suffered for our salvation, whom God gave for our sins. All we who are called Christians serve Him and follow Him as the Prince of life and the Giver of salvation.' The proconsul pressed him, 'Let it be put on, or you are a lost man.' Maximilian replied, 'I will not be lost. My name is written with my Lord.' The proconsul persisted. 'Think how young you are, and become a soldier. It suits a young man.' Maximilian stood firm. The proconsul said, 'In the holy service

of our lords Diocletian and Maximian Christian soldiers also
perform their service.' Maximilian answered, 'They must know
for themselves what is suiting. I am a Christian, and I cannot
do anything blasphemous.' The governor asked, 'What
blasphemies have soldiers to perform?' The veteran's son only
replied, 'You know yourself what they have to do.' The
governor at last broke off the interrogation, and gave judgment, 'Since Maximilian in his impious heart has rejected the
sacramentum of military service, he is to be put to the sword.'
Maximilian was executed, and buried beside the martyr bishop
Cyprian. 'I am a Christian, and cannot do anything blasphemous.' No doubt Maximilian was thinking of the camp
cult of the imperial standards, which was part of the soldier's
military duties. But very different things were also required
of a good soldier of the emperor. We see this from the fate of
the soldier Dasius, who also died a martyr's death in the
reign of Diocletian. The account of his end first describes
the military custom of commemorating the golden age at the
winter solstice with a great masked festival in honour of
Saturn. The central figure was the so-called king of the Saturnalia, a soldier chosen by lot a month previously, who for
thirty days could eat and drink and do as he pleased, then
during the time of the festival was arrayed in the royal robes
of Saturn, performing all manner of follies, and finally,
says our account, at the conclusion of the festival was
slain in honour of Saturn. The origins of the Saturnalia
and the concluding sacrifices go back to remote antiquity,
but in the late empire the celebrations were wilder than ever
before.

The account goes on to describe how the lot fell on the
Christian soldier Dasius, who refused to take part in the
detestable orgies and said, 'It is better for me to be a sacrifice
of my own free decision for our Lord Christ, than to be
sacrificed for your idol Saturn.' A remarkable dialogue then
took place before the judge.

The governor addressed Dasius, 'Pray to the emblems of
our lords the emperors, who maintain peace and give us our
pay, and day by day in all things consider our good.' Dasius

replied to this military catechism of the imperial religion with
the Christian soldier's catechism, 'I repeat, I am a Christian,
and my war-lord is no emperor of flesh and blood, but the
Emperor of heaven. I am paid and fed by Him, and His
ineffable generosity makes me rich.' The governor repeated,
'Fall down, Dasius, before the sacred images of our emperors,
which even the barbarian tribes honour and serve.' Dasius
replied, 'I owe obedience to none save the one, undefiled and
eternal God . . . , who will arm me with the strength to overcome and destroy speedily the raging of the devil.' The
governor shook his head. 'Do you forget, Dasius, that every
man is under the imperial power and the holy laws?' But
Dasius could not be moved, he was sentenced to death and
led away to be executed.

Before him walked a ministrant with a vessel of incense,
part of the camp cult. Well-meaning comrades tried to persuade him, at the eleventh hour, to offer incense for the
emperors. Then, in the concluding words of the contemporary
account, 'the blessed Dasius seized the vessel and scattered
the incense to the winds, trampled on the shameful and
sacrilegious images of the blasphemous emperors, and
made the battle-sign of the adorable Cross of Christ on
his brow, through whose power he stood firm against the
tyrants'.

Such was the state of affairs in the army. In civilian life the
situation was much the same, for it was part of the duties of
every official and of every loyal subject to take a share in the
worship of the emperor. This general obligation was sharpened
and extended in the spring of 303 by a decree from Rome
which inaugurated persecutions of unprecedented severity.

Twelve-year-old girls were tried and martyred in Rome and
in Spain. Elsewhere Christians were bound hand and foot,
packed into cargo-boats, and cast adrift. In Asia Minor the
persecution became practically a military operation of the
heavily-armed legions against the unarmed soldiers of Christ.
One contemporary account described events in a little Phrygian
town which was completely Christian. The imperial troops
surrounded and besieged the town, and made preparations for

a proper siege. But no one recanted, the whole population confessed its Lord and Saviour in a loud voice. The troops set the besieged town on fire, and burnt it to the ground with all its inhabitants, men, women and children.

But no one individual knows all the affliction that came upon the Church in these years. We can only describe a few particular events, military reports of the last great battle between Christ and the Caesars.

In those days of affliction the apocalyptic spirit was greatly quickened. In the words of a Greek writer on the martyrs, echoing the words of Jesus: 'When the world is about to collapse, evil does not cease, but becomes worse and worse.' The African Father, Lactantius, searched out old oracles and Sibylline sayings about the fall of Rome, and spoke of the last tribulations which were about to come. 'The empire is breaking up, and its power is distributed among many emperors. Rome still stands, keeping chaos at bay. But the signs of the time show that the collapse of all things is not far away.' Bishop Victorinus of Pettau in Styria wrote a commentary on the Book of Revelation, which is the oldest expository work of the Latin Church, and is full of passionate references to the history of the time. He preached about Antichrist and the millennium, until the emperor's minions seized him.

In Thessalonica, the Christians Agape, Eirene and other women and girls refused to sacrifice to the emperor's gods. The imperial governor had them brought before him and explained to them, 'Everyone knows that all must submit to worship our emperors and lords. . . . Since Agape and her companion in their impiety have offended against the oracles of our august emperors and lords, I have condemned them to be burnt. Eirene and her companions, being minors, are to be cast into prison.' Shortly afterwards the young Eirene appeared again before him, and was commanded to deliver up the Scriptures, as well as to betray the names and addresses of her fellow-believers. She refused, and was handed over by the governor's command to a public brothel. But there no one touched her, or even injured her by a word. For the third time she was brought before the governor, and con-demned to die at the stake, like her older companions. She died with psalms and hymns on her lips.

In North Africa the governor asked the Christian Crispina, 'Do you know what the holy law says? . . . I shall have you executed unless you freely submit to the decrees of our emperors and lords. I know how to break your obstinate spirit. Even you must know that the whole of Africa has offered sacrifice.' Crispina refused. The governor made an-other attempt. 'Must I compel you to learn true reverence and to keep your life?' Crispina replied, 'That is no true reverence for God to which people are forced against their will.' The governor tried to propitiate her. 'Surely it is not blasphemy to obey the holy decrees? Join in the Roman worship, which our invincible emperors and lords—and we ourselves—also acknowledge.' But Crispina was immovable. The governor uttered sentence of death. 'I condemn you to death by the sword, in accordance with the heavenly rescripts of the holy law.' Crispina cried, 'Blessed be God whom it has pleased to free me from out of your hands.' She made the sign of the Cross, and so died.

It may be seen how profoundly the official language of the time had been influenced by the imperial philosophy. In the time of Decius an imperial edict of persecution was simply called 'the decision of mercy'. In the days of Diocletian it was called 'the divine oracle', 'the heavenly command'. It was a world of violence and deceit from which those young Chris-tian women took their leave with hymns of praise and thanks-giving—'Blessed be God who has freed us from out of your hands.'

Crispina's martyrdom took place in December 304. Some months later the great imperial change-over took place. In the West Constantius made an end to the persecutions. In the East Galerius increased their severity. In 311 the dying Galerius also called a halt—in order to win the intercessions of the Church for his recovery. In January 313 the victorious Con-stantine made Christianity a legal religion in the Roman empire. 'Let this be so', runs the imperial edict, 'in order that the divine grace which we have experienced in such manifold ways, may always remain loyal to us, and continue to bless us in all that we undertake, for the welfare of the empire.'

It is the end of the old Roman empire and the beginning of the *imperium gratiae*.

XV

IMPERIUM GRATIAE

'THE Caesars too would have believed in Christ, if either the Caesars had not been necessary for this world, or if Christians could have been Caesars.' So writes Tertullian on the threshold of the third century (*Apology*, 21). The history of that century proved that the world needed Caesars who were Christians. For the history of the third century is the final self-contradiction of the *imperium naturae* and a single cry for the *imperium gratiae* which had to come if mankind was not to drown in its own blood.

The assertive propaganda of the pre-Christian imperial philosophy can be nowhere better studied than on the imperial coins. One can also trace the silent and victorious course of Christianity on the official coinage; and in recent times surprising information has come to light, of which I shall say something here.

I

When Tertullian wrote his famous words about the incompatibility of empire and Christianity, there were already circulating in the eastern parts of empire the first imperial coins showing the sign of the Cross. Richard Delbrueck has recently drawn attention again to the copper coinage of Abgar the Great of Edessa, who has been unduly neglected in recent generations.

Abgar's father, Manu, in the latter years of his reign struck copper coins with the obverse type either of the emperor Verus or king Manu himself with a plain tiara, and reverse his Aramaic names and titles. Abgar the Great followed this tradition. His first coins were of copper, with his own likeness

on the obverse, with a plain tiara, and the Aramaic royal
inscription on the reverse. Then came coins with the head of
Commodus on the obverse, and Abgar himself on the reverse,
again with the plain tiara. Then came the change which is of
special interest to us. Again the coins have the type of Commodus on the obverse, and Abgar on the reverse, but now
his tiara is adorned with a jewelled cross. In the reign of
Septimius Severus Abgar continued to issue the copper coins.
The obverse type has the head of the new emperor, and the
reverse as a rule Abgar with the tiara. Sometimes the tiara is
unadorned, sometimes it is decorated with a great jewelled
cross. But on most of the coins, instead of the simple cross,
there appears a crescent ornament in different settings, with
three stars, or two stars and a cross, or one star and two
crosses, or even three crosses. The latest coin in this series
clearly shows a half-moon with a cross in the centre and a
cross to right and left. Abgar lived and reigned, and struck
coins, during the reign of Caracalla, but reverted to the unadorned tiara. His son Abgar Severus seems to have continued the tradition, but the minting of coins in Edessa ceased
suddenly in his time, while Caracalla was still reigning.

These are the numismatic facts. They provide the needful
clarity for the otherwise confused chronology of Abgar's reign,
and combine with literary records to give the following picture.

Edessa was the capital of a small East Syrian kingdom, which
was ruled over by Arabic kings and was then under Roman
suzerainty. As early as late-apostolic times Christianity of a
very liberal kind seems to have taken root. Syria was the classic
land of eclectic religion. A Syrian letter of the second century
impartially associates the crucified King of the Jews with
Socrates and Pythagoras, as in a similar way the empress Julia
Mamaea put the portrait-bust of Jesus in her gallery of divine
men along with Abraham, Orpheus and Apollonius of Tyana.
In the reign of Commodus king Agbar the Great became a
Christian, under the influence of the friend of his youth,
Bardesanes, made his faith the State religion, and placed in
his palace an 'original portrait' of Christ, which presumably
served as a model for the likeness in Julia Mamaea's pantheon,

and later was taken to Constantinople. On his coins the jewelled cross appeared. At that time Commodus was ruled by his favourite wife Marcia, who was well-disposed to the Christians, and he seems to have taken no offence at the ornament of the cross on his vassal king's coins. Then Abgar brought the highly educated Bardesanes to his court. At that time the much-travelled Tatian returned to his native Syria and gave the Church there the first Harmony of the Gospels, a work whose influence reached far into the Middle Ages. Edessa became the first Christian capital of ancient times.

Meanwhile, after years of struggle Septimius Severus reached the imperial throne. Apparently Abgar had been for a time on the wrong side, until in the year 195 he made formal submission to the final victor in the imperial struggle. The tiara on Abgar's coins was now ornamented (as a measure of caution?) in a way susceptible of different interpretations, pagan as well as Christian. For the sun with a half-moon (and other stars) was a favourite ornament in the pagan world round Edessa. It adorns the famous horoscope relief of the sun-lion of Commagene on the Nimrud Dagh, the mountain at whose foot the town of Edessa lies. We find it also on the tiaras of neighbouring princes on the most various coins of the Euphrates valley. We know, besides, that Abgar's court theologian Bardesanes was very interested in astrology and the mythology of the stars and praised Christ as the Son of the moon and the sun, and as the first-born Brother of the stars. Nor is it long before we hear of the sun-sign of Christ between the morning and the evening stars, and elsewhere we come upon cosmological speculations about the Cross. The symbolism on the crown of the king of Edessa could therefore be emphasized in one direction or the other, according to the exigencies of the times, without harm to theological scruples in that land of eclectic religion. Even in the West, moreover, it is not rare to find Christ glorified as the Sun of salvation and to have the cross or the Christogram represented as a star, a diagonal cross, a form which only the initiate would understand.

About the year 202 Abgar paid a State visit to Rome, where he was received at the court with great pomp. He was in touch with Hippolytus and other Christian leaders in Rome, and when he reached Edessa again he installed a bishop who had been consecrated in Antioch, which was loyal to Rome. The first Christian world historian, the learned Sextus Julius Africanus, worked in the royal archives in Edessa. The king himself corresponded with the Roman bishop. It was from this time that Abgar seems to be reckoned in the ecclesiastical tradition as a full Christian. This may be the reason for the traditional confusion about the date of his conversion. The coins too confirm the fact that after his journey to Rome there was a move to greater clarity and definiteness in the court theology of Edessa. For the image with the great jewelled cross perhaps comes from the last years of Abgar's reign under Severus, while the picture of the half-moon and the three crosses certainly does.

Under Caracalla a sharper wind blew. The tiara was again devoid of ornament, at least of any significant ornament. In April 216 the Roman emperor put an end to the modest kingdom on the Nimrud Dagh, and transformed Edessa into a military colony. Twelve months later Caracalla was assassinated in Edessa on the steps of the temple of the moon. Edessa remained a Christian city, and became more and more the centre of a flourishing church life of Syrian characteristics but of world significance. 'Here there arose, alongside the European, the Eastern form of Christian culture, which stretched from the Mediterranean to Ceylon and China' (Abramowski).

The tiara of the minor king of Edessa with its emblem of the Cross is in more than one respect a forerunner of the imperial helmet which the first Christian emperor wore four generations later and put upon his coins. We shall have to speak of this later.

II

In the third century innumerable coins of consecration were issued on the death of emperors and empresses. One may see, for instance, how the glorified empress ascends to heaven on an enormous mythological peacock, and the inscription (*consecratio*) announces that Her Majesty has been received into the circle of the gods. In the catacombs of the same period the graves of Christian women had simple plaques with a cross or a Christogram, the name of the deceased, and the words (coming from Jewish sepulchral epigraphy), 'In Peace'; for example, *Lucilla in Pace*. In the sixties of the third century the empress Salonina, the consort of the much harassed emperor Gallienus, died. A consecratory coin was struck with the inscription, AUGUSTA IN PACE. It is the first imperial coin with a Christian formula, and has a threefold significance for us.

First, it confirms the ancient tradition that Salonina was a Christian, and indicates that she did in fact provide the impulse for the emperor's policy of tolerance after the catastrophe of her father-in-law Valerian's persecutions.

Second, it shows that Christianity became popular at that time in the form of an other-worldly belief. In an age of nihilism and tumult, of plague and assassination, of barbarian invasion and dreams of world peace, the words on the empress's tombstone are like an echo from another world. There is rest at hand.

Finally, the bearer of that other-worldly belief was a woman, an empress. Salonina had her precursors. There was Domitilla, the Christian mother of the last Flavian emperors, Vespasian and Domitian. There was the 'god-fearing' Marcia, the favourite of Commodus who interceded for condemned Christians. There was Julia Mamaea, the empress with the ideals of a universal religion. Towards the close of the third century examples multiplied: the consort of Diocletian was a Christian, as was his daughter. Constantius Chlorus had two dissimilar wives, first Helena, an innkeeper's daughter, then Theodora, an emperor's daughter. Both were, or became, Christians. Helen was the mother of Constantine. Theodora had a daughter with the Christian name of Anastasia, and a coin of Theodora's from the year 328 (or later) has the reverse type of a cross.

III

In the year 307 the emperor Maxentius, the brother of Theodora, struck a group of gold coins, which promise that

Rome, so much attacked and threatened, will be preserved. The goddess Roma is enthroned in a temple whose pediment is adorned with various symbols. For example, one series depicts the she-wolf, the ancient coat-of-arms of the city of Rome. Another series has the cross. The eternal city is to fulfil its historical mission and promise in the sign of the Cross.

The coin with the Cross was only discovered a few years ago by Italian and German investigators (Lodovico Laffranchi and Hans von Schoenebeck). It roused the greatest interest among the experts. For it is the oldest imperial coin with the Christian emblem.

Though of course it did not imply a personal announcement by the emperor, it was probably issued with his approval. It cannot be called an official confession of Christianity, but it may well be understood to imply an official policy of tolerance, which was ready to give free rein to Christianity, and to tolerate the Cross beside the she-wolf of ancient Rome.

Maxentius had a sound Roman dislike of the deification of the emperors, and refused to give divine honours to his own father, Maximianus Herculius. It is therefore possible that he had some sympathy for the Christian refusal to worship the emperor. But he was not the only emperor to make this change. Constantius Chlorus sabotaged Diocletian's programme of persecution from the start. His son Constantine and Constantine's co-emperors Galerius and Licinius formally revoked Diocletian's edicts against the Christians in the year 311. Maxentius, Constantius, Galerius, Licinius, Constantine—these men were by no means all of one accord, and they engaged in a life-and-death struggle with one another. This means that the cessation of persecution was not a subjective whim on the part of an individual ruler, but was an objective political exigency which no clear-sighted statesman could avoid.

So the little Roman coin with the tiny Cross of Christ is the symbol of a historical decision. After a three-hundred-year war with Christ, after a violent and fearful finale of five years, in which the greatest power of the ancient world concentrated all its forces for the extirpation of the Church of Christ, the Caesars laid down their weapons before Christ.

IV

Galerius died in the year 311. In the autumn of the following year Maxentius fell in battle against Constantine. From
that time Constantine controlled the empire, and was the
mightiest ruler of the world. At the beginning of 313 he issued
an edict in Milan, permitting the free exercise of their religion
to the Christians, 'in order that the Godhead, whatever may
be the case with It and with heavenly things, may be gracious
to us and to all who live in our empire.' The same year the
first coin of Constantine bearing the Cross was issued. The
idea of the *imperium gratiae*, which had begun to make its
appearance in the days of Abgar of Edessa, was now being
put into effect on a world scale. We witness the remarkable
spectacle of the transformation, step by step, of the coins
which were the most intimate documents of imperial self-
glorification and demonic Christomachy, into symbols of the
victory of Christ and His all-conquering glory, power and
grace.

In the year 315 Constantine struck a significant silver medallion, which has survived in only one good example, in Lenin-
grad, and has only recently been properly examined and
appraised, by Richard Delbrueck and Andreas Alföldi. It has
a portrait-bust of the emperor in full armour, wearing a helmet
with the name of Christ in the centre, on his left arm a shield
with the Roman she-wolf, and above it a sceptre with a cross-
shaft, on which is set a globe of the world. What is the meaning of these symbols? The politician of tolerance, who laid
down his weapons before the Galilean, has become the knight
and general and emperor of Christ, dragging the world on
his back 'in the Name of Him who died upon the Cross'.
We know that the idea of divine right is older than Christianity
itself. But here the idea has been revolutionized by its connexion with Christ the Crucified and Exalted. The Cross of
Jesus Christ is henceforth the sign of reconciliation over the
whole sphere of politics, and the heavenly emperor is the
image of all earthly rule.

Constantine, admittedly, had his own idea of the meaning

of the divine right of the ruler—different, at least, from the legends about him. He understood by it not only that the emperor was installed by God, but also that God maintained him on the throne by His grace, no matter the guilt in which the emperor was entangled for reasons of State. The guilt of Constantine was perhaps greater than that of any other ruler. The story of the assassinations in his family has recently been investigated, and from this one can see how ruthlessly he engaged in the struggle for power. The first Christian emperor was no saint, but a great statesman who was aware of the inherent tragedy of politics with its involvement in sin and violence. This very awareness made the grace of God in the Cross of Christ the *conditio sine qua non* of his political life, which played an increasing part, subjectively as well as objectively, in his whole career.

In the same year (315) the building of the triumphal arch was begun, which, above the pictures of his political triumphs, the lapidary inscription, INSTINCTU DIVINITATIS—'impelled by divine power'. Also about that time his colossal statue was set up in white marble in the basilica on the *forum Romanum*. The emperor was enthroned like a Pharaoh in super-human proportions—the statue was about thirty feet high without the socle. He gazes into the distance with that trans-cendental look which we find in the most typical work of the third century, for example, in the marble bust of Decius. But it is no longer the shadow of the coming destruction of the world, but the splendour of the *civitas Dei*, which lies across that face. In his eyes one no longer sees the flicker of an apo-calyptic end, but a visionary readiness, a divine certainty of his calling and of the future: *instinctu divinitatis*.

In the year 317 a coin was struck showing the emperor once more in full armour, wearing the helmet with the monogram of the name of Christ which he probably wore in 312 in the decisive battle with Maxentius, and on his arm a shield with the image of the mounted dragon-slayer.

In 325 Constantine opened the Council of Nicaea, and invited the assembled church fathers to celebrate the twentieth anni-versary of his reign. Bishop Eusebius of Caesarea thereupon proclaimed him as the fulfiller of all imperial hopes and of the biblical promises of a king. The following year the emperor founded his new capital of Constantinople, and there struck the coin which may be regarded as the last document of the great struggle between the rule of the emperors and the rule of Christ. It shows the standard of Constantine with the monogram of the name of Christ, triumphantly raised above a pierced snake. The legend is SPES PUBLICA, a formula with a long and significant history, which we might venture to paraphrase as 'The hope of all history'.

In his great palace in Constantinople Constantine had himself represented as the knightly hero in the armour of Christ, conquering the demonic dragon. The mosaic portrait, which we unfortunately know only from ancient descriptions, was a symbol of the first Christian emperor's conception of his calling. He was the warrior of Christ against the powers of hell. The picture alluded to the great victory over Maxentius at the battle of the Milvian Bridge, to which Constantine owed his supremacy. The coin, on the other hand, alludes to the future—*spes publica*. The figure of the earthly emperor has quite disappeared from the picture, and only the standard of the divine emperor is shown, the symbol of Christ Himself.

The meaning of this symbolism is that the emperor can only fight the old dragon, the devil or Satan, in his historical manifestations, but Christ attacks the devil in his very self. The emperor can only throw the devil again and again, but Christ will make an end of him, absolutely and for ever. The emperor's achievement is never more than an interim solution, pointing symbolically to the final work of Christ. So the emperor's kingdom is in the last resort nothing but the prayer, 'Thy kingdom come'. So we may understand the coin to mean that the Cross is the *ultima ratio* of all imperial politics. The victory of Christ over the Caesars is summed up in the confession of the first Christian emperor: the *imperium* of Christ is our hope for all history.

The symbolism of the coin belongs to a twofold tradition, whose correlation is the most expressive form of the theological axiom that the earthly emperor is the image of the heavenly.

For thousands of years the dragon-slayer had been a recurrent image in the Near East. In an Egyptian catacomb it may be seen in a Christological form and with a biblical interpretation. A youthful, beardless Christ is trampling a lion beneath one foot, and a dragon beneath the other, with a snake on one side and an ichneumon on the other. The words of Ps. 91.13 are beneath the picture: '*Super aspidem et basiliscum ambulabis, et conculcabis leonem et draconem.*' In recent years in an Old Syrian monastery chapel the fragment of a relief has come to light on which Christ is triumphing with the cross-sceptre over the beasts of the devil. The same motif is to be seen on Roman lamps, frequently also on monumental pictures in the Ravenna of Theodoric, from where it passed to the Germanic north, to reappear on Carolingian ivory tablets, on Ottonian miniatures and Early English sculpture. In Old High German texts, too, Christ as the dragon-slayer is a favourite theme of Early Germanic Christology.

The imperial dragon-slayer is the weak image of the divine dragon-slayer. He appears on coins of the fifth century (Honorius, Valentinian III), with sword and sceptre with Christ's monogram, crowned by the heavenly hand, and with his right foot on the defeated beast from hell. This type was a favourite on coins struck in Ravenna, and its effect is still seen in the reliefs on the graves of Renaissance emperors. In the coin of Constantine, therefore, with the standard of Christ above the dragon of hell, the whole history of the Western imperial idea is proleptically indicated.

On an Old Syrian relief the divine Hand is handing a bow to the emperor with which he will subdue his enemies. On the recently uncovered wall-paintings of the synagogue of Dura, which were made about 245, the Hand of God is seen above scenes of Old Testament history. 'The Hand of God was apparent in the battle', wrote Lactantius, a year after the victory of Constantine over Maxentius. About the year 330 a gold medallion of Constantine represented the emperor with raised finger, crowned by the divine Hand. And on the coin of consecration which was struck after his death, Constantine is shown ascending to heaven in a quadriga, as at other times Caesar or Helios, Elijah or Christ. The divine Hand which had graciously guided the emperor on all his ways reaches out from heaven, and now receives him at the end of his earthly career.

V

The best summary expression of the Christian motifs which run through the symbols and images of Constantine's proclamations (which like the tiara coins of Abgar are not always wholly unambiguous) is to be found in the address to the assembly of the saints composed by a contemporary at Constantine's bidding. Once more, at the close of the imperial history of ancient Rome, the advent hymn is quoted which was composed at the beginning of Roman imperial history and since then had accompanied the generations of emperors like an unsettled question—the Fourth Eclogue of Virgil. This time it is quoted in a Greek text, *Interpretatio Graeca*, which comes very near to the *Interpretatio Christiana*:

> The Divine Virgin returns,
> And the Golden Age.

Who could this Virgin be save she who conceived by the Holy Ghost? And the King is to return who is the longing of the whole world, by his Advent lifting the world from its collapse. 'What remains of our guilt will be destroyed by him, and the world will be freed from perpetual fear.'

> Come then, lad, oh come,
> And smilingly greet thy Mother.

Virgil becomes the official prophet of Christ, and the Sibyl the official prophetess of His Advent—and their interpreter is none other than the emperor himself. He removes the divine radiate crown from his own head and lays it before the Child in the Manger.

When he deals with the Christomachy of his predecessors, the emperor of Christ is brief and brusque: 'How great is the vanity and arrogance of earthly power, that mortal men should dare to wage war with God.' He had a different ideal, the image of the ruler who goes the way willed by God, in the sober conviction that it is the way which offers the best future for himself and his peoples. So out of his acknowledgement of Christ's Advent there grew a will to shape an empire in which every Advent hope capable of historical fulfilment could be realized. 'Freedom is saved', said the emperor, 'the sanctity of agreements has been restored, the foundations of a lasting peace have been laid.' Were these any more than the phrases and ideas which we have encountered from the time of Augustus onwards? Yes and No. The ancient expectations were now indeed to be fulfilled, but in a new way—by the spirit of the new age penetrating the renewed empire; and the spirit is that of grace. 'True community and humanity; punishment which aims at the betterment and not the destruction of the guilty man; treatment of men in the service of salvation and not the service of cruelty—and mercy to all who have been struck down by fate.' Constantine promised no golden age, as the emperors and court prophets of the past had done, but an age of grace, an empire which practised forgiveness, because it was founded and depended upon God's forgiving act. His last metapolitical testament is an impressive monument, like the words on the triumphal arch:

'Impelled by divine power I began my work. For it is God's work to guide everything to the best fulfilment, and it is for man to be obedient to God. That is the most holy service which our hands can perform, and which we owe to God in pure and transparent faith. And with the work of our hands prayer and intercession must be joined, that what is begun for good may reach a happy conclusion.' It is like the voice of Cromwell, when Constantine alludes to the wars and battles in which Divine Providence was revealed, in which God heard the prayers of His servant Constantine. 'For true prayer is an invincible power, and no one who beseeches heaven in the fear of God misses his goal. For God is always present in

His grace. Men indeed are subject to error. . . . Therefore all who fear God must give thanks to the Saviour of all for our salvation and the fortunate state of public life, and with humble prayers and unceasing requests reconcile Christ with us, that He may continue the work of grace which He has begun.'

XVI

THE FALL OF
THE ANCIENT WORLD AND
THE EUROPEAN MISSION
OF THE CHURCH

WHEN Attila invaded Italy in 452 and was marching on
Rome without meeting any resistance, the Roman Bishop Leo
met him in Mantua at the head of a small embassy, and succeeded in preserving the capital from the storm which was
about to break over it. An eyewitness gives this account:
'Attila received the delegation with all honour, and was so
pleased to see the high priest that he declared himself ready
to make peace and to return over the Danube.'

The event is symbolic. For the service performed by the
bishop of Rome for the sake of the capital of the old world
is the same service as that which the Church of Christ performed for the whole classical age. The old Church loved to
describe itself as the Ark—and rightly so. For in fact it saved
the essential elements and cultural goods of the ancient world
in the Great Flood of late antiquity.

This event, the crisis and rescue of classical culture, may
be studied in a few random examples, which speak for themselves, without need for much commentary. We shall take
the crisis and rescue of faith, courage, truth, beauty, purity,
marriage, mercy, joy, freedom, and the European concept
of empire.

I

Herodotus tells of two Spartan noblemen, who alone remained standing in the palace of the Persian emperor, when

all the courtiers and diplomats and generals cast themselves to the ground before the divine majesty of the emperor. 'It is not our custom to worship a mortal man.' It was the protest of young Europe against the old Asiatic deification of the sovereign. But a few centuries later the same Europe worshipped the Roman emperor, for belief in the Olympic gods had collapsed. 'What shall we worship if the worship of the emperor's image ceases?' asked a Roman politician of the third century. But in that very century faith in the emperor also collapsed. Men worshipped him, but no longer believed in him. They knew that he had come to power through assassination, and would fall by the same means. The twilight of the gods, unbelief and nihilism were the marks of the age.

But there was a little group of men who said, 'We do not worship mortal men, but the eternal God alone.' They were not the last Spartans but the first Christians who spoke these truly European words. They spoke these words as evidence before the Roman judge who tried to convert them to emperor-worship. 'I have sacrificed to the emperor. Do you also sacrifice,' said the judge to one of them. Then a Roman officer, himself still a pagan, interrupted and said to the pagan judge, 'What? Will you make out of a man who believes in God one who does not believe?' It was the witness of an impartial observer. Here was the Church in which European men learned belief again.

II

The courage of the Spartans was held before the youth of later centuries as a brilliant example. Philosophers wrote moving treatises about the art of dying and the exalted school of heroism. But the generations which honoured the heroes were surprisingly deficient in men of character. It was not the art of dying which was practised, but the art of advancement.

The exception was to be found in one little circle, that of the Christians. Men like the philosopher Epictetus or the emperor Marcus Aurelius spoke of it with vexation and fury: there were the men who knew how to die. One of these men was the martyr Bishop Cyprian. The imperial governor had

him brought before him, and asked, 'Where are your companions in office?' Cyprian replied, 'Your laws have with
good reason forbidden denunciation. I am therefore not able
to name my companions. But be assured you will find them
at their posts of duty.' Cyprian was first exiled, then soon
afterwards again brought before the judge. Then he wrote
his farewell letter to his people. 'The emperor's minions are
on their way. I await their coming. What has still to be
arranged we shall do in common with God's counsel, before
the judge sentences me for my confession. May Christ preserve and keep you in His Church in grace.' Cyprian was
condemned to death. The executioner appeared. Cyprian paid
him twenty-five pieces of gold, bent his head, and received
the death-stroke. So died the old Romans in the brilliant days
of the Republic, as Christian bishops now died in the character-
less days of the late empire. In the Church men learned again
the meaning of heroism.

III

In the year 399 B.C. Socrates died as a martyr to the truth.
'I will obey my God rather than you.' But the spirit of Socrates
became more rare with each century. 'What is truth?' asked
Pilate, and shrugged his shoulders, and did what was demanded
by State expediency and his own advantage. And of the 'philosophers' of the second century A.D. a contemporary writes,
'Your hypocrisy betrays the blindness of your hearts, however
dense the throng of words in which you take refuge.'

The Christians were an exception. They took eternal truth
seriously once more, and died for it in the midst of a world
of political truths, of official untruth, of public deceit. When
the Christian philosopher Justin gave his testimony to the
truth before the judgment-stool, the judge wanted to help
him. 'You are of the opinion, then . . . ?' Justin answered
quietly and firmly, 'It's not my opinion. I know.' These men
deliberately raised the standard of truth which had been set
up by Socrates, but had been betrayed long since by his
unworthy imitators. Bishop Phileas was called on to deny his
faith. The Roman judge addressed him, reminding him of his

wife and children who were present in the court, awaiting the decision. Phileas refused to recant. 'I will not injure my soul. It is not only Christians, but heathens too, who have regard to their souls. Take Socrates, for example. When he was being removed for execution and his wife and children were standing there, he did not draw back, but went unhesitatingly to his death.' Again and again the apologists and martyrs of the Church allude to the fate and the legacy of Socrates. 'The same world which once persecuted Socrates later persecuted Christ too, and now it persecutes us.' An ultimate metaphysical opposition between the truth and the world was disclosed, which was expressed by Tertullian in the Apocalyptic and Johannine tradition as follows. 'The truth knows that it has no home on earth, and is a stranger in a hostile world, and that its origin, its home, its hope, its validity and its future are in heaven.' A Church which took the truth so seriously in a relativizing age, was bound to become the refuge of the spirit and the nursery of learning. So the treasures of ancient culture were brought into the ark of the Church, and the oldest university in the world was founded by the Church.

IV

The most genuine cult of the classical world was the cult of beauty, the glorification of the harmony of spirit and blood, form and substance, ideal and reality, heaven and earth, the celebration of the beauty of man (plastic art) in beautiful surroundings (architecture), of a beautiful microcosm (sport, dancing) in a beautiful macrocosm (the harmony of the spheres, music). The beautiful picture of the world, and the beauty of man, broke up in late classical times. No essential difference was made by the appearance of romantic stragglers, Antonius the apostle of Dionysos, Nero the dilettante, Antinous who died young, Julian the fanatic, the faded blossom Hypatia.

But in a poor hovel on the Jordan a 'lost child' poured an alabaster jar of perfumes almost £100 in value over the feet of the doomed Son of Man, and He called that extravagant homage a 'beautiful' deed. God loves and affirms beauty, and restores its original meaning: it is a service to the glory of God. So in the dark catacombs early Christian art flourished. The most beautiful objects in the beautiful cities of the *imperium sacrum* were the basilicas raised in the name of Jesus Christ. The Church which saved classical culture also laid the foundations of an art which was to flourish for a thousand years.

V

In ancient times there was no lack of moral preachers who proclaimed the ideal of purity. Their efforts were without success. Immorality became the rule, not a secret vice but open practice, applauded and publicly encouraged. They 'not only do the same, but consent with them that practise them', wrote Paul in the time of Nero (Rom. 1.32). Tacitus confirms this fifty years later, in the last brilliant epoch of the empire. Roman society was rotten in body and soul.

In this situation Paul said, 'Be not fashioned according to this world' (Rom. 12.2): these are basic words for a Christian morality which does not aim at being a generalized morality but an exception, the morality of a closed circle which does not aim at producing holy men, heroes of virtue, and Pharisees, but sees sin as sin, takes it seriously, and therefore produces a spirit of wholesomeness, power and purity.

VI

In classical times there were instances of fine marriages: Aspasia and Pericles, Porcia and Brutus, Octavia and Antony. When the black lists were published during the Roman civil wars, when every bond of loyalty and honour was dissolved, and brother betrayed brother, friend slew friend, hundreds of Roman matrons shared death with their husbands as a matter of course. The most Roman of all marriages, that between Augustus and Livia, was celebrated at that time. For more than fifty years the simple house on the Palatine, where Livia ruled, was the centre of the world. For fifty-two years she was the good spirit of that house, and the only person who could influence the master of the world. She could do this because she neither idolized him nor upbraided him. Suetonius relates that the last words of the dying emperor were words of gratitude for this marriage. 'Farewell, Livia, and remember our marriage.' But there were other marriages, even then, and the social crisis of the late empire was intimately bound up with the crisis in marriage.

In that apocalyptic age the spirit of classical marriage found a refuge in early Christianity, and beneath the sign of the Cross a new kind of marriage, based on metaphysical foundations, was made out of the old. For there is no deeper community between man and man than that which is found under the sign of the Cross; nor any stronger community, for it is not of this world, and therefore mighty beyond death. The Early Church illustrated this community of marriage in its account of the end of the wife of the apostle Peter. 'When the blessed Peter was forced to watch his wife being led away to her death, he rejoiced because she was being called home, called her by name, and said, "Wife, think of the Lord." ' Eusebius, who relates this, adds his comment: 'Of such a kind was the marriage of the blessed fathers, and their love in the face of death.'

VII

In the midst of the hopeless conflicts of her house, and the tragic conflict of might and right and guilt and revenge, Antigone declares, 'Not to hate but to love is my destiny.' The tragedy which consumed the House of Oedipus became in later ages the tragedy of all mankind. The office of Antigone was taken over by the Church.

The Church did this in the name of the crucified Christ. It knew of the murderous spirits which slumber in mankind and which had broken out and driven an unhappy generation into a war of all against all, and it showed, or rather it went, the only way which could lead out of the indiscriminate slaughter: the way of mercy, of forgiving, helping, sacrificial love. It 'went through a valley of tears and dug wells'. The masses in the great cities of imperial times were never able to understand the Christology of the Church properly. But they did understand that where the word of forgiveness was preached and lived a new and saving way was disclosed, a last hope. Five hundred years after the death of Christ it was possible for the two contending parties in Constantinople to bury their old quarrel with the words: 'Let friends live, and enemies live, and sympathy live: long live mercy between friend and foe.'

VIII

Man does not cling so much to life in itself as to a certain form of life. If this form is destroyed he loses his joy in life. This is true of men of the classical age as well as of modern men. By means of a centuries-old culture they had succeeded in making out of life a work of art, they had constructed in the midst of the world their own world in which they were happy and at home. It was this world which broke up in the late years of the empire, burying beneath its ruins everything that had made life beautiful and worth-while. The horsemen of the Apocalypse had broken loose, war and plague and inflation, the devil himself. The end was at hand. There was no purpose any more. A little happiness, and love, and power, every general an emperor in turn—and then the Flood. The triumph of death was the chief theme on the sarcophagi of the third century, and written across all the portraits of the time is the same signature of hopelessness. 'We don't see the way.' Those with a sense of responsibility fought with tragic resolution against this spirit of decay. Theatres and games and festivals were organized in unprecedented number, grain and wine and money were distributed, and coins were struck with such words of guidance as FELICITAS and HILARITAS. But meanwhile the Germanic tribes were breaking through the frontiers, and the old order was tottering to its end. One con-temporary account compares the sick gaiety with the effect of the 'Sardonian root', a poisonous plant which forces a convulsive smile across the face of the dying. 'In the face of imprisonment who can think of the circus? Who can laugh on the way to execution? We play while we fear slavery, and we laugh while we fear death. One could almost believe that the whole Roman people had tasted of the Sardonian root, for it is dying, and it laughs.'

Through this century of death and intoxication went a body of people with new faces showing a new joy. They move across the ruins of the past to a new future: *vexilla regis prodeunt*, the banners of the King go before us. The King was Christ, and Cyprian wrote to the 'soldiers of Christ', who in the year of the plague, 250, swore an oath on the standard of the Cross: 'You know that the fall of this world is only the sign of the coming Kingdom.' Here is the secret of that apocalyptic movement, with its certainty about the future. Where others saw only the fall of the old world, their world, the Christians saw the dawn of a new world, their world, which they greeted from afar.

IX

On their way to the Persian capital the Spartan nobles reached Asia Minor, where they were conducted by the Persian governor through the splendid palace grounds. Then, at table, he turned to them, 'Do you like what you have seen? This is how the emperor rewards his faithful servants. You too may have this.' The Spartans only said, 'Only he who does not know how sweet freedom is, can speak thus.' The Greeks fought for this freedom, knowing that it was the basis of their human dignity, of their whole life and culture; and in so doing they fought for one of the basic concerns of Europe. But their passion for freedom was their political destruction. The Romans murdered Caesar in the name of freedom, and produced Augustus, who proclaimed imperial freedom. Augustus recognized, and in a reign of half-a-century convinced the peoples of his empire, that freedom and authority must go together, that the synthesis of freedom and authority was the historic mission of the European empire. But under Augustus's rule there were millions of slaves, for whom the evangel of freedom meant nothing. A hundred years later there were millions of Roman citizens who were economic slaves. After another hundred years the emperor was addressed in the same style as the slave addressed his owner, '*Domine*'. What was left of freedom fell sacrifice to the Germanic conquerors. 'The sword of the Goths, swinging with the fury of Bacchus, lays Roman freedom low', is a lament from that time.

The Church watched this tragedy of Europe with compassion. It gave new power to the old European reserve in the use of the word 'Lord', and brought its reserve into the very heart of the empire. 'I can call the emperor *Domine*', wrote Tertullian to the emperor Septimius Severus, 'but I remain a free man of God before him.' Nevertheless, the Church did not dabble in politics. But it made history. For it preached of the God who loves freedom and rules over a creation which has been made free. It preached of the God who loves Europe, because it is the place of freedom, and loves it so long as it remains true to its mission. And it put this God before the rulers of Europe as the image of kings and the ideal of political rule. This was its decisive action. 'This is the supreme excellence of the Roman emperor, that he rules not over slaves but over free men, that he loves freedom also in those who serve him.' In the Germanic epoch the Church continued to proclaim the ideal of the 'free empire', and prayed for God's support that after the conquest of the enemies of peace Roman freedom would serve Him faithfully. Centuries later the Marquis Posa held before the tyrant Philip as his model the Christian image of God: 'Look at His glorious Nature, it is founded on freedom, and how rich it is through freedom.'

X

Aristotle, the tutor of Alexander the Great, once said, 'The northern peoples (the *Germani*) are politically too ungifted to make history.' His pupil Alexander was the first European to acknowledge the classical idea of empire. And the culmination of the political greatness of the ancient peoples was the creation of the Roman empire, the union of the Mediterranean peoples in a single European society under the aegis of the Roman eagle.

This achievement was nowhere more honoured than in the early Church. And it remained true to this European idea and mission of the empire even during the century of violence, when the *imperium Romanum* itself had lost any faith in it. And when *Roma Aeterna* and the *imperium aeternum*, together with the dogma of the *aeternitas Augusti*, collapsed in the storms of the *Voelkerwanderung*, it was the Church which took over the inheritance, the task and the idea of the Western empire. In the eternal City it was the Pope who took the place of the emperor as guardian of European order and western tradition; it was Pope Leo who went to Attila, and to many others, for the good of Rome and the Roman world. It was then that the Church grew in stature, with the assumption of a quite new task. It became the tutor of the young Germanic peoples in the European idea—those 'unpolitical' peoples of whom Aristotle had spoken so scornfully. Only a century after the great wandering of the peoples there arose out of their midst the first great imperial statesman of Germanic blood and Christian faith, Theodoric the Great. And three hundred years later Charlemagne, the pupil of Augustine, created the Western empire, Christian Europe.

In this way the ancient Church understood its European task. 'We want to stand upright amid the ruins of the world, and not lie on the ground with those who have no hope', wrote Cyprian. That is the spirit of the Church which survived the catastrophe of the old world, saving both itself and the best gifts of Europe: upright amid the ruins.

CHRONOLOGICAL TABLES

Before Christ

	IMPERIAL HISTORY		HISTORY OF PALESTINE
3200	Beginning of Greater Egypt	3200	Fortification of Jericho
		3000	Fortification of Megiddo
2600	Accadian Empire		
2000	Babylonian Empire		
1750	Hittite Empire		
1550	Egyptian Empire		
		1468	Pharaoh Thutmosis III conquers Megiddo
1350	Decline of Egypt under Amenophis IV	1350	The Hebrews threaten the cities of Palestine
		1200	Israelites in Transjordania
		1180	Philistines on the Palestinian coast
			Joshua conquers Jericho
1150	Assyrian Empire	1150	Israelite victory at Megiddo
		1000	David conquers Jerusalem
		701	Assyrians besiege Jerusalem
670	Assyrians control Palestine and Egypt		
600	Neo-Babylonian Empire		
		586	The Babylonians destroy Jerusalem
539	The Persians under Cyrus conquer Babylon		
		538	Cyrus permits the Return of the Jews from Babylon
334	Alexander's campaign in Asia		
		332	Palestine part of Alexander's empire
175	The Syrian Empire under Antiochus IV Epiphanes		
		168	Worship of Zeus in Jerusalem
63	Cicero Consul Conspiracy of Catiline Birth of Augustus	63	Pompey conquers Jerusalem

IMPERIAL HISTORY	HISTORY OF PALESTINE
44 Assassination of Caesar	
	37 Herod I conquers Jerusalem
31 Battle of Actium	
27 Augustus reforms the Empire	
17 The Secular Games	
9 Augustus sets up Altar of Peace	
The Augustus inscription at Priene in Asia Minor	
8 Closing of the Temple of Janus	8 Fall of Herod I
7 The Augustus inscription at Philae in Upper Egypt	7 Beginning of the Census in Palestine
	Jewish Resistance movements and Messianic prophecies
	Birth of Jesus
6 Tiberius goes into solitude	4 Death of Herod I in Jericho
	Varus in Sephoris and Jerusalem
2 Exile of Julia	

Anno Domini

IMPERIAL HISTORY	CHURCH HISTORY
2 Death of Lucius Caesar	
4 Death of Caius Caesar	
14 Death of Augustus	
Tiberius Emperor	
15 Sejanus becomes Prefect of the Guard	
	18 Caiaphas becomes High Priest
	26 Pilate goes to Jerusalem
27 Tiberius goes into solitude	27 Battle of the Standards in Jerusalem
	28 Baptism of Jesus
	30 Provocatory Coins struck by Pilate
31 Fall of Sejanus	
	32 Crucifixion of Jesus
	36 Fall of Pilate and Caiaphas
37 Caligula becomes Emperor	
41 Claudius becomes Emperor	
	48 Apostolic Council in Jerusalem
54 Nero becomes Emperor	
59 Murder of his mother Agrippina	
64 Burning of Rome	64 Persecution of the Christians

288

CHRONOLOGICAL TABLES

IMPERIAL HISTORY	CHURCH HISTORY
65 Suicide of Seneca	
68 Suicide of Nero	
70 Vespasian's Advent in Rome	70 Destruction of Jerusalem
79 Titus becomes Emperor	
Eruption of Vesuvius	
81 Domitian becomes Emperor	
88 Insurrections in Mainz and other places	
95 Execution of Titus Flavius Clemens	95 John exiled to Patmos
96 Assassination of Domitian	96 Relatives of Jesus appear before Domitian in Rome
Nerva becomes Emperor	
	135 The Catastrophe of Bar Kochba
	179 Abgar the Great becomes King of Edessa
193 Assassination of Commodus Advent of Septimius Severus in Rome	
	202 Martyrs in North Africa and Egypt
211 Caracalla attempts to murder his father and brother Death of Septimius Severus	
212 Caracalla murders his brother Geta and rules alone	
217 Assassination of Caracalla Suicide of Julia Domna	
227 Artaxerxes founds the neo-Persian Empire	
	249 Cyprian becomes Bishop of Carthage
250 Outbreak of the fifteen-year Plague	250 Decius's Edict of Persecution
251 Invasion of the Goths in the Lower Danube	
256 The Persian King Sapor conquers Antioch	
	258 Valerian's Edict of Persecution Martyrdom of Cyprian
259 Gallienus defeats the Alemanni at Milan Valerian defeats the Persians at Edessa	

CHRIST AND THE CAESARS

IMPERIAL HISTORY		CHURCH HISTORY	
260	Valerian taken prisoner by the Persians	260	Edict of Toleration by Gallienus
268	Assassination of Gallienus Claudius Gothicus becomes Emperor		
270	Death of Claudius Gothicus Aurelian becomes Emperor		
272	Aurelian defeats Zenobia	272	Aurelian gives decision against Paul of Samosata
275	Assassination of Aurelian		
276	Probus becomes Emperor		
282	Assassination of Probus		
284	Diocletian becomes Emperor		
286	Carausius in Britain		
293	Assassination of Carausius		
296	Advent of Constantius Chlorus in London		
		303	Diocletian's Edict of Persecution
		304	Martyrdom of Crispina
305	Abdication of Diocletian		
307	Constantine becomes Emperor		
		311	Constantine's Edict of Toleration
312	Constantine's Victory over Maxentius		
		315	Constantine strikes Coins with Monogram of Christ's Name and the Cross-Sceptre
		325	Constantine at the Council of Nicaea
326	Founding of Constantinople		
		452	Meeting of Leo and Attila
525	Justinian marries Theodora		

The dates are given only for general orientation, and many of them are disputed.

INDEX OF PERSONS

INDEX OF PERSONS

Made in the USA
Columbia, SC
29 October 2020